Essentials of Automated Acquisition

Essentials of Automated Acquisition

C.K. Padmajam

Ess Ess Publications

4837/24, Ansari Road, Darya Ganj,
New Delhi-110002
✆ : 3260807, 3201533
Fax : 3274173
E-mail: essess@del3.vsnl.net.in
url:http://www.essessbooks.com

First Published 2002

ISBN : 81-7000-329-6

Price : Rs. 675 /-

Published by:

Ess Ess Publications

4837/24, Ansari Road, Darya Ganj,
New Delhi - 110 002
Phone : 3260807
Fax : 3274173
E-mail : essess@del3.vsnl.net.in
url:http://www.essessbooks.com

Laser Typesetting:
Mukesh Graphics
L-2/8, Mangolepuri, New Delhi
Ph.:7924405

Printed at :
Print Line

Contents

Preface

The library is the place where individual needs for knowledge and information are met through the collective provision and interpretation of resources. The technological developments put the individual consumer directly in touch with a global information marketplace create an apparently barren future for this particular public service.

Today, libraries automated rapidly, the possibility of record sharing and distribution increased exponentially, and users had catalogues which were current, potentially well-maintained, and amenable to a much wider range of search strategies. Now the computer is moving out of the office, into the home and on to the road as the growth in electronic communication brings the library catalogue direct to a screen near you. The electronic evangelists believe that all this points to the sure and certain fact that the internet is the library of the future.

The ideal underpinning the electronic information revolution is that the ability to plug into a worldwide web of unregulated and uncensored digitized information will empower the individual against the institutions — economic, social and political — that control our lives. If the ideal became reality, we would find the individual interacting with the computer in total isolation from our crumbling communities.

Acquisitions automation is becoming more sophisticated and at the same time electronic publishing is adding an entirely new dimension to acquisitions service. These two developments are bringing about major changes in acquisitions, in terms of both process and organisation. The future is in the way libraries adapt to the electronic environment that is increasingly surrounding them.

An exploration of the impact of acquisitions automation signals a shift toward a distributed acquisitions environment in academic libraries of the future, as opposed to the centralised approach prevalent today. This shift will bring about a redefinition of both the process and the organisation of acquisitions.

Much progress has been made in recent years in the development and enhancement of automated acquisitions systems. At one time the focus of development was on replicating manual ordering and receiving routines within a comparatively isolated context. The integration of the acquisitions component with other internal library systems and with external bibliographic utilities was considered ideal but not reality.

This publication will constitute a meaningful contribution to contemporary literature in the area of library automated acquisition. It will be useful and valuable for both students and researchers, as well as professional librarians, documentationists, information technologists and communicators.

1
Introduction

Acquisitions is the core activity for acquiring information necessary for a library to fulfil its service function of providing information to its clientele. Automation of acquisitions has been slow in development. There are a number of reasons, two of which are the complexities of acquisitions tasks which have demanded time and expense in development of systems, and the evolving organisational structure in the performance of the acquisitions tasks.

In a 1985 survey of 28 libraries, it was interesting to learn that only seven libraries used an automated acquisitions system but 75 per cent had an online catalog. Of those libraries with automated acquisitions systems, six had automated ordering, four used automated serials check-in and two, automated binding. Automation itself will cause further changes in the organisational structure of acquisitions, something which the in-house systems and early vendor-developed systems have indicated. There are very labour-intensive tasks in acquisitions which require much typing and filing.

In the current period of library financial retrenchment and with smaller percentages of the operating budget going to acquisitions, there has been tremendous pressure on acquisitions personnel in the acquiring of materials. Just a few years ago, all acquisitions work was performed manually. In general, it is still performed manually. Out of desperation and a desire to provide online acquisitions information service to the library's clientele a fair number of libraries developed in-house automated acquisitions modules. Some of these are still in use; however, their efficiency varies greatly. These were developed mostly as an interim step until turnkey systems became available. A majority of these systems are in batch mode and operate on a general purpose mainframe computer. Most of these early systems were not comprehensive acquisitions systems in their development because of technological, financial or political problems.

Automation of acquisitions has received less attention than other library functions. Although there are many elements that enter into the slow development of the automation of the acquisitions function, two of those reasons are the non-realisation of the service benefits of the acquisitions function, its complexity, and the lack of a uniform organisational structure for performing the acquisitions task. "The move toward integrated systems is belated in some ways since acquisitions automation in libraries is now more than two decades old. But it is now coming very quickly and will play a very significant role in our future activities." This statement was made in 1980 by one of the most knowledgeable librarians in the field of automation.

Acquisitions automation of a sophisticated sort began in the mid-1960. As we near 1990, there are several automated acquisitions systems in the market, a few of which interface with a library's system if the library uses the same system for other library functions. There are others which perform most of the tasks needed in the acquisitions operation but which do not interface with a library's online catalog. Now that other service functions have been automated and are in the process of becoming highly developed, attention is focusing more on the automation of serials check-in and acquisitions functions for fully-integrated library systems. However, software vendors have not been willing to devote the time and expense necessary to develop the complicated software to handle the complex tasks of acquisitions.

Until recently there was little available in vendor or network-supplied acquisitions systems or services. There are systems on the market for both functions; however, these are rare considering the length of time that has elapsed since the beginning in the mid-1960s. Several well-known systems available are NOTIS, GEAC, INNOVAQ. Several of the other early acquisitions were the Baker and Taylor BATAB system of 1969, WLN in 1978, CLSI, and OCLC. NOTIS, first operational in 1971, included both acquisitions and cataloging. Serials receiving was designed into the system as an integral part of acquisitions.

Although automated acquisitions functions are a giant step forward, when software cannot interface with a library's online catalog, it deprives a library's clientele of valuable information. The traditional tasks of acquisitions have included participating in collection development activities, serving as liaison with academic faculty in selection, bibliographic searching, ordering receiving and checking in all materials ordered, payment authorisation, and mail receipt and distribution. In some libraries, other activities include receipt and acknowledgement of gifts, binding and book repair, and disposition of discards.

Although there have been arguments for decentralised acquisitions, to achieve efficiency and accountability, ordering, receipt and payment must be monitored by a single entity.After bibliographic searching and order information are entered into a part of a library's database, the interim file must be given a final review by acquisitions prior to ordering. After revision by acquisitions, the record then may become part of the online catalog/database and searchable by normal index keys. This would provide for centralised management of bibliographic and financial information and may also assist in the transition from manual to an automated environment. In a 1984 survey, it was reported that 57 per cent of responding libraries stated that monograph and serial acquisitions are organisationally separate and at one time, proponents of serials departments argued that advanced bibliographic skills were necessary to handle problems with title changes, frequency changes, and claiming. According to the 1984 survey, integrated acquisitions areas performed somewhat less of preorder searching and did more work in marking, editing, and so on. In this survey, of 28 libraries, 19 respondees performed the functions of bibliographic searching, ordering, receiving, check-in, and payment. Eleven received and distributed mail, ten handled discards, and only six performed the binding function. It is interesting to note where some libraries have dispersed some of the traditional acquisitions functions in other library areas. For instance, at one library in California, the acquisitions librarian has the title of Collection Development

Librarian; ordering and receiving are performed in that department. Monographic materials are searched, verified, and ordered by the order section, a division of the cataloging department. A separate serials department handles ordering, receiving and check-in of all serials. However, the cataloging department catalogs all serials. At a college in New York, bibliographic searching is performed in the cataloging department and payments are authorised by a separate payment department.Mail receipt and distribution is performed by the department that handles payments and, binding, although formerly in the cataloging department, is now part of public services. The binding unit is near the area where all currently received periodicals are shelved.

Other acquisitions functions have been dispersed to various other areas of the library, but the library is now planning to return all ordering and receiving and check-in to a single acquisitions department. These are only a few, medium to large-sized, libraries that have chosen different ways of fulfilling the acquisitions function. However, the overwhelming majority of libraries responding to the 1985 survey maintained the acquisitions functions in the traditional way by an acquisitions department with a librarian as head. Twenty-two libraries responding to the survey employ one or more professional librarians in acquisitions with a range of one to ten. Forty-one per cent believe the greater part of acquisitions tasks is professional, 35 per cent believe the greater part of acquisitions tasks is business or management-oriented, and 23 per cent believe that acquisitions tasks are evenly split between professional and business-oriented tasks. When this question was posed differently, 68 per cent felt acquisitions tasks were an even combination.Twenty-two acquisitions librarians responding to the questionnaire participate in selection of materials for the library, act as liaison with other librarians who participate in collection development, make budget decisions, and negotiate with publishers and vendors. Fifty per cent of the acquisitions librarians believe that collection development differs from acquisitions, that collection development is the actual selection of materials and collection measurement, the analysis of and policies for these functions. The same 50 per cent believe acquisitions is the function of physically acquiring materials and participating in collection development. Four respondees believe collection development and acquisitions are the same function. In 81 percent of the libraries, librarians other than the acquisitions librarian participate in collection development and 54 per cent of acquisitions librarians serve as liaison with academic faculty in collection development. With decentralisation, "the role of acquisitions librarian would require greater coordination and communication with other library areas."

Automated acquisitions module is designed for batch processing and runs on the IBM 3084. The database used is IMS and the program is primarily written in COBOL. Much typing and filing is eliminated with the use of this system, and, also, by the use of only a few vendors from whom to acquire library materials instead of ordering direct from thousands of publishers. After entering orders into a database, they may be edited, status reports added and receipts recorded. Bibliographic searching is performed by using an online bibliographic utility and transferring the information into the acquisitions database by rekeying. Orders are edited by the acquisitions department, part of which includes assigning a search code for duplication, a fund check code, a claim date, and a vendor code. These are then verified the first part of each week and mailed to suppliers. The acquisitions department monitors each fund account by accessing a separate accounting database. Upon arrival, all materials are checked in on the acquisitions database. Status reports are also entered into the online order record. However, none of this information is available to the public service area.

Although the biggest advantage in using this in-house developed acquisitions module is the termination of some paperwork, other benefits have been the automatic claiming and batch printing of purchase orders. However, batch processing of these purchase orders slows the process of ordering. The whole ordering process requires three full weeks.

During the evaluation process of automated acquisitions, the participants were temporarily assigned to the acquisitions division, where three OCLC terminals and one printer had been installed. The group was to determine the potential for improving the existing acquisitions and accounting procedures in the library. To accomplish this task, the group was:

1) To search, order, and receive firm order monographs;

2) To encumber and expend funds;

3) To catalog books received.

The unusual inclusion of cataloging in this work configuration derived from the need to explore efficiencies of a single record concept. All this was to be accomplished in as few terminal sittings as possible.

After the evaluation period, library administrators determined that the OCLC Acquisitions Subsystem should be fully implemented. A new department was formed from the nucleus of the test group, excluding the library assistant from processing. This group became the automated acquisitions department whose responsibilities include:

1) Searching, ordering, and receiving firm order monographs,

2) Searching, ordering, and receiving first issues, backfiles, and replacement issues of serials,

3) Searching, ordering, and receiving special format items such as maps, AV materials, and software,

4) Encumbering and expending funds,

5) Producing regular fund reports.

Cataloging books immediately on receipt was not feasible because the cataloger had to log off the acquisitions subsystem and log onto the order to process the books. This change of mode negated any timesaving benefits which could be gained by processing the book upon receipt. Also, the time-consuming task of verifying AACR2 headings when cataloging slowed the process even more.

Several points must be stressed when discussing the evaluation period of the test group.

First, a major reason for the success of the test and the implementation was the fact that the staff involved were included in the planning. Administrators sought staff input from the inception of the idea through its implementation.

Second, thorough and ongoing training was provided. Professional staff was available to answer questions as they arose.

Third, the staff could see the value of the new system in terms of making the acquisitions process more efficient and effective. If the staff "buy in" to the new system, the implementation will be accomplished much more smoothly. Predictably, there were problems.

One problem cited in the test group was the use of too much OCLC and bibliographic jargon with staff who were not familiar with the terms. Time has made many of these new terms familiar and common to automated acquisitions staff. Production time slowed down briefly because the group of twelve were sharing only three terminals. Until specific procedures could be worked out, certain bottlenecks occurred. The professional staff had to be available constantly for questions until the self-confidence and knowledge base of the test group developed.

After pre-order searching is done by the Resource Development Division personnel, the request card is given to a clerk in acquisitions (NAD/Maps Clerk on organisation chart). This clerk uses established guidelines in determining the best source for materials to be ordered. Although OCLC has an extensive vendor file, the Name Address Directory Clerk must often enter new vendor records. Once the record is entered, it is available to any OCLC user with NAD authorisation. The NAD number is then written on the request card and the card is placed in a "To Be Ordered" box by the OCLC terminals. The cards/orders are processed on a first in/ first out basis. Rush items are given to a terminal operator to be ordered immediately.

The ordering clerks and student workers search the OCLC database for the most appropriate bibliographic record on which to order the item. If not found on the database, an "O" (Ordering) level record is input by the library assistant II. This "O" level record can be used by other libraries for ordering purposes, but cannot be used for cataloging except by libraries with authorisation to update "O" level records.

Libraries are allowed to update their own "O" level records to full cataloging records.The ordering process is fairly simple once the appropriate record has been located. The fixed field area is changed to show STATUS: ordered; FORMS: (number of copies for the library), (number of copies to be sent to the vendor).

The Name Address Directory number is typed into the SOURCE field, and the DESTIN is filled in with the appropriate three character code abbreviated from the full address of the receiving section. The orders are transmitted via DX (direct electronic transmission) to the vendors, or the printed action forms are printed once a day, and mailed to the appropriate vendor, based on the NAD number entered on the record.

The receipt process is also quite straightforward. The Monographic Receiving Clerk opens boxes addressed to the Monographic Ordering Section. Ideally, there is a copy of the action form in the book or the purchase order number for each item is typed on the invoice. The clerk then pulls the request card from the in-process file and places it in the item to await terminal processing.

At the terminal, the Clerk retrieves the record by purchase order number and begins the receiving process.

The STATUS: is changed to "receiv" or "recprt" (received partially). The EXPEND line is filled in to indicate the fund to be used and the amount actually on the invoice. OCLC provides subfields in the EXPEND line to show the number of copies received, postage, and handling charges.

The Acquisitions Subsystem automatically multiplies or adds the appropriate subfields and places the total cost in subfield f. An INVOICE line is filled in to show the invoice number, date, and date expended. A RECEIPT line may also be filled in if a set is only partially received or if other receipt information seems necessary.

When the information is complete, the terminal operator taps [UPDATE] and [SEND] and the appropriate fund is immediately adjusted. The Receiving Clerk also flags the books as to the type of bibliographic copy she discovered and the book proceeds to Resource Development for pre-catalog searching. Some DLC books are given to the Library Assistant II in charge of Monographs/Special formats for copy cataloging.

Following certain processing division guidelines, she is allowed to "quick catalog" monographs to be located in the stacks which have straightforward LC call numbers and no series statements. The receiving clerk also stamps the invoices with several stamps: date processed, date received, Fiscal account number, media type, and initials the date processed stamp. If the purchase order number does not appear on the invoice, it is also written above the date processed.

Special formats, such as AV materials and maps, are ordered and received by the same clerks because many of those items have additional paperwork. For purchase requisition items, the OCLC order is updated rather than produced, 'because the order must be processed via a bid from the central purchasing office.

Serials also have special requirements. The same purchase order number is retained on the record until the vendor for the item changes or the maximum of seven screens are filled with data. Then a new purchase order number is initiated. New EXPEND and INVOICE lines are added yearly, and the RECEIPT lines indicate the year or volume paid for.

After monographic items are cataloged and the permanent shelf list cards are filed, processing staff change the STATUS: to "complit." Six months later the order record will be purged from the online system; serial records remain indefinitely.

OCLC allows an unlimited number of funds to be tracked online. Funds can be encumbered and expended on title records, and the accounting program will automatically adjust the fund accordingly. Lump sum expenditures can be processed on individual funds. At any point in time, the fund record can be retrieved to look at the allocation, encumbrances, expenditures, free balance, and cash balance. Encumbrance and expenditures limits can be set in rupees or in percentages, so that if an order will overencumber a fund, the screen will display a warning that the fund is overencumbered. Over-encumbrances can be overridden on the system, but over-expenditures cannot.

Because a moment-by-moment update of the financial information is available, acquisitions personnel creates a method of down-loading the name of the fund and the one line which contains the current status of the fund: allocation, encumbrances, expenditures, free balance, and cash balance. This down-loading is accomplished on an M300 and manipulated on an IBM-XT using Lotus 1-2-3. The result is a three-page summary fund report and an extended version which reports on the activity in every fund requiring review by the bibliographers in resource development.

The OCLC acquisitions subsystem allows the printing of claim and cancellation action forms by simply changing the status of the record to "clmmat" for claiming materials, "clminv" for claiming missing invoices, and "cancel" for cancellation of orders. Not all correspondence can be accommodated by the OCLC Acquisition System, but it does reduce the number of letters to be typed. The extensive use of PCs has further automated the acquisitions division.

Advantages and Disadvantages of OCLC ACQ are given below:

Advantages:

— The staff time has been saved by automating the accounting process and the ability to view current fund balances as necessary.

— OCLC provides offline products, such as the monthly Fund Commitment Record and the Fund Activity Record. Available on microfiche or paper, the activity on each OCLC fund is reported. The list is arranged alphabetically by fund name, and, within each fund, the arrangement is by vendor and then by purchase order number. For archival purposes and various management and problem-solving purposes, these off-line products are invaluable.

The ability to view the on-order file from an OCLC terminal. Library staff and patrons can search by title and determine whether a needed item has been ordered.

— All cataloged material and on-order materials are on the same system. When an order is being placed, the terminal operator can look in the upper left corner of the screen and determine at a glance whether the title has already been acquired because TXA will appear there if the item has been cataloged. If the item has already been ordered, but not received, the order record will be retrieved.

— Reduction of repetitive keying made possible by the OCLC database. Since the bibliographic data is often already on the screen, only the ordering information must be input. A related advantage is the "constant data" feature. A constant data screen can be set up with ordering or receiving details which apply to several items. By utilising this feature, the same information can be overlayed onto the order display, thereby saving many keystrokes.

— Only three lines need to be added to each title screen if the vendor remains the same. This serial expenditure advantage is further enhanced by "constant data" because many of the multiple-item invoices are quite lengthy, so the invoice information and fund name remains the same on each record.

Disadvantages

— The expense of using OCLC acquisitions.

— Tesponse time is one common to all OCLC users The response time fluctuates from micro-seconds to several minutes depending on the use of the database, and so on. This factor makes it difficult to estimate time needed to accomplish work.

— One must log off the acquisitions subsystem and log onto the cataloging subsystem in order to edit the bibliographic record and produce catalog cards. This aspect of the system originally caused the acquisitions division to decide against integrating copy cataloging with receipt of materials.

2
Effects of Automation

In a changing world, librarians have a responsibility not only to know about the ways in which libraries can use the techniques of automation, but also to be aware of the changes automation can bring to library service in the near and perhaps the more distant future. It is easy in this twentieth century to strive for change simply for its own sake, just as it is even easier to strive for retaining the status quo.

Those librarians whose task it is to decide for or against the particular change of automation need especially of be on their guard against these two attitudes. They need to make their decisions in the light of facts; facts about their libraries as they are now; what services are provided to what people by what library staff and at what cost, and similar facts about any proposed system of library automation.

A library has no different from any other office or factory considering the use of a computer to perform a given job of work most economically. Where the difference does arise, however, is in the concept of a library's service. A factory may charge a certain price for its products and so, hopefully, make an overall profit on its operations. In such circumstances a computer can be shown to act either to increase or to reduce profits.

But there are few libraries today which exist in order to make a profit for their owners, and few are required to balance an income from subscriptions against their expenses. How, then, can a price be set against the service which a library can provide, and how can this price be measured so that automation may be seen to be justified? An answer to these questions can be found in two ways.

Firstly, any industrial librarian knows that his job is to satisfy his company's information needs. He, a specialist in information work, can supply information to company employees more efficiently than they can obtain it themselves, and so the value of his library's service can be expressed in terms of minutes and hours of saved time, and hence in monetary terms. An analogous argument can be used of the reader service functions in university and public libraries.

Secondly, the value of a library's service can also be expressed quantitatively in terms of the chief librarian's bargaining power at meetings of the library committee, and so in terms of the hard cash voted to him to enable him to run his library.

It is possible, therefore, although difficult, to express the value of automated library systems in quantitative terms and so to compare an automated library with its conventional counterpart. The decision to automate or not to automate can then be taken in the full light of the facts. That this decision seems frequently to have been taken in ignorance of the facts does not invalidate the argument, nut serves merely to throw into clearer relief the well-known truths that librarians are, as a class, busy, that libraries struggle for enough money to buy all the books they want, let alone finance a proper automation feasibility study, and that it is much easier to obtain money to buy computer equipment than to buy books.

Furthermore, once the computer is working in the library it is seldom difficult to show that improved standards of service have resulted, even though it has probably not been possible to reduce the staff required, and even though the library's total overall expenditure will almost certainly have risen.

The final situation then in most cases, will be that improved library service has been bought at a price. If the librarian has been able to justify this to has committee, then, according to my argument, the automated system has at least "broken even".

We must look a little more closely into the reasons why a librarian might consider using a computer in his library in order to improve its working in some way. And the first kind of reason, which we shall term emotional, is one unfortunate outcome of the automation revolution through which the advanced nations of the world are now passing.

According to the emotional argument, computers are modern and efficient, a library which uses a computer in some way must necessarily also be efficient and forward-looking, and almost certainly therefore a "good" library. It is indeed true to say that those libraries which have introduced computer systems are modern and forward-looking. The automated systems may well be efficient and the library may be a good one. But it is certainly not necessarily true to say, as the emotional argument does, that if a library uses a computer then it will be all these things. That this reason exists at all, even if only as an attitude of mind, is a direct result of the false glamour ascribed to the computer and the shallow thinking and writing of those responsible for automating aspects of library routines. If, as seems likely, computers will fill a necessary role in libraries in the future, now is indeed the time for some libraries to experiment with ways and means of enabling computers to take their proper place in library work. These experiments should yield both qualitative and quantitative results. So far there have been too many of the former and too few of the latter kind.

A computer is an electronic machine for manipulating symbols. For out purposes, we can readily make this definition more meaningful if we say that a computer can be regarded in many ways as being like a clerk. And if it is a clerk, then we may be able to use it to do clerical work in libraries more quickly, accurately, and more efficiently than it is done at present. It might even be possible to teach it some professional or intellectual jobs. Being a machine it should not tire under heavy work loads, and in fact, should become more efficient as the work load increases so that as library grows this can be accommodated without proportionate increases in staff.

From what we know about computer applications in other fields, we should expect automation to be feasible only in larger libraries or in cases where a number of smaller libraries combine together to form one large unit for processing purposes. However, we know also that computer time is growing steadily chapter as newer, more advanced machines are devalued, whereas the time of human clerks is becoming steadily more expensive. So we predict that automation will gradually became feasible in smaller libraries. This trend will be accentuated somewhat by the emergence of very small, cheap computers, but it must be remembered that many library applications require a large machine.

Growth of on-line techniques, which are particularly suited to some areas of library work, will make it realistic for libraries to expect to have on-line access to a large and powerful machine, rather than consider purchasing a small machine for their own use. We are now witnessing the gradual birth of widespread cooperation among libraries, founded upon the fact that modern techniques of electronic data storage, processing, and transmission make possible the speedy and accurate exchange of bibliographic date.

New concepts of bibliographic control and library service are emerging as a direct result of computer applications to library work. A well-established set of procedures exists, leading from the point we have now reached, that of having stated in general terms the advantages which might be expected to accrue from using a computer, to that of installing, testing, and running an automated system in a library. To follow all these procedures faithfully might seem pedantic, perhaps unnecessary in many circumstances, but it is necessary if the job is to be done honestly, avoiding emotion, cultivating reason, and working in quantitative terms.

Because procedures will be enumerated and discussed in one particular way, it does not mean that this is the only way, or that different combinations and distributions of these procedures might not result in very different patterns of overall working; only that the basic ideas must follow one another in this way. The first step towards introducing an automated system is to carry out a feasibility study. This may be done at any level of detail, but the purpose is to ascertain whether or not a computer can be used to do a particular job more efficiently than heretofore.

A computer was not ledge that many such studies have shown that a computer was not really needed at all, and that the information gained from the feasibility study was sufficient to improve the existing system so as to make it more efficient than the automated one first contemplated. It is during the feasibility study that systems analysis takes place. The system, be it the whole library itself or only one department, is analysed; its method of working is systematically taken apart piece by piece, so that in the end all the pieces are known and understood, as are the ways in which they fit together to make the whole.

If only one department of the library is being investigated, the relationships between it and the other departments, and the library itself, must also be known and understood. Measurement will also take place so that the final result of the study can be in quantitative terms. Numbers will be counted; the numbers of items bought, catalogued, lost, circulated, damaged, and the way these number may be expected to change in the future will be discovered. Also counted will be the number of people needed to do the various jobs in the system, and the time to do each jobs in the system, and the time to do each job will be measured.

It is very important that the end results of all this library activity be calculated or estimated. This can be difficult because it is not easy to apply a measure to a student reading a book, a chemist pleased with a morsel of information, or a housewife experimenting with new dishes described in a cookery book borrowed from her local public library. It must be attempted, however, because any automated system, as we have seen, is likely to alter the pattern of service offered by the library, and this is as important in the final evaluation as the numbers of books ordered each week, or the time it takes to discharge an overdue book. From all these measurements the costs of the present system will be calculated. They will almost certainly be expressed as unit costs—the cost of cataloguing the "average" book, or answering the "typical" reference question.

Together with details of the services performed by the present system and in particular any difficulties and problems associated with it, any aspects which are like to become unsatisfactory in the light of future developments will be indicated, and all will be used by management to make an educated decision about the introduction of automation.

Because the introduction of computerised operations is not the only, and not necessarily the best solution to the problems that will have been brought to light, the next stage of the study is just to find the best solution, automated or not. It is highly desirable, therefore, that the study should be carried out by persons who have no direct interests in seeing that a computer system is installed, perhaps even using a particular make of computer. They should be perfectly free to advise on the optimal course of action.

Like wise, the investigators should have considerable experience of similar studies, and be well informed on all data processing and work study techniques. Needless to say there is a great shortage of such people. Feasibility studies, therefore, are not cheap and so are often skimped or omitted entirely.

If the introduction of automation is indicated, and this is the only case that really concerns us here, then the second stage of the study will involve the selection of a computer and the various necessary ancillary items of equipment and stationery needed by the system. There are considerable differences between the different makes and metals of computer on the market, so that the selection of the machine most suited to the purpose on hand will have a marked effect on the final operating efficiency of the system. The end result of this second stage of the study is a broad system specification. It will indicate the hardware or machinery required and, in general terms, how everything will work. The throughput or work load handled will be given, as will the estimated costs.

Staffing requirements will almost certainly be different from those of the old system, for keypunchers will replace clerks and it will be necessary to have a senior staff member, with data processing experience, in charge of operations and one or two programmes may be required on a permanent basis. Staff requirements will be very different where a library installs a computer for its own use, from the case where it merely uses a short time each week or someone else's machine.

Because computers work in ways radically different from human beings, the flow of work in an automated system can differ quite considerably from that in the corresponding manual system. Old departmental barriers can therefore be broken down of the introduction of automation, as similar processes in different departments are combined and as duplication of work is eliminated.

The overall organisational structures of the library can be materially altered, and this will be appreciated and stated in the feasibility study.

Once an automated system is considered in any detail it is apparent that it offers a range of possible products and services considerable winter than does a conventional system. The compilation of all kinds of statistics is but one example of this. A library can expect, therefore, to expand the scope of its operations by introducing mechanised routines, and it is desirable either that the team doing the study include a good knowledge of library service among their skills, or that one member of the library staff work closely with the team, in order that the full possibilities of winter operations are realised.

From the final report of the feasibility study it should be a comparatively simple matter for the library management to decide on a course of action. Only in the largest libraries would a feasibility study be likely to indicate clear overall cost reductions through introducing automated methods.

In other libraries the situation would almost certainly be that at the present time a computer-aided system would cost more but would bring additional advantages. It is up to the management to decide whether these advantages justify the increased costs, bearing in mind that, in time, costs will tend to change in favour of automation. If we assume that a decision is made in favour of automation, where does the library go from here? The answer is that the next stages in this idealised introduction of mechanisation will depend very considerably on the extent of the automation which is planned, on the organisational framework of which the library is a part, and no what we can term the library's computing environment. The procedures for implementing an automated circulation system, for example, will be different from those required by a system embracing all a library's technical processing routines.

In a university environment the library would expect to make use of a central university computing facility rather than purchase its own machine or use the services of a commercial bureau. This will affect not only the type of machine used, which is likely to be better suited to mathematical than to library work, and the languages programs are written in, but also, because programming may well be done in the computing laboratory, it will affect the staffing requirements in the library.

The overall computing policy of the organisation of which any library is a part will also affect such factors as, for example, the frequency with which computer runs can be made, or whether on-line working is, or is planned to be, available, and so be an important factor in the design of the library system.

In large organisations it not infrequently happens that a library in another division or department has already automated some of its functions. It may be possible to take these programs over just as they stand or with only small modifications. In the majority of instances, however, the library's computer system will have to be created from scratch. This stage—system design—can be regarded as consisting of two main parts, although in practice they can so merge together as to be indistinguishable. The first part involves floe-charting the ways in which the system will work, and then in more detail, the several operations and decisions performed by the computer in working the system. The second part, which is the job of programming, carries on in more detail and converts the flow charts into a sequence of computer instructions—a program. It is quite possible for one person, or one group of persons, to carry out both of these two steps, in which case the distinction between them is obscured. Alternatively, the second step, which has more of the character of straight forward routine than the first, can be performed by a programmer. In either case it is absolutely vital that at the stage of system design proper (step one) all the implications for the library of the various detailed decisions and operations which will be included in the final program are fully understood. This requirement can be achieved, as during the feasibility study, by having as senior library staff member work with the system design group, but, ideally, the system designer or designers should themselves be experienced librarians.

Few people, even nowadays when their great worth is appreciated, are at the same time experienced librarians and knowledgeable and up to date in computing matters. If it is vital that an automated library system be designed with all its implications for librarianship in mind, it is, at the very least, highly desirable that the programs are written so as to make the system as efficient as possible from a computing point of view. So library systems are very often designed as a cooperative venture between library and computing department staff in order to assemble together the necessary skills and expertise. The work is often done as a sideline, or even in staffs' own time. That so much sound work has been more rapid and more quantitative analyses made had these methods of working been less common. Where it is difficult to find the time to design and implement automated system, the detailed analyses and comparisons necessary for its full justification and evaluation naturally tend to be skimped or omitted. Overall impressions are substituted and, as a result, the library profession wherein the arguments of emotion can flourish.

The languages in which computer programs for library routines are written are important subjects for discussion at the present time. For mathematical, commercial, and other special kinds of work, a number of high-level programming languages have been defined. These make it easy for the programmer because the programming language can be quite similar in form and content to the language ordinarily used in the particular discipline. The price paid for this programming facility is a less efficient use of machine time. This is unimportant in one-off jobs, but it becomes a major factor in library systems where a program is run frequently.

A further advantage of high-level languages is that they can often be run on many different makes and types of computer; on all machines, in fact, for which a special translating or compiler program has been written. This takes each instruction in the high-level language and converts it into the necessary number of detailed machine instructions for the computer concerned.

Programs written in high-level languages can thus be exchanged widely, to the overall conservation of programming manpower. Because of the machine inefficiency of high-level languages, library programs tend to be written in what are termed low-level languages. These make better use of computer time but, being less similar to natural language and requiring the use of quite detailed instructions, make greater demands on the programmer's time and ability. They are generally applicable to only make or series of computers, and so do not permit free exchange and utilisation of programs. In a situation where computing power is at a premium, library programs will tend to be written in low-level languages at the expense of programming manpower.

Where programming manpower is at a premium, the tendency will be to use high-level languages at the expense of computing power. Present trends are beginning to indicate that, in future, library programs will be written in high-level languages and exchanged freely in order to save the very considerable effort which would be entailed were each library top design and program its own systems.

When a program, has finally been written, it must then be tested, or "de-bugged", to remove as many as possible of the errors which the fallible human system-designers and programmers will have written into it. This is generally done by running the programs with test date to simulate as many as possible of the circumstances that are likely to arise in real-life working.

It is at this stage that the value of an experienced programmer is most apparent. He will have written fewer errors into the program to start with and will be able to discover more readily why things go wrong when they do, and be able to put them right. Programming skill in this respect is particularly valuable when working with low-level languages. After this stage the program is ready to being work with real library data, nut it is usual to place one more safeguard against error in the machine system by working the new system in parallel with the old for a few months. After this period, if everything is satisfactory, the support provided by the old system in event of failure of the new is removed and the automated system, having been thoroughly tried, takes over full responsibility.

Machines, of course, like human beings, are not infallible and they do from time to time make mistakes or break down. A "safety net" must therefore be provided so that in the event of machine failure no data is lost and the system can carry on, or safely suspend operations until the failure can be rectified. Such a safely suspend operations until the failure can be rectified. Such a safety net can be provide with a coarse or with a fine mesh, the latter being more expensive. A coarse-meshed net, commonly termed a "fail soft" subsystem, permits only limited degree of confusion and disruption of operations to result from machine failure.

A net with fine mesh, a "fail safe" subsystem, constitutes an analogous set of producers with allow operations to continue normally with, hopefully, no confusion. The sort of net employed in each situation will be determined by the importance of the particular system and the value to be placed on keeping the relevant records intact. For example, a library could not possibly allow any of its shelf list records to be accidentally destroyed, while it would be of little consequence if overdue letters for student book loans were not sent because of machine failure.

Once an automated library system is working satisfactorily, it becomes important that it should continue to do so. Procedures in the event of machine failure are only one aspect of this general problem. Equally important is the need to establish a good working relationship between the library and the computing department so that the desired standard of library service is maintained.

A library system usually demands that a computer run be made at a stated time each day, week, or month. For example, where a university library has introduced a computerised circulation system, it is necessary that an updated printout of books on loan should be available in the circulation department each day. If anything cases this printout to be delayed, then the work of the circulation department will be hindered.

In fact, in the case of circulation control it is true to say that the whole justification of an automated system hinges on the daily printout being available at the right time each day. Library work must often therefore receive high priority in the computing department, and this can be difficult to achieve. In some organisations, however, computing policy, and thus the order of priority of the different users, is determined by a special computing committee and not by the head of the computing department.

If the library can put a sufficiently strong case to such a committee, then the necessary degree of priority will be guaranteed and, consequently, the desired quality of library service ensured. In some instances the first move towards library automation comes from within the computing department, and then this difficulty should not arise if the importance of priorities is emphasised by the librarian from the early stages of the project.

The correct note will be sounded, if, instead of speaking simply about "changes" in computer science, we use the word "improvement" and say that improvement are continually and very rapidly being made to computers and the ways in which they can be used. This it is certain that within a few years of introducing a particular automated system, improvements in computers will make it possible to redesign the system for a more modern machine so as to extend the scope of what is being done and to do it more cheaply. Of course it may well happen that the particular computer used by the library will not have been replaced so quickly and improvements which would be made possible by a newer machine cannot be made. It is unusual for a given computer to remain in service for more than 10 years, and after 5 years newer machines will being to make a change very desirable. The implications for libraries of this state of flux are very considerable, especially since, until recently, libraries have exhibited only a very slow rate of change.

Librarians, despite or perhaps because of the conservations they display in relation to changes in libraries, show a remarkable interest in the very latest computing techniques that are either still in the early experimental stages or no more than ideas in designers' brains.

These future developments invariably hold out the promise of solving all the world's problems of bibliographic organisation, and, perhaps not unnaturally, librarians grasp eagerly at them. But when the full implications of such developments are pointed out in terms of the sacrifices and changes each library would have to make in order to adopt them, then the former panacea can become less attractive.

Once a program has been implemented in a library it will not be long before the need will become apparent to make small additions and changes to it. These must be done by a programmer and will sometimes involve considerable alterations in the whole structure of the program.

Where automation in a library has progressed beyond an elementary stage, it will become very desirable for the library to have a programmer on its permanent staff and perhaps a more senior person, a systems analyst, as well.

An embryonic data processing department will have been created within the library because of this requirement for constant minor change and improvement. It will have responsibilities in all the conventional library departments where automated routines have been introduced and must have the authority to see that any changes are made in such a way that they satisfy the requirements of efficiency laid down for the system itself.

Once such as department of data processing has been established, a library will be in a good position to keep abreast of advance in computer science and will be able to modify the library's own systems from time to time to take fullest advantage of changes in the facilities offered in the computing unit where the library's work is done. Being actually on the library's own permanent staff, members of the library data processing department will be able to take full account of the librarianship aspects of their work.

This is the ideal situation, and where a library is introducing automation on anything more than a very limited scale, the establishment of such a department should be given high priority.

In order to complete this picture of libraries and automation it is necessary to try to look a short distance into the future, to see what development are likely to come about in computing and how libraries will be able to use them.

Because of the rapid rate of change in the field of automations, such future knowledge becomes essential if one is fully to understand the present situation and to know how to plan for library systems which will become operational in a few years' time.

There is one fairly recent development in this which should be of the greatest importance in the future. And because here is something which is with us now, holding potentially great possibilities for the future, it is possible to speak with some certainty.

There now exist in Britain a number of working parties, each active in some areas of the field of library automation. Each owes its existence to the fact that a number of library automation. Each owes its existence to the fact that a number of libraries are cooperating and pooling their resources to speed progress.

Some of the working parties are designing systems for a particular make of computer, while others have no such limitation. Some are concentrating on the problems of one particular type of library, while others consider all types of library. It is beginning to seem likely that when these groups finally produce viable systems each will be adopted with little or no change by several libraries.

One group in particular is designing a book-ordering system in such a way that it includes most of the features required by libraries and can readily be altered to cater for special individual preferences. This cooperation will be of the greatest importance in future.

Now, and always, it makes possible savings in programming effort and speeds the introduction of automation where this has been shown to be justified. When cataloguing data in machineable from become more generally available, for example, its use by individual libraries will be facilitated where numbers of libraries are using identical or similar cataloguing systems. The situation will be similar where a new technique or piece of equipment becomes available to a group of libraries which are using one type of computer.

A new improved program need be written once only to be capable of adoption by all members of the group. Once a group of libraries have automated all or some of their activities and have proved this to be an advantage, other libraries will find it to their advantage either to adopt the common systems as they stand or with the minimum possible alterations. Among university libraries at least, programs will be made available freely. It is much easier to talk of library cooperation in this way then to achieve it in practice.

Although all libraries are the same to the extent that they buy, catalogue, store, and lend books and other material, they do differ considerably in that they buy different kinds of books, catalogue them in different ways, and serve many different types of readers. Accordingly, libraries have developed in many different ways, and rightly so.

But it is nonetheless true that when comparing the various methods of performing a given job, the differences tend to be in matters of detail, and that underneath is a large area of common practice. This makes it reasonable to expect that cooperating libraries will be able to accept large segments of automated systems as they stand and will need to later only details. It is true that some apparently trivial differences in points of detail can make the adoption of a whole system impossible, but such cases are the exception rather than the rule. There is a very broad spectrum of different types of library, each with different needs, but it should be possible for the whole spectrum of needs to be satisfied by there or four major types of automated system.

Three such divisions of the spectrum of libraries might be as follows:

a) Small libraries, having simple cataloguing needs and buying straightforward material from limited number of suppliers.

b) Medium and large libraries, buying a wide range of materials from all parts of the world, with cataloguing needs more complex than type (a) but not so demanding as (c). Full control of circulation is needed and individual treatment, particularly as regards cataloguing, is required for special collections. Most university and public libraries would fall into this class.

c) National and other very large libraries with complex acquisition procedures for all types of library materials. Fully detailed cataloguing is necessary for very large catalogues which may have to be related to the production of a national bibliography.

Despite our understandable attachment to our differences, we accept standardisation because of the clear advantages it offers. The greatest pressures towards standardisation will come in the area of cataloguing as a result of advances in the practice of librarianship that are associated with the introduction of automation. Three events are combining together at the present time which are potentially capable of effecting very great changes in library practice throughout the world.

Firstly, the Library of Congress Shared Cataloguing Program is extending the scope of the Library of Congress printed catalogue card service to include all material from western European countries. Secondly, the introduction of standard book numbering in Britain, besides facilitating the acquisition of books by libraries, provides a unique tag for each book which can readily be handled by computer, and enables cataloguing copy for new books to be recorded by the British National Bibliography from 3 to 6 weeks before publication. If standard book numbering is adopted by other countries, and there is good reason to hope that it will, be then the cataloguing copy provided by the Library of Congress shared Cataloguing Program will also be available a similar period before publication. The third event, or rather programme of events, is the Library of Congress MARC (Machine-Readable Cataloguing) Project. When this has been fully implemented it will make the cataloguing copy, collected in advance of publication by the Shared Cataloguing Program, available to libraries in machineable form.

The format of these machineable catalogue records is designed to facilitate the exchange of cataloguing copy between libraries and to enable individual libraries to modify and adapt the records to their own particular needs. Such modification can be of two kinds, programmable and non-programmable. Programmable alterations can be performed automatically by the computer when the machineable catalogue record is added to the library's own internal records. They included standard abbreviating operations on headings, descriptions, and classification number, and the reformatting of entries. The basic idea behind such programmable alternations is that they are standard.

Non-programmable alterations involve human intervention and are needed whenever part of a catalogue record must be changed to some form that cannot be derived by algorithm from the original record. All such alterations cost money and the non-programmable ones will be the more expensive of the two kinds. Centrally produced cataloguing copy, of course, has been with us for some time, and it has been bought by many libraries, especially in the United States.

Two drawbacks have prevented its more widespread use; the comparative slowness of the service and the low percentage of libraries' total acquisitions covered. Both these disadvantages should expect to have approximately 70-80 per cent of their new acquisition covered by the Library of Congress service.

Librarians have long realised the advantages of central cataloguing service and have been aware of the great waste of effort when books are catalogued in each library where copies are bought. Now it is likely that this long-standing dream will soon materialise. Another librarians' dreams may also be realised over the next few decades as a result of this cooperation in cataloguing: the national catalogue given the holdings of all libraries in the country and also containing entries for all new books as they are published, able to be searched by computer from remote on-line terminals, appears to librarians to solve very many of the problems that they have today. There are very great obstacles of the problems that they have today.

There are very great obstacles to be overcome before such a catalogue can be made a reality, but work being done now leads one to expect that it will eventually come to exist. Machineable copy for all new books it almost with us and the investigations now in progress 9 on how to convert the entries in the British Museum catalogue to machineable from should enable a very large corpus of existing catalogue material to be included in the national catalogue. The very real difficulties in programming a machine catalogue search by author and title, cased by inconsistencies in cataloguing, can be overcome by standard book numbers for new books and for old ones.

Direct access computer memories are rapidly increasing in size and should cause no serious problems. The remote on-line techniques are already with us. The advantages of such a catalogue are considerable. Primarily, it will give the locations of material listed in it and remove almost all the inefficiency and frustration from existing systems of inter-library lending. As such, it will be a major adjunct to national scholarship.

Libraries will be able to extract cataloguing data for new acquisitions directly from it by means of on-line consoles. This act will automatically indicate a location in that library for the items concerned. Local catalogues, whether printed on paper or kept only in machine memory, will list the most frequently used material only.

Thus, great savings will be realised in catalogue printing costs or in machine memory storage devoted permanently to library catalogues. Uniformity in cataloguing practice will be further encourage. It is questionable, however, whether such a catalogue will be searchable by subject. From this point on, libraries' dreams of the future begin to bring the handling of textual material within the scope of systems of automation.

Facsimile transmission of photographs is an everyday occurrence in the newspaper industry where speed is all important and where the volume of information is comparatively small. Transmission of printed pages by these means is practicable and economical over short distances where there is a high traffic density, but up to the present there has been little demand from libraries for higher transmission speeds than those provided by sending photocopies through the post. Prophecies of libraries where the codex and the printed page have been replaced by digital storage devices and where a computing facility has taken over the task of literature searching is very exciting and attractive, both to librarians and to those scholars who really are overwhelmed by their century's information explosion.

Although many people would regret the passing of the codex and although the combination of the printed page, the codex, and the library is embarrassingly efficient as a machine for storing data and providing rapid random access to it, there is no doubt that many research workers would welcome real assistance with their information gathering problems.

Good assistance would be provided by a skilled librarian, but in a world where skilled people are in short supply it is likely that some machine system will eventually take over this task. The techniques that such a machine would use may be quite different from those now used in libraries, but the end result would be the same.

Our task as librarians is both to design these techniques and to see that we do not hinder their adoption, where appropriate, by arguing from emotion. One such technique, now with us, may be that of bibliographic coupling, and certainly the methods now being developed for machine processing of natural language texts will have an important role to play in the operation of this future automated library.

Automation has affected most library processes to some extent, and in many cases has influenced the development of library policy. The effects may be seen in four general areas:

1) Extent of cataloguing information presented to the users
2) Choice of information given
3) Arrangement of information
4) Typographical presentation of such information.

Librarians, however, have bemoaned the "upper-case mentality" of computers and related machines since their use in library work began. The resulting catalogues were certainly less attractive and less readable than the printed or typed cards with which most people were familiar. Within a few months of Clapp's talk, however, the situation began to change. It did cost a substantial amount in computer processing time, however, which led to its abandonment by Atlantic University.

Photocomposition machines, which did not share this handicap, later became available, and in some cases offered the additional advantage of a wider variety of type faces and images than older printing techniques. Microform catalogues and computer terminal displays have encountered the same problem, but both have now advanced at least to the stage that acceptable upper and lower case characters in the Roman alphabet are available. Non-Roman alphabets and nonalphabetic characters are still a problem, but the capacity for providing these exists if the demand becomes sufficient.

Changes in the extent of cataloguing information presented to the user under each entry have been mainly deletions rather than additions, and such changes are most frequently seen in book catalogue projects. Virtually every descriptive element has been eliminated or abbreviated in one project or another. The Boeing SLIP catalogue restricts author's forenames to one and represents the others by initials; other catalogues give only initials, with no forenames.

The University of Rochester catalogues limit the main entry to twenty-one spaces, with necessitates a substantial amount of abbreviation in corporate authors. Collation is perhaps the most frequently abridged set of elements. Standford and Florida Atlantic give pagination only, and many catalogs give no collation at all. Notes and tracings are also frequently omitted, with the exception of series and contents notes in a few cases.

The ONULP (Ontario New University Libraries Project) catalogs, however give full tracings under main entries, as does the National Library of Medicine Current Catalogue, the latter because other medical libraries use the catalogue as a source of cataloguing information. In many catalogues the amount and type of abridgement varies according to the type of entry involved.

Normally the main entry is reasonably full, and most abbreviation or abridgement takes place in added entries. In the Los Angeles County catalogue, however, the subject entries are more complete than the author entries, because the subject entries include an annotation.

The practice of abridging entries has been justified on several grounds. Undoubtedly it began, especially in catalogs produced with unit record equipment such as the University of Rochester listings, because of the eight-column limitation of punched cards and the printing limitations of tabulators. As Weinstein and George have noted, "the one-to-one, punched card/printed line relationship, and line-length/field-length compromises, all encourage brevity of entry.

However, the elimination of data elements also reflect a desire to cut costs. Simonton has viewed it "as a reflection of the traditional policy of many of these libraries of shortening the bibliographical record for more economical processing." Another justification is based on the shorter life expectancy of the book catalogue as compared to the traditional card catalogue:

> As [card] catalogues serve as the basis for the permanent record and their cost can be prorated over several decades the need for a careful description of the many facets of a book is quite properly justified. In the case of a book is quite properly justified. In the case of catalogue supplements, however, where the record will serve quite likely for only a few months, any attempt at detailed description of the book cannot be justified.

Many catalogs of special libraries have provided additional subject headings, however, taking advantage of the ease with which machines can reproduce entries under various headings. Most book catalogs also reproduce title entries for all items in the catalogue, not just those with "distinctive" titles, and as mentioned in the discussion of the Boeing SLIP catalogue some also "permute" the titles so that they appear several times for each work, under each significant word in each title.

The choice of main entry has long been a critical issue in cataloguing policy and in the development of cataloguing rules, but with the advent of machine-produced book catalogues the need for the concept of "main entry" may be questioned. When catalogue cards were printed or typed by hand, it made economic sense to produce only one card, with the data arranged in a standard format under a "main entry," and then to reproduce other cards as needed, typing only the added headings required after the "unit cards" had been duplicated.

Computers, however, can rearrange data in any fashion deemed appropriate, so this rationale is no longer applicable. Despite this fact, many book catalogs continue to follow the unit card and main entry concepts. The ONULP catalogue, for example, print the author under each title entry, and then repeat the title a practice that would appear to have no justification except for mechanically reproduced catalogue cards. A few book, catalogue projects have abandoned this anachronistic practice and reproduce entries under various headings without any attempt to designate one as the "main" entry, even though the entries under each heading are still "unit" entries. Abandonment of the main entry concept, it should be pointed out, also means abandoning and attempt to designate the person or body primarily responsible for the intellectual content of a work, but clearly it makes the choice of entry less critical, particularly in difficult case such as conference proceedings, where the choice between conference title, sponsoring body or editor may be little more than arbitrary.

The greatest effects of automation on cataloguing practice to data has been in the arrangement of entries in relation to each other. Virtually all book catalogs are divided catalogs, abandoning the so-called dictionary arrangement that interfiles all types of entries in a single sequence. The type of division is not consistent from one catalogue to another. Some have separate author, title, and subject sections; some combine author and title entries in one catalogue with a separate subject section; and at least one combines titles and subjects, with the author entries separate.

Regardless of the method of division, however, two principal reasons are usually given for the arrangement: users make different uses of subject entries as opposed to author and title entries, according to a number of user studies, and the filing or sequencing of entries can be simplified if all types of entries are not interfiled. The latter reason is normally the more urgent when automation is involved.

Catalogues can be divided without being automated, and if ease of use were the only justification for division there would be no reason to attribute the popularity of the practice to automation. Filing, however, is another matter, and simplification of filing for automation purposes is undoubtedly the main reason for the predominance of the practice. Computers can sequence and arrange data with extreme speed and accuracy if given explicit rules for doing so, but traditional library filing arrangements are a mixture of alphabetical, chronological and other sequences presumed to be "logical," with numerous general and specific exceptions. In addition to the complexity of the rules, many of them are based on the ability of human filers to recognize information that is only implicit, not explicitly stated, and computers can work only with explicit data.

At least five categories of difficulty may be identified:

1) Information in the headings must be ignored or removed in order fore computers to sort it acceptably. Honorific titles such as "Sir" in proper names are also commonly disregarded, so that "Drake, Sir Francis" files as "Drake, Francis."

2) Information that is implicit must be made explicit. A common example is "U.S.—History—Civil War," which as a subdivision of "U.S.—History" files not alphabetically under "C" but chronologically, as if it were "U.S.—History—1861-1865." This category of problems is perhaps the most difficult for computers to deal with because there are no clues for most such instances, sand the number of "as if" situations in most current filing practices is large. It is also the least defensible. "Dr." is filed as if were spelled "Doctor" or "Doktor," depending on the language of the text, nut if the reader does not know the rule, or has only a title such as "Dr. Jacob Dubs" to go on, he may miss the entry entirely. "Mrs.," and presumably "Mac," although McKenzies insist they are not Mackenzies. Numbers are a special example of the "as if" problem; they file as if spelled out (again depending on the language of the text) at the beginning of titles, but file as numbers, in numerical sequence, in headings for numbered conferences, series and so forth.

3) Information in headings must be rearranged in order for machines top sort it into the desired sequence. "Charles II, King of England" must be

read as 'charles, King of England, II"—or actually, since there is also a numeral in this case and the second category of difficulty comes into play, as "Charles, King of England, 2."

4) Exceptions must be made to alphabetic order. Some rules require that entries beginning with the same word or phrase be sub-arranged not alphabetically by the next filing element but by bibliographic function (authors, then subjects, then titles, for example), or according to the type of entity the heading describes (persons), then places, then things).

5) Punctuation is even a problem, because of complications introduced both by the machines and by filing rules. Computers regard punctuation marks as character just as letters and numerals, and sort them into a certain order (differing to some extent by brand of machine) unless programmed to do otherwise. Extra spaces inadvertently inserted by humans will affect machine filing order as well. Existing rules differ on the treatment of certain marks, for example, whether "Brewer's Dictionary of Phrase and Fable" should be filed as "Brewers" or "Brewers," and "Mott-Smith" as "Mott Smith" or "MottSmith."

The ideal solution to these various problems is unclear, but attempts to solve them in automated catalogs have produced a significant amount of change as compared with manually filed catalogs. Most projects have used a combination of four basic approaches:

1) Continue to follow present filing rules, using people to assign additional codes to headings as necessary

to allow computers to arrange the headings as desired.

2) Abandon present filing rules, and use the arrangements produced by the computer's sorting sequences with a minimum amount of change.

3) Change the headings themselves as necessary so that computers can arrange them in accordance with very simple filing rules.

4) Attempt to program computers so that they will arrange headings automatically, either by present filing rules or by modifications of them.

Florida Atlantic University used the first approach in its book catalogue, the first edition of which was published in 1964. "Nonfile" symbols were used to indicate to the computer that portions of an entry were to be ignored in filing. Determination of when the symbols were to be added and actually adding them were of course operations performed by human beings. A considerable amount of manual coding was performed in the University's main card catalogue. Entries were sorted not on the text of the entries themselves but on separate "sort keys" composed of a total of 100 characters, 80 from the filing element (the author, added entries or subject headings) and 20 additional characters from the title, which was used throughout the catalogue for sub-arrangement of entries under each heading. An obvious disadvantage of extended use of sorting and filing codes was noted at Stanford: the technique requires manual maintenance of authority files, very careful inputting, and very careful editing and proofreading.

Few projects have attempted the second alternative, because of the radical differences from traditional filing that would result, but a number of catalogs have used the third approach—changing the headings so the computer would arrange them in accordance with simplified but more or less traditional filing rules.

Usually such projects have taken a strictly pragmatic approach, solving the simplest problems and ignoring the others. The Baltimore County book catalogue, first published in 1965, is an example. Initial articles, titles of honour and such designations as "ed." or "comp." were omitted from headings during input, which of course meant that they were ignored not only in filing but also in printing.

Abbreviations, numerals, and symbols such as the ampersand were written out. Some titles were rearranged, e.g., titles of annual reports were input as "annual report," followed by the date. In all other cases, the computer sequencing was accepted as it came.

The foremost advocates of changing headings to produce the desired sequence have been Theodore Hines and Jessica Harris. In 1963, Hines urged that "filing should be a purely mechanical operation which can be reduced to a straight forward arrangement of sorts and nuls. The filer or program should not be expected to expand or interpret entries for filing purposes. These functions should be shifted to the formation of entries." Publication of the Hines-Harris code created a storm of protest. One reviewer warned, "This little book seems likely to do more harm than good. The end it proposes may be laudable, but the means are not. The book rests on the proposition that what is awkward for the machines must be eliminated and the simplicities of the machine system imposed on non-machine processes." Another criticized the proposal for failing to make efficient use of the computer: "Entries are arranged only after the format has been decided by a human.... If we must spend professional time in this manner, what, then, is the advantage of using the computer?"

The fourth approach, which is the extreme—attempting to program the computer to follow traditional rules as closely as possible— was taken by William R. Nugent of Inforonics, Inc., in a study commissioned by the Council on Library. Resources. Unlike most proposals which advocated sorting abbreviations and similar exceptional cases "as is" rather than "as if," Nugent proposed a system of "substitution notes" which would continue traditional "as if" filing. Extensive rules to permit arrangements by category (under Bible entries, anonymous classics, and corporate authors, for example) were also suggested. In not every case, however, was Nugent happy with his assignment to propose ways of "programming the LC Filing Rules."

> If one set out deliberately to destroy the simple precision of numerical hierarchy, little worse could be done than to insist that numbers be ordered by the spelled out equivalents of their spoken sound. In this writer's view, the present filing rule should be quickly replaced by one in which all cardinal or ordinal numbers, whether in alphabetic or numeric from, would be ordered by their elementary numeric from.... As this is unlikely to occur with any haste, it will probably be necessary to write programs to covert the numeric portions of entries to alphabetic from.

He then pointed out that it would be necessary to devise further rules to ensure consistency, because "1810" could be written out as "eighteen ten," "one thousand eight hundred ten" or "one eight one and the existing LC Rules convert such numbers "to differing forms by application of some unspecified and doubtless unprogrammable subtlety." This kind of problem of necessity led Nugent to propose various types of manual coding as well as elaborate programming.

Perhaps the most thoroughgoing and thoughtful consideration of the entire range of automated filing problems is in a series of papers by John C. Rather, Chief of the Technical Process Research Office in the Library of Congress. In February 1970 Rather distributed a working paper entitled Filing Arrangement in the Library of Congress Catalogs within LC and to a limited extent outside it, setting forth a series of principles and basic approaches. Consensus within the Library led to public distribution of a full set of rules with the same title the following year.

In 1972, the principles and basic approaches were elaborated in print, accompanied by an abridged version of the rules. They have since been used as the basis for a computer program to arrange MARC records and produce a variety of book catalogs for LC. Since they are also being considered for using in automatic preparation of the National Union Catalogue, their significance is obvious. Rather is eloquent on the dangers of changing headings merely because of the filing difficulties they present in automated systems. The complexities of catalogue headings and their arrangement are not attributable primarily to the rules that govern them; they arise from the varieties of materials being catalogued and the size of the catalogue being maintained. The need to differentiate names in the catalogue while still conveying intelligible information about the name result in forms of heading that indubitably present difficulties of arrangement.

The fundamental conflict between the function of headings as units of intelligence and their function as filing guides cannot be underestimated, but the integrity of the heading must necessarily take precedence over any attempt to structure it so that it files "automatically." Or, to put the matter succinctly, headings do not exist merely to be filed. Rather thus eschews revision of headings for the sake of filing convenience, but he also advocates abandonment of the "as if" or "file as spoken" tradition, and for essentially the same reasons. Variations in form among name and subject headings are an essential part of the structure of a file arrangement; they should not be ignored in filing. It is illogical to construct a heading on way and then to file it as if it were constructed another way. The three basic principles of his code are

1) Elements in a heading should be taken in exactly the form and order in which they appear.

2) Related entries should be kept together if they would be difficult to find when a user did not know their precise from.

3) A standard set of fields should be established for each major type of filing entry.

The first principle "emphasizes the way a heading looks, not how it sounds," the second "preserves important values offered by the present arrangement of the LC catalogues," and the third "applies the legal precept 'De minimis non curat lex' (the law cannot take care of trifles) as a way of preventing the proliferation of special rules."

Since Rather's rules have already met with general acceptance at LC and been used to produce several book catalogs, and since a computer program already exists to arrange MARC entries following these rules, their influence is likely to be evident in cataloguing practice for some time to come. Another important influence on the arrangement of cataloguing information has been the use of on-line techniques. By 1968, Stanford University's on-line BALLOTS project had evolved a technique of filing machine-readable catalogue entries not by any of the usual rules, but in an arbitrarily arranged file with indexes by various bibliographic elements, such as author, title, topical subjects, and so forth.

The significant and important aspect of the technique, however, was that the position of each entry in the author and title indexes was computed directly from the data itself, using the first three letters from the author's last name and the words of the title. The computer, of course, followed the same procedure in retrieving the index entries on command. In effect, the actual filing arrangement of the "catalogue" was transparent to the user. This technique of "derived keys" was being studied by several researchers at about this time. Nugent described four different "compression coding" techniques, and Kilgour and Ruecking reported the results of separate tests using various combinations of characters from author and title entries for retrieval purposes.

In 1970, Kilgour and two associates analysed the effectiveness of derived keys varying from four to eight characters in length for retrieval of name and title entries taken from a sample of 132,808 entries. They concluded that a "3,3" key—that is, the first three characters of the author's last name and the first three character of the title-would retrieve five or fewer entries 99 percent of the time. Further experiments with titles only produced similar results. The results of this research led to the use of 3,3 keys for name and title searches and 3.1,1,1 key for title-only searches in the design of the Ohio College Library Centre (OCLC) system, and the technique has been one of the major factors in OCLC's success. The implications of this practice, while perhaps not immediately obvious, are nevertheless enormous. In effect, when the user names a key of six characters, he designates what Kilgour has called a "micro-catalogue" of five or fewer entries, on average, or twenty or fewer entries 95 percent of the time. Because ten entries can be displayed on the screen of the on-line terminal used by OCLC participants, and twenty entries require only two screen displays, the desired entry is easily chosen. "Such a catalogue," comment Kilgour, "makes it necessary to include bibliographical embellishments required for entries in huge card or book-from catalogs," and of course it also makes unnecessary the solution of the filing rule problems discussed earlier. Nor are the implications of such on-line techniques necessarily limited to OCLC participants, at least not for long.

3

Digitisation in Libraries

The technological advances are discernible in the hardware materials used in the machine and its operational processes. The computer designed in different periods by using advanced technology has been specified by the term 'generation'; e.g., the pre-1959 computer is called the first generation computer; the computer designed between 1959 and 1964, the second generation computer; the computer of the period between 1964 and the late seventies, the third generation computer; and so on.

In different generations, the material used in the computer have been changed for each and every part of machine—the memory, the arithmetic and logic unit, input/output processes etc. In the first generation computer, dating prior to 1959, vacuum tubes were used and all functions were performed in the central processor unit. In the second generation, dating from 1959 to 1964, transistors were used. These had considerable effect on the computer which gradually became smaller in size and lesser expensive in cost. The third generation computer was built with integrated circuits by making use of microelectronics for the components introduced in 1964. The magnetic media were used for the memory storage. The fourth generation computer came into being in the late seventies using advanced microelectronic concepts to get further circuit densities. The new circuits were microscopic. The size became smaller still and the cost, less expensive. At the same time, the capability for storage and performance of the operational systems increased greatly.

Modern technological advances had an overall impact on the computer hardware in all aspects-the machine, operations and the cost. The primary impact on the machine was the diminishing of size. The earlier computer was large enough. The weight of ENIAC was 30 tons. It consumed much electricity and produced much heat. The second and the third generation computers became smaller and smaller as a result of the use of electronics and microelectronics.

There are more than 50,000 integrated circuits in a modern computer, but the size is smaller than that of the earlier computer. The size of a modern computer has been reduced considerably by using a wafer-like material—the silicon chip. It is possible to pack over 2,00,000 components in one square inch of the silicon chip. It is expected that smaller chips will be able to accommodate even more components in future. The chip is an extraordinary material for the computer hardware, because of its low cost, compact electronics and capability to embody the logic and the memory units.

A large number of microelectronic circuitry can be fabricated on a small chip which lead to 'very large-scale integration' used in a modern computer. A chip can store a very large amount of information, and so it is known as the memory chip. A microprocessor is the 'computer on a chip' combining memory with logic functions. Using the chip the computer is becoming cheaper and more powerful, day by day. A computer stores a large quantum of data in the memory, much in the cache memory and performs complex operations for various computations. So, it should be perfectly reliable. The vacuum tubes were not so reliable. The transistors had also certain flaws. They sometimes broke off from circuit boards. The chip has no soldered wires and each circuitry is more compact. So, the failure points are almost nil, and it has become most reliable.

Furthermore, it is tiny and the electronic signals can move through it very quickly and thus save time. The probability of failure or committing mistakes is almost nil. Moreover, self-repairing computers are also being produced. The sophisticated magnetic media and the silicon ship brought about a major break-through in the storage of data and information.

The magnetic media like the magnetic tape of offline service and the magnetic drum or disc for online service can hold more information than their counterparts in the earlier computers. Magnetic cores are proved to be efficient storage media requiring less space and working with greater speed. They are inexpensive and compact in size. Millions of magnetic cores can be accommodated in a small cabinet. Random access is provided much faster. The time for access to documents can be measured in nanoseconds. The early chips could perform work with greater speed than magnetic cores.

The large scale integrated (LSI) circuit storage elements were used. In modern chips, very large scale integrated (VLSI) circuits are being used. It has increased the storage capacity in a comparatively smaller space. Computers are becoming smaller in size, but of larger storage capacity owing to the advancement of hardware technology. The speed in operation has become faster and the output, of greater reliability because of reduction in size. Now, least time is required by electronic pulses to travel because the distance is shorter in modern hardware. Thus, the speed of the processor has increased. The calculation time in the 1970's increased several hundred times more than what was in the 1950's. More than a million of calculations can be made in a second. The speed of the early computers was measured in milliseconds, i.e. thousandths of a second; the second generation speed was expressed in microseconds, i.e. millionths of a second and the next generations of computers in nanoseconds, i.e. billionths of a second. It does not come within human perception.

The computer job of ten hours in the 1950's came down to a few seconds' hob in the 1970's and now the very same job can be performed in the tiny fraction of a second. This can be done also in a time-sharing and multiprogramming operation.The new innovations in hardware technology, particularly storage media, microelectronics, VLSI, etc., have reduced the cost of the computer. Not only the cost of machines is reducing, but the cost of maintenance and operation is also being reduced because of the low consumption of electricity compared to that of the earlier computers.

The cost of computer instructions has also been reduced because of greater speed. As the computer capability is increasing more and more, so the cost is becoming lesser and lesser. A wide range of general-purpose and special-purpose computers is being used in libraries. Computers are also available in various sizes and with various systems adaptable to various specific-purpose applications. Mainframe computers, mini-computers, microcomputers, microprocessors etc., are the types which can be used in libraries. These can be used independently or in interconnected systems with master-slave relationship or network relationship. Computerisation may be implemented as an integrated system with a mainframe computer or part by part with mini-or microcomputers to be interconnected in future. Such alternative make library automatic financially viable.

Planning and management also become efficient, cost-effective and result-oriented. Mainframe computers are usually host systems for several libraries or information centres. These computers are time-sharing and multiprogramming, and an usually multiprocessors, being composed of many computers including microcomputer. All these operate in a connected way under the control of a central operating system. Modern mainframe computer are capable of address and several billion positions or more of memory with hundreds of registers. These are more than 32 bits in length. The channels between various parts of such a computer are capable of carrying upto 5 million bits of detain one millionth of a second.

A mainframe computer has microcomputers to control specific hardware devices, such as printers, disc drives etc. These also help transfer of memory from one device to another through the bus. These microcomputer have central processing units with the large scale integrated memory system like the read-only memory or the programmable read-only memory or the programmable read-only memory.

Random Access Memory (RAM) is a general-purpose memory to store data and programmes. It requires electric power to hold the content intact. So, it is known as volatile memory. In RAM, the location of the specific circuit is possible and can be accessed directly in the middle of the chip. One need not examine each circuit starting at the beginning and moving forward one by one.

While the chip is composed of specific circuits designed to execute a single programme, it is called Read Only Memory (ROM). Expect the designed programme, no other programme can be held by ROM. The entire chip must be replaced and redesigned for any change in the programming. But ROM is very much useful for any specific application, and when it is to be produced in large quantities.

The large scale integrated memory can be used for specific applications known as Programmable Read Only Memory (PROM). In PROM, chips are used singly for programming by breaking connections between circuits. PROM is very useful for specific programmes and can be used for specific routine programmes.

The disadvantage of PROM is that once a programme is recorded in the chip, it cannot be changed or revised. So a method has been devised known as Erasable Programmable Read Only Memory (EPROM) which is constructed not by breaking circuits, but by activating circuits between specific values within the chip and later de-activating the circuits with high intensity ultra-violet light.

The chip for EPROM can be programmed over and over again without being replaced. The instructions programmed in ROM, PROM and EPROM can be held for years together, and are known as non-volatile memory. The programming languages viz. BASIC, COBOL, FORTRAN, PASCAL, PL/1 are available for microcomputers.

All the programming languages have their specific fields of application for different purpose. In library applications, Beginners All-purpose Symbolic Instruction Code (BASIC) is most widely used. The advantages are that it is easy to learn; and the programming is rather simple.

Moreover, the scope is wider and all the terms used in the library are programmable with basic. With the knowledge of a few commands and by manipulating them judiciously, one can construct fairly sophisticated programmes with basic. It is possible to create numerous routines, subroutines and subcommands with BASIC.

The usefulness of BASIC in library applications lies in its capability to handle strings. It is not always possible to determine the lengths and the characters for bibliographic data, and so, the undefined length area of a string allows flexibility in data input. The original BASIC was limited in scope and command. But basic has been much developed since then.

Now it is available in two modes-interpreted and compiled. The interpreted mode is better at the initial stage. It is slower, but helps the programmer to do his hob correctly. The compiled version is sophisticated and meant for advanced users.

While the age of the library management system has blossomed precisely because there are libraries, these other technologies are the product of a wider market. That we can exploit systems which have a large consumer base gives security to what we do—if two or three library management system suppliers cease trading panic could ensue, whereas if two or three CDROM database producers pull out, what do we care? There are plenty left. However, if we have some minimal 'clout' in the LMS market we have very little in this wider world.

Before we get too euphoric about the future of these technologies within libraries we should remember that it will only look rosy so long as the products run in parallel with out business and we can prove our intermediary role in of value to the customer. The clutch of technologies which cover electronic information delivery include CDROM, online access to remote database hosts, videotex/teletext and automated community information. They are all well known applications some of which have been around for years—online access must soon be celebrating a quarter of a century of service. That does not mean that every library uses them or that in those that do the systems form a major part of the service.

Public libraries are still very much about lending material for home use—how often are you reference librarians asked whether it is possible to borrow a reference-only item? However, information as a commodity has always been vital to our service and with the growing demands of students and others, it is unlikely to diminish in the near future.

If the face of public libraries is to change radically during the next ten years it is probably in the area of electronic information delivery that we will make it happen.

These technologies have literally the potential to give the power of information searching to the customer rather than through the librarian to the customer. That does not mean we are an endangered species if such a situation comes about—the systems will need to be managed, exploited and the customers trained. It does mean that our roles may change. That is the real challenge of electronic information delivery.

In the last survey hyperbole was necessary to describe the impact that the CDROM had made on public libraries. Like the compact disc in the audio market, the CDROM has been the high flier of the late 1980s and will continue to change the way that we operate as librarians well into the 1990s. Just to remind you, before looking more closely at the data from the present survey, in 1987 two libraries indicated that they were considering using CDROM while in 1989, 49 were actually in the thick of it.

A variety of databases were being used, but all were using Bookbank which was the catalyst for most libraries. In four years the number has gone up 50 times, since 1989 it has more than doubled. Any way you look at it, CDROM is a popular delivery system for information and is likely to continue its sweep through public libraries.

The data are pretty self-evident, there are increases everywhere. Northern Ireland scores a full house while all other authorities show a rapid take-up. Only Scotland and the Non-Mets lag behind the 60% and over which is seen elsewhere. We commented last time that the size of these two exceptions might create barriers to buying the system and that still seems to be the case; although the relative cheapness of the hardware and the real savings and benefits of using Bookbank, for example, continue to raise question marks about these discrepancies.

There are in the end only two possibilities. Either the scale of operations in these two types of authority is such that resources cannot be found for what elsewhere is spreading like wild-fire or, the nature of demand means that other priorities must take precedence.

Looking closely it is not clear that all authorities are using Bookbank, although the vast majority are. Indeed it may well be that those who did not report its use felt that it was not worth mentioning! The data also show, however, that a wide range of databases are now in use, ranging from those of local relevance, such as the Northern Echo, to national newspapers, official publications, British Standards and the odd encyclopedia.

Selection tools remain a popular sue for the CDROM equipment and alongside Bookbank we now find Bookfind (from Bookdata), American Books in Print, BNB and the British Library Catalogue. Respondents were asked to indicate whether the systems were staff only or made available directly to the public, without staff intervention.

Of the 101 total, 66 indicated that their systems were staff only while nine report direct use by the public. That leaves 26 who said nothing about access. From the databases the 26 'question marks' are using I am pretty sure that they are not providing public access, which means that only about one tenth of CDROMers are allowing customers to get their hands on the technology.

Of the nine allowing public access, a fair smattering (five actually) are providing it to the Northern Echo, evidently a strong catalyst to encourage public access. This balance of 10% public access to 90% of authorities using staff as intermediaries is in marked contrast to the developments taking place in university and polytechnic libraries where CDROM networks are seen as an essential means of giving the customers what they want.

For a whole variety of reasons we in public libraries are taking a different approach. The case for CDROMs as selection/bibliographic aids is won, the case for purchasing databases to support reference and information services looks set to be a victory, but, perhaps because of the diversity and differing levels of customer ability in public libraries, direct access is not yet seen as the highest priority.

We certainly hope that we are not, since it is costly to provide one PC and CDROM drive per database and, if there are fewer PCs than databases, switching disks in and out all the time is a pain. The evidence from the academic sector is that the task is labour intensive and leads to disks 'disappearing'.

With the jukebox well out of harm's way and a menu of databases to choose from at the terminal the process is much simplified. We are confident that the benefits of direct public access and the provision of networks will appear in the returns when this survey is undertaken again.

The breakthrough will come when three criteria can be met.

First, that jukeboxes can be readily connected to the big networks supported by library management systems so that the richness of CDROM databases can be exploited at terminals far and wide. So far, experiments have hit a number of problems of software compatibility and lack of intelligence on the networks and these problems have kept the breakthrough from coming, but come it must.

Second, search software can provide a standard query language which is applicable to all CDROM databases so that the user once trained can sue any system, and finally, that reasonable pricing structures can be negotiated with CDROM publishers for networking agreements.

Online access to remote database hosts has been around for a long time. It must have been in use outside esoteric research labs for twenty years and many public libraries have been providing online access for upwards of ten. In some ways the potential of online access is not unlike that of CDROM—providing the ability to search very large stores of data—with the added advantage that the information can be as up to date as today. The risks of incurring high costs through long searches has damped any enthusiasm for providing direct public access to hosts, but online access remains an important tool to those librarians involved in the provision of information services.

Pricing structures which do not discourage the occasional user and the wide availability of microcomputers have seen a steady increase in use over recent years. What used to be a hit-and-miss affair using dedicated terminals and devices called acoustic couplers has become a simple and reliable matter of hitting a few keys.

However, we suspect that a continuing subjective feeling that searching online is expensive and complicated has created some barriers and the growing availability of databases on CDROM which incur no cost at point of use has influenced decisions on whether or not to use online searching.

There is no conclusive evidence that the two methods overlap significantly, however subjective evidence suggests that an important use of CDROM is the formulation of search strategies which can then be used during an online search. Also, it would appear from a recent report on the 1991 International Online Information Meeting that demand for online hosts continues to grow despite the popularity of CDROM databases.

Turning to the data from this current survey, there are now 107 authorities using online searching. That is a 10% increase over the figure in 1989, which was 97. Looking at the percentage changes since 1985, we can see that there has been a slowing down in the increase—the change between 1985 and 1987 was 30% up, and 1987 to 1989, 13%. The majority of those libraries who see online searching as an asset to their services have already begun using the technique and that the increases seen in the past are tending to plateau.

Whether the remaining 60 authorities suffer a financial barrier, a psychological one or simply do not believe that online searching is relevant to their services cannot be evinced from the data available. However, as we shall see below, the nature of the databases most used implies use by libraries who prioritise bibliographic and business information as important. Perhaps the non-users have set other priorities for their services. The fact that only 25% of Scottish authorities use the technique influences significantly the overall total.

Non-mets are also at 25% but they are only four in number, yet Scotland, with the largest number of authorities, lags far behind. We cannot claim an in-depth knowledge of Scottish library services, however elsewhere in this review we will see that they tend to plough a separate furrow in their use of IT. The other data show manly steady increases and no decreases, from which we may conclude that once adopted, online searching has lasting value to service delivery.

A trend which previously proved of interest is the method of access used to search online hosts. Trend is an important word in this context since, on occasion, the replies received from the questionnaire needed some interpretation.

When compared with 1985, the data from the current survey reinforce patterns which were noted in 1989. The fairly even mix of dedicated terminal, Prestel and microcomputer which existed in 1985 has been routed by the micro which now stands head, shoulders and keyboard above all other access methods.

Not really very surprising when you come to think about it since the micro has been widely adopted as the access medium for those who operate outside our world. Modem boards can be fitted into machines and there is bags of cheap software around to be played with. Insofar as online searching can be a suer-friendly business, the micro can facilitate it since it is possible to set up dialling and log-in codes for rapid access, and the micro can still be used for so many other things.

The other significant feature of the data is the steady increase in the number of authorities using the circulation system as the medium of access. While five is a very small figure when compared with the micros, there are some interesting implications in the decision to use the library management system for online searching. First, most of the new systems allow you to do so, and have done for some time.

There is nothing particularly fancy about it, but for very good reasons most libraries have shied away from doing so. While in principle it should be a good thing to provide online access in a variety of locations, where the information is really needed, it requires trained staff to use the systems effectively and untrained staff can run up some hefty bills in no time at all. Use can be limited to defined terminals, but the strategy which has been to focus online searching to key locations where specialist staff, capable of knowing for certain when online should be used, are on hand.

Without doubt, the use of the library management system as a delivery medium holds great potential and we will be very surprised if more libraries do not take the plunge. Certainly if the complexities which remain in host interfaces can be reduced so that infrequent users have a chance of getting in and out more quickly, there is every incentive to widen the network, and that is precisely the value of the library management system 0 it has a wide network of terminals.

The truth of these comments becomes more clear when the total terminal population is considered, rather than the use of the medium alone. What we have been looking at so far is the number of authorities using each method, rather than the number of terminals used by each.

The major use for online searching is clearly business information. The two aspects of online searching which can be considered here relate not to the technology or the range of services available, but how they are delivered to users. The first factor is the costs which are passed on to users and the second is the management of the service—staff skilled in the techniques and how it has changed traditional provision. Charging policies ought to tell us a great deal about the priorities of libraries and their responses to changes especially those outside their control, whether from competition or from the comments of the Minister for the Arts!

Back in 1989 made some observations about the reasons for the high level of certain replies. Discretion, for example, could be an excuse for saying one thing and doing another—telling everyone that certain categories of user are charged, or charges are levied when a search is requested, while not bothering because of the hassle of recovering the money. No comment, on the other hand could be an excuse for doing almost anything; anything that is except charge. The use of online searching has grown up in a tradition where it is the exception to levy a fee for a service at point of use.

The whole point of public goods is that they are funded from individual contributions (rates, taxes) which bear no relation to level of use made by that individual. The management of the service includes the organisation of specialist staff and the changes which have resulted from the development of online searching. There is just as much need to have highly trained staff undertaking searches as there has ever been.

Despite developments in the design of user-friendly interfaces, online searching remains a special skill, both in the knowledge of command languages and in the formulation of suitable search strategies. It is likely to be a long time before access is provided to customers without the need for a trained intermediary, since cost rises and effectiveness falls if the searcher is not properly trained.

Libraries were asked to indicate numbers of locations of trained staff and 86 provided replies, as opposed to 78 in 1989. As with all questions demanding more than a yes or no reply, we must be cautious about making too many assumptions from the data. The evidence provided in the replies shows that all but a very few authorities focus their online services in key locations—usually reference libraries, business information centres and the like.

The average number of trained staff in each authority is something over four, a slight increase on 1989, but remains fairly stable. It seems that whatever changes may face public libraries in the next few years, this is at least one service which will continue to require 'gatekeepers' to make it fully effective. Changes in the form of other services resulting from the use of online searching was the last question asked on this subject. Again, since the data re textual rather than precise responses, only general conclusions may be drawn.

Despite that, the replies add some detail to the overall picture of online searching in public libraries. Fifty seven authorities commented, compared with the 39 who did so in 1989. Of those 28 implied in their reply that online searching had enriched the range of services available.

Eight libraries reported that printed sources had been cancelled and ten that there had been no significant change; either because online had been used for so long that no-one could remember what life was like before, or online was such a new acquisition that there had not been time to see any impact. On the other hand, two authorities reported dramatic changes to the scope and method of service delivery.

While online searching involves only a few staff and demands small amounts of the budget, it is an important and emotive topic. The trend which has emerged over the past four or five years is for the databases to form part of services to business and now, for those services to be viewed in many places as 'suitable cases for charging'.

The CDROM/online searching duopoly should be a key focus for our attention over the next few years and will, I am sure, be the subject of further research. Indeed, a recent report from the Centre for Communication and Information Studies at the Polytechnic of Central London reports research which looked in much more detail at the actual pattern of database use by analysing bills from a range of authorities, and interviewing a sample of users in great detail.

The general trends reported above are echoed in the research results and the report is well worth reading to gain a clearer picture of what the future may hold.

Turning to videotex and teletext we are in the realm of technologies which have been around for some years, have become well established, to the point where we are beginning to see them superseded. We can remember a time when there was much talk about Prestel (videotex) as a major medium of information delivery. Organisations were clamouring to be a part of a readily accessible and widely spread public network.

Today Prestel is still around, but many new systems have arrived which are Prestel-like in their utility, but have much more power to exploit data resources. Such systems are now used in private viewdata networks, closed user group systems providing information using the format of Prestel, but managed by some local information provider.

Teletext, an information system available on broadcast television networks such as Ceefax and Oracle has never been a critical element in publicly provided information services since the data cannot be manipulated locally and is usually of momentary interest—news, racing results, etc. Moreover, it is common for home use television sets to be sold with Ceefax and Oracle decoders as standard. The trends for teletext and videotex show a situation which has matured to the point where use has levelled off and appears at present to be falling slightly.

Private viewdata, on the other hand, is growing steadily in popularity as a medium for the delivery of information tailored to the local community.

In six years there has been an almost threefold increase in the systems in use and we may expect this to continue since often these systems are developed as corporate information systems, sometimes managed by the library service, sometimes not and while libraries may find themselves low down on the corporate IT programme private viewdata systems may not.

Analysing use at the level of the authority provides only a general picture of developments and that to establish more clearly the impact made it is necessary to consider the penetration of systems within individual authorities.

Respondents were asked to report the numbers of terminals used on each of these systems and, in addition, to show whether their use was seldom, steady or constant.

These data support earlier points about the fall in the popularity of videotex and teletext as information systems in libraries. Not only has there been a fall in the number of authorities using the systems, but the number of terminals provided has also dropped—videotex almost to the level of 1985, teletext below it. Of course, mean numbers are just that, and the actual distribution shows that in a few authorities there are relatively large populations of terminals.

Wiltshire, for example, reports 38 for videotex. In contrast, not only has the total number of authorities using private viewdata risen, but the mean number of terminals shows a 23.5% rise. Not surprising since if private viewdata is the means of delivering community information, as it usually is, then terminals should be as widely available as possible.

Having descended from the level of total use, to penetration within a library system, we can finally consider how much the systems are used. The questionnaire invited comment on whether the use of each of the three system was seldom, steady or constant. We must exercise some caution. One person's steady is another's constant and we can only draw limited information from these data. Also, use is likely to vary from terminal to terminal so the single comment may not reflect reality where more than one is in use. Steady is the most frequently cited option, except for videotex where seldom is top. We do not think there is much value in a detailed analysis of these data since their objectivity is questionable, but we can give a personal opinion.

Videotex is not used much since alternative sources of information may provide speedier access. The cost of teletext is unaffected by use since it is broadcast with the TV signals. Leaving terminals lying about for people to play with, therefore carries no risk of large bills. Safe for the customer to come in and tinker with. Moreover, many customers will now know more about the resources available on teletext than the managers providing it.

Automation of community information highlights one of the paradoxes of information technology. It is very easy to start—just buy a micro and printer, some database software and off you go—but it can be very hard to keep the data comprehensive and up to date. Anyone who has had much to do with computers knows that the data are the most valuable commodity, much more valuable than the hardware or software that can be replaced at the corner shop. Creating any database takes time, maintaining it takes time, and time is money. Community information has always been an attractive product to automate since so much of it is in the form that can readily be fitted into database software products.

Clubs, societies, business organisations and the like are the lifeblood of the community information database and are maintained in some form or other by the vast majority of libraries. Indeed, comprehensive community systems are something unique to libraries; you certainly can't buy them at Smiths.

Not surprisingly then the number of libraries automating community information continues to grow. 1987 and 1989 has been matched in the past two years by a total increase of just over 19%. The rend which was apparent between 1985 and 1987, use of the micro and word processor, has now changed. This time the micro, still the most popular medium, remains unchanged at 38 while use of the library management system shows the most significant growth, up by 75%.

It is also not unexpected that private viewdata continues to increase since we have already noted in this chapter that the number of authorities providing the medium continues to rise. One question which comes immediately to mind, however, is if 40 authorities reported use of the system under the videotex/teletext section above, but only 18 report using it for community information, what are the other 22 doing?

Just the same question had to be asked in the last survey and suggested that the problem was one of interpretation—that the authorities might not be managing the private viewdata system and therefore thought that it should not be reported under the community information banner. Whether that is true one cannot say. Certainly the prime purpose of private viewdata networks is to deliver information of relevance to the community.

While considering the method of processing, it should be noted that a further five libraries indicated that they were actively investigating the automation on their community information files, and by now they may have done just that. That gives a potential total of 102 authorities who use IT for community information or 60% of the 167 country wide.

Micros and word processors have been around for so many years, have at least 40% of the libraries in the country not started to automate the community information files which they certainly must have. With common sense, transferring manual files to a micro can save time and make the product much more useful. Mail merge makes remainders easier and with multiple indexing possible, more variety of presentation is not a problem.

A micro/printer set up is not pricey and there are so many examples of applications that not to try seems swimming against the stream. To see whether there was any pattern to this reticence we looked a bit more closely at the 66 libraries without automated community information. An interesting fact emerged—that nearly half of the 66 were authorities of the same type. Twenty seven of the 41 Scottish authorities (66%) have yet to do anything about automating their community information; only one of the four Welsh Non-Mets has done so and none of the Northern Ireland libraries has started.

Elsewhere, the most likely authority type to find automated systems is the English county where 85% have automated their community information. London, the Mets and the Welsh counties range from 74% uptake down to 63%. You will remember that Scottish authorities were also behind on the library management system front and one can only repeat that perhaps they have set different priorities or lack of resources places severe restrictions on the acquisition of technology. Conversely, English counties are large organisations with disparate service points and the benefits of using IT for community information has clearly been recognised. Lastly, the questionnaire sought details of how the information is actually made available to customers.

There are three possibilities—online, hardcopy and a mixture of both—online in some places, or for staff use, hardcopy elsewhere, or for the customers. The trend which was reported in 1989 was towards more data to be presented online rather than in printed format and the 1991 data confirm that this trend has continued during the intervening two years. Online as the only means of delivery has increased by more than a third and online/ hardcopy has also edged up. On the other hand hardcopy has fallen by something over 10%, having remained unchanged for the two years before. It is a pity that ten libraries did not give any indication of dissemination format since, had they, the data might have looked different. Nevertheless, from what we have it seems hat progress towards direct public access for customers continues. Hardcopy should not be dismissed as an anachronism just yet since there are many occasions when it is useful to send the customer away with a list to browse through—doing that online in the library has implications for the number of terminals provided. The benefits of online access include the freedom of the customer to search in their own way without an intermediary and sometimes the opportunity to search the database from the comfort of the office or the front room.

4
Acquisition Systems

The library is the place where individual needs for knowledge and information are met through the collective provision and interpretation of resources; technological developments which put the individual consumer directly in touch with a global information marketplace create an apparently barren future for this particular public service. In the drive to increase productivity and improve economic strength, the private sector has invested heavily in technological development. Within the public sector too technology has been used to increase productivity and efficiency, but with the primary objective of improving the value of the service provided to the public.

Libraries, automated rapidly; the possibility of record sharing and distribution increased exponentially, and users had catalogues which were current, potentially well-maintained, and amenable to a much wider range of search strategies. The collections could be used more effectively, and the library increased the value of the service it provided. The computerized catalogues, though, unlike their print and fiche predecessors, were only searchable at the library. Now the computer is moving out of the office, into the home and on to the road as the growth in electronic communication brings the library catalogue direct to a screen near you. The electronic evangelists believe that all this points to the sure and certain fact that the internet is the library of the future.

The Internet is a 'good thing' because it is free, because it is accessible to anyone and everyone, and because it is essentially anarchic and libertarian. The ideal underpinning the electronic information revolution is that the ability to plug into a worldwide web of unregulated and uncensored digitized information will empower the individual against the institutions — economic, social and political — that control our lives. If the ideal became reality, we would find the individual interacting with the computer in total isolation from our crumbling communities.

Information is the result of the application of human understanding and interpretation to the transmitted communication. Until that happens, until the digitized information is actually processed by the human brain, it lies as stagnant as an unread journal article or a video collecting dust on a shelf.

Librarians are currently faced with hordes of information-hungry readers anxiously awaiting their next information fix and begrudging the fact that they have had to venture away from their computer screens to get it. For most users of the library, the visit is an enjoyable, social experience and for many it is part of the shared ritual of the life of the community which the library serves. This is not to suggest that there are not collections whose users do require information on demand, and those collections will naturally be held and accessed in the way which most conveniently answers that demand. That said, all but the most specialized, data-based libraries gain enormously from the physical building that houses their collections, and those gains are practical and psychological for both the individual and for the community.

The infoage, which places so much emphasis on individual interaction with electronic information, has paradoxically brought us the cybercafe, where people meet to talk, drink coffee and use and discover the multitude of facilities available on the Internet. In one of the first examples of the breed to be found in the United Kingdom, the cybercafe is housed in an area lined with books. Some entrepreneurs at least have discovered that not only is information-seeking for leisure purposes a more pleasant activity when carried out in the company of others, but also that books in themselves create a calm, peaceful, secure environment. Surely it would be inconceivable for libraries willingly to abandon circumstances which are so conducive to fulfilling their objectives and which are one — of their greatest assets?

Similarly, when they first entered the United States market, the booksellers Waterstone's quickly discovered that they had to adopt three of their North American rivals' most successful sales tactics — coffee, music and conversation — if they wanted to really bring in the customers. The introduction of a 40-seat cafe in their new Chicago store led to a marked increase in traffic. While libraries rush to the cold embrace of the virtual library, others in the hardheaded world of business have seen that people need people.

Access to electronic information within a physical environment which contains a variety of information sources in a variety of media, each best-fitting different user needs, gives the best of all possible worlds. Librarians have known and understood this for years and must not lose sight of that reality. The provision of information is only one of the responsibilities of the library, and the way in which the library provides information has always been handled in a different way from that in which it provides access to knowledge.

An insurmountable obstacle to putting book-level works into electronic form for anything other than purposes of transmission is apparent to anyone who has attempted to read a document more than a few paragraphs in length directly from a computer screen. It is an unpleasant and unsatisfactory experience, physically and mentally.

In their book *Future libraries,* Walt Crawford and Michael Gorman have done librarians an inestimable service in presenting the technical evidence for this single, critical fact in a well-documented and incontroveitible form. There is no possibility of computers being used for the kind of sustained reading required to follow a narrative or a reasoned argument. Computer screens are excellent for displaying unconnected pieces of information, but the inability of the user to glance at what precedes and what follows the text displayed on the screen — much less the ability to see what happens several 'pages' away — is a serious hindrance, as is the impossibility of adopting a relaxed posture or reading 'on the fly'.

Any general library which chooses to go down the path of providing leisure or research textual materials in electronic form must do so on the understanding that readers will find these next to impossible to absorb intellectually. The library will be obliged either to ignore this fact, or to provide a hard copy at the time of use. The first option would be an act of gross unprofessionalism, the second of gross environmental and economic vandalism. Many librarians believe that information technology has radically altered the library profession, and that the burgeoning electronic online services mean we will have to completely rethink our perceptions of what a library is and the role of librarians in this new setting.

Librarians are told that they have a bright future in the 'Information Age' if only they will adopt the role of information brokers. Some may see the role of information technology in libraries as a case of the tail wagging the dog. Nonetheless, this idea of the librarian as information broker follows logically from moves over the last 20 years to rename librarianship as information science and libraries as information centres.

In his book *The myth of the electronic library,* William F. Birdsall has placed librarianship in the 'people centred' professions, together with other public service professionals such as teachers and social workers. In contrast to the doctor or lawyer, who is paid to apply specialist knowledge, the aim of such professionals is to help the clients to help themselves. The librarian can also be seen as working to achieve a social result, by assisting the individual in achieving his or her aspirations and enhancing the good of the wider community in so doing.

The electronic library presents a mirage of salvation for our hard-pressed services. For librarianship, it is perhaps the ultimate expression of the trends of social fragmentation, economic globalization and the dominance of the market. It is also the idea upon which librarianship, it, a mixture of panic and despair, have seized as the answer to falling budgets, and attacks on professional cohesion. Computer application in library and information field has made phenomenal progress in industrialised countries where hardware, software and communications facilities are well developed. In view of their technological advancement, they are able to computerise their entire library and information system in the country, with great success.

Besides improving services and operations for a better performance, libraries are able to evolve effective computer networks, towards optimum utilisation of resources and facilities. International programmes like UNISIST/UNESCO, Universal Availability of Publications (UAP) and Universal Access to Information (UAI) of IFLA and a few others have helped in promotion and coordination of information services through out the world. IDRC, Canada, EEC, Brussels and similar other have helped developing countries to strengthen their information infrastructure.

Global information systems, characterised by decentralised input, centralised processing and decentralised distribution, such as INIS, AGRIS, and DEVSIS have been evolved towards universal bibliographic control and dissemination of literature. Major producers of secondary information services have become international information/database centres for their respective subjects/disciplines. International information network/centres such as Lockheed/DIALOG, SDC/Orbit and ESA/IRS hold 100 or more databases in several disciplines and offer online services to users through out the world. Communication networks like

TYMNET, TELENET and ESANET offer communication facilities to international information centres that offer database services.

Towards promoting cooperative endeavours, regional networks like ASTINFO, RINSCA and TECHNONET and specialised networks like AIBA, INNERTAP, SEAMIC and others have come about. These are all useful international efforts in transborder flow of information and in diffusion of knowledge through out the word.

The library networks in USA are in a most advanced level of development. The favourable factors responsible for successful development of library networking in USA are long tradition of cooperation among libraries, introduction of library automation as early as from 1960's, advances in information science during 1970's and 1980's and introduction of MARC format by the Library of Congress in 1968.

The experiences of USA in library networking are valuable to our efforts in designing the INFLIBNET. Three foremost bibliographic utilities and networks in USA are the Online Computer Library Centre, Dublin, Ohio (OCLC), Research Libraries and Information Network, Stanford, California (RLIN) and Washington Library Network, Olympia, Washington (WLN).

In addition, there are networks of different types, levels, etc. The library networking is based on three major areas of technology, viz., creation of bibliographic information in machine readable format for storage and retrieval, hardware/software for database use and services and telecommunication mechanism for transmission of information. The major point of success of library network depends upon availability of machine readable catalogues in the constituent units. A great progress has been made by USA in this regard. The latest trend is to use CDROM technology for storing the catalogue data.

The OCLC, established in 1967, and has a staff of 812 persons is a non-profit organisation and supports resource sharing among more than 6,700 libraries in USA, besides countries in Europe, Saudi Arabia and Australia. Its union catalogue database contains 13 million records; some 30,000 records are added every week. With the steady growth of OCLC, there has been a progressive decline in the amount of original cataloguing to be done by the participating libraries.

The system hit rate has increased from 66 per cent in 1971 to 94 per cent in 1983. The details about telecommunication system, input sources. RLIN, established in 1978 and which has as staff of 81 persons, supports the cooperative programmes of Research Libraries Group, comprising 36 major libraries and other research institutions. It maintains 6 databases online.

The catalogue database holds more than 20 million records. WLN, established in 1972 and which has a staff of 51 persons, provides, more than 250 libraries in seven states of USA, online computerised services to promote resource sharing and automated library functions.

The bibliographic file contains more than 3.5 million catalogue records. UNISIST II, Main Working Document defines Information Network as a set of interrelated information systems associated with communication facilities, which are cooperating through more or less formal agreements and institutional agreements, in order to jointly implement information handling operation, with a view to pooling their resources and to offer better services to the user. They generally follow identical or compatible rules and procedures.

Automated library acquisition systems are designed to handle the considerable amount of paperwork involved in buying books. Typically they print purchase orders; maintain book fund accounts and print book fund reports of various types; provide information on orders outstanding, and sometimes on works in process—that is, books received but not yet catalogued; prepare vouchers or checks to pay for the books. Many also print other reports derived from the order information; one system described below, for example, produces 32 separate products. These may include lists of orders by order number, by author, by country, by language or by any other element of data that has previously been coded and entered into the system; claims or cancellation notices to be sent to a dealer when the book has not been received within a predetermined period of time; and notices of the original requester of a book that it has been ordered or received. Some of the more elaborate systems also provide for such functions as conversion of foreign currencies to dollars; automatic checking for possible duplicate orders; reordering from a second vendor if the first cannot fill the order; computation of such dealer performance measures as average length of time to fill an order, or average discount; and provision of information for cataloguing or circulation functions.

Acquisition systems also vary in other respects:

1. By type of material handled (most handle monographs, but many do not handle serials)

2. By type of orders handled (many do not handle standing, blanket or approval orders, or gifts and exchanges)

3. By type of payment possible (some cannot accommodate payments in advance, deposit accounts, or memberships)

4. By type of language representable (most cannot deal with nonalphabetic languages such as Chinese, and many do not provide for diacritics)

One of three major technical catalogues are:

1. Those based exclusively or primarily on unit record equipment

2. Off-line, batch-processing systems using computers

3. Online systems using various types of remote terminals for communication with a computer

The typical punched-card or unit record acquisition system uses a keypunch, a sorter, a collator, and a tabulating machine such as the IBM 402, 403, or 407. Cards are punched with order information, and are then sorted and passed through the tabulator to print orders. The punched cards are then placed, with the help of the collator, in the file of cards used for previous orders, to create an order outstanding file; this file may also be printed out in list form on the tabulator. When the books are received, the price paid for each item is punched into one of the cards, which then serves to update financial records, and in some cases to write vouchers or checks. The public libraries of Decatur, Illinois and Lake Country, Indiana provide early examples of such systems. Decatur began late in 1959 with an inexpensive set of equipment (the IBM Series 50) costing $ 375 per month, and used it to produce not only purchase orders but 14 other products as well, including accounting records, statistics, shelflist cards, and book cards.

By 1963/1964, the cost for machine rental, material, and equipment had risen to $798 per month, but payroll, budgeting, and circulation functions had been added, the total staff of the library had been reduced, and the library was operating on less money then it had five years previously. Among university libraries, the University of Missouri, St. Louis University, and the Joint University Libraries of Vanderbilt, Peabody, and Scarritt were early pioneers with punched-card systems.

The Missouri system was unique in its use of an IBM machine no longer being manufactured, the "Cardatype," rather than the customary accounting machine. The Cardatype combined a typewriter-like keyboard and printing platen with the ability to read unit record cards, punch them, and perform modest computational chores.

Data entered though the keyboard, read from punched cards, or computed in the arithmetic unit could be utilised in the production of printed orders and other records, and as many as four additional typewriter units could be attached to the central unit, each preparing distinctive documents.

The application at Missouri is an excellent example of a unit record system in which the same punched cards are used repeatedly to produce various products. The Cardatype, used at the beginning of the process to prepare purchase orders, also produced temporary cards for the public catalogue, Library of Congress card orders, order records, and report slips. A collator was used periodically to search the file of cards for the books on order, and if items were not received within a specified period of time the same cards were used to produce cancellation notices or claim notices.

If the items were reported out of print, the card could also be used to request quotations from out-of-print book dealers, in which case a copy of the request from was again placed in the public catalogue as well as in a desiderata file.

In the St. Louis University application, the order date was recorded in so-called "Julian" or "shop" date from—that is, the number of the day of the year—and this was used to trigger claim notices. The files were so arranged tat if the items ordered were not received within ninety days of the time ordered, a claim notice was automatically produced. After operating for several years, the system was abandoned for lack of sufficient volume to justify its cost.

The Joint University Libraries system handled fund accounting, produced orders for Library of Congress catalogue cards as well as for books, printed lists of books on order and in process, and produced temporary cards to be field in the public catalogue.

A special card punch, the IBM 526 summary punch, was connected to the 402 tabulator so that when purchase orders were printed, cards could be punched with the total amounts of each order for use in encumbering funds. The system was converted to a computer operation in 1966 using IBM 1401 and 7072 computers, and is still in operation at this writing.

Numerous special libraries had also begun such systems by the mid-1960s, typically using company equipment for a few hours per week. The one at IBM's Watson Research Laboratory is of particular interests. As books moved from one step to another, the appropriate cards were manually shifted. Three times a week, an IBM 407 tabular was used to print the file, creating a

"Processing Information List," or "PIL," which made information on the processing status of any item readily available. The system was later transferred to an IBM 1401 computer, with "recent additions" in one list and the other five categories combined in a second list, still called "PIL."

The status of each item was noted in columns corresponding to the five categories, with "Julian" or "shop" date shown for the day each item moved into each category. By observing which column had the most recent date, one could see at a glance the status of each item. The computer was programmed to identify items which stayed too long in one category, and produced notices of items that required claiming or exporting. "PIL" lists, increasing in sophistication of typography and production, were to become a common feature of later systems until superseded in the 1970s by terminal displays of the same information.

As general-purpose computers become widely available in the 1960s, off-line, batch-processing computerised systems became the most common and popular form of acquisition system. Most such systems still use punched-card input, feeding order information into the system in a way not greatly different from unit record systems, but once data input has taken place information is normally transferred back and forth between magnetic tape or magnetic disk files without the necessity of repeated manual handling of cards. The typical acquisition system of this type, in addition to printing orders, automatically updates the file of information on orders out standing, encumbers the necessary funds and updates the appropriate financial records, stores the bibliographic information for later use, and gathers statistics.

Two public library systems are of interest as examples of the transition from unit record systems to computers. Both used a Univac machine, the 1004 Card Processing System, which had capabilities about halfway between he unit record systems and a small computer as the IBM 1401.

The Suffolk County (New York) Cooperative System began with an IBM 403 tabulating system in 1963, and switched to the Univac 1004 a year later, adding tape drives for storage. A unique feature was the use of mark-sensing pencils to record and input some elements of data, such as the list price and discount in lieu of keypunching the information.

The magnetic tape drives allowed the system to store fiscal data and bibliographic information for production of catalogue cards. The Nassau County (New York) Library System began with a similar system in 1964; the system was transferred to a Univac 1005 with magnetic tape drives in 1968 so that order and other reports could be printed faster and the information for them stored more conveniently.

By far the most popular computers for acquisition systems in the mid-1960s, however, were those in IBM's 1004 series, particularly the 1401. The University of Illinois at Chicago Circle began using a 1401 for an off-line acquisition system in 1964, incorporating the "Processing Information List" feature pioneered at the IBM Watson Research Library.

The UICC was arranged not strictly alphabetically, but according to a computer-generated code work composed of the first four letters of the author's last name, the author's initials, and the initials of the first two words of the title. Order were printed on three-by-five-inch slips, which were manually sorted by vendor and attached to vendor and attached to cover letters for mailing. Pennsylvania State University implemented a similar system the same year, using a 407 tabulator as well as a 1401 and a 7074 computer.

A unique feature was the use of "change cards," five cards punched with the order number each time an order was prepared, and later used to report changes in the status of a book on order or in process. These cards were placed in cardboard packets and kept in a manually arranged file; if the status of an order changed, one of the card was withdrawn, a code for the change was written on the card, the card was sent to a keypunching section where the code was punched in the card, and the card was then used by the computer to update the master magnetic tape record of orders outstanding.

Codes were established for some twenty-five different changes, including "not yet published," "out of print," "book in cataloguing," and "processing completed." In addition to a listing of orders in process, with the status of each order shown, the system produced daily lists of books requested by faculty but not yet ordered for each university department or separate fund, about 250 lists in all; when the system was later redesigned, however, this feature was dropped. Perhaps the example of an off-line batch-processing system of the mid-1960s is the one at the University of Michigan, implemented in 1965 on an IBM 1401, converted a year later to a 1460 and soon after to an IBM 360, and still running strong at this writing. A ten-part order form is generated, which includes slips for the official and public catalogues.

The orders outstanding file is automatically updated, but instead of printing it out the university now produces it on a computer-output microfiche (COM) for both economy and ease of handling. Entries for Slavic language works have "Slavic" punched at the beginning of each entry, and orders for music recordings similarly begin with the word "Recording" in order to create separate sections in the list for such works; other entries are alphabetised through the first 83 characters.

The Michigan system is one of the few projects for which good cost figures are available. About a year after the initial implementation, an analyst from outside the library evaluated the system in terms of both overall efficiency and costs. The results indicated that the system did indeed perform efficiently and economically; almost fifty percent more orders were handled by the automated system than by the previous manual system, and the cost per order, when like activities were compared, dropped by seven cents over a two-year span.

The librarian principally involved with development of the system has cautioned, however, that "while the information gathered was informative, it can, at best, only be considered as a guide since it is impossible to compare accurately an existing system with something that might have been." In the same year that Michigan's systems was first implemented, Washington University in St. Louis designed a system to control technical processing routines after books left the Acquisitions Department and until they had been fully catalogued and processed.

Building on Penn State's "change card" idea, the system was designed to generate "process control cards" that could be inserted in IBM 357 terminals along with a plastic prepunched "badge" indicating the particular change in status to be recorded: for example, that the book has been received, or reported not yet published, or cancelled, or forwarded to a particular cataloguing station, or to the card preparation unit, or (finally) that the book was under central of the public catalogue and could be removed from the system. The information would be automatically recorded by a high-speed card-punch (an IBM 1034) in a remote location, and then be transmitted to the computer.

Two years earlier, in 1966, Yale University packed up the idea of "process control" and used it in the design of an acquisition system that later served as a model for the automated acquisition system at the Library of Congress. As implemented at Yale, the technical processing "monitor" checks the status of each order during each day's run, and notifies the library of orders delayed past a predetermined length of time, and of other actions that need to be taken as a result of changes in status. The system represents an improvement in communications for off-line systems, presaging the later development of no-line system; the insertion of prepunched cards in remote terminals eliminates the necessity of manually punching the information in a data processing department and carrying the cards to the computer, and the computer "talks back" by automatically printing action reports regarding particular items when needed.

One remarkable thirty-two different outputs were originally produced by the Yale system, including notices to requesters of the status of their orders and large in-process and order number listings, both 'of which were changed to microfilm form in 1971 because of their size and cost. First implemented on an IBM 6094-7040 "direct-coupled system," the system was converted in 1972 to run on an IBM 360 Model 67 and a short time later to an IBM 370 Model 155. IBM 357 data collection devices are still used for recording status and location of items, and IBM 826s are used to prepare order forms while simultaneously punching the same information into cards. Other example of batch-processing off-line systems in university libraries are legion. By 1966, the Joint University Libraries system had converted to a 1401 and the University of Missouri had converted its unit record system to a 1440 computer, in this case not a university computer but one used solely by the library.

In California, the Honnold Library, which serves the six Claremont Colleges, implemented a computerised acquisition system using an IBM Model 40. The fullest bibliographic information available was entered as early in processing as possible, and a book catalogue was produced as the final step in the system. The University of Maryland, which had a unit record system modelled after Missouri's, Converted to an off-line system using several computers in succession, most recently a Univac 9300. Other Ivy League universities were not to be outdone by Yale. Harvard implemented a successful system in 1967, Cornell in 1968, and Columbia between 1968 and 1971. The Harvard system automatically edits order information for obvious mistakes such as lack of vendor, unusually high price, and invalid fund coding before producing orders.

Prices need not be in United States dollars, since the computer has been programmed to convert all foreign currencies into dollars at the current rate of exchange, which can be altered daily if needed. The system checks the outstanding order file periodically, and claims are automatically produced if orders have not been received in the time specified by the selecting librarians; if an item has still not been received after two claims have been produced and a third survey of the files made, the order is automatically cancelled. The Columbia system is remarkable particularly for the size and power of the equipment used: two IBM 360s, a Model 91 coupled with a Model 7, one of the most powerful complexes in the world at the time it was installed. Input is prepared on IBM Magnetic Tape Electric Typewriter (MTSTs) and converted to machine-readable from on a Digidata System 30 converter.

Records for materials in all Roman alphabet languages and in transliterated Cyrillic languages are handled by the system, as are microforms, maps, and speech records, but not serials; and material received through purchase, blanket order, standing order, gift, exchange, deposit, and cooperative acquisition programs are all included. As in the Yale system, the flow of materials in monitored through acquisitions and cataloguing departments and until catalogue cards are field in the public catalogue. About 65,000 order are processed annually for a impressed annually for a impressively low 93 cents per order.

Acquisition system differing from others in its extensive use of paper tape was implemented in 1968 at the University of British Columbia. Friden Flexowriters were used to punch the paper tapes as a by-product of such activities as typing orders, processing invoices, and receiving books. The paper tape then served as input to a PDP-11 computer which, in conjunction with a Honeywell 200, did the processing. The usual orders outstanding lists, claims, cancellation notices, and fund reports were produced, as was a list of current accessions, later discontinued for lack of user interest. A system originally developed in 1968 at Florida Atlantic University for use on an IBM 360 was transferred to Arizona State University and implemented there, on a Honeywell 200, in 1971.

Of later off-line, batch processing system, one in particular may be noted because of the unusually small size of both the system and the institution involved. This is the acquisition system implemented in 1971 on an IBM 360 Model 30 at Parkland College, a two-year community college in Champaign, Illinois. The system has required the addition of an extra staff member for keypunching, plus $170 per month for a model 129 keypunch, $400 per year for punch cards and magnetic tape, and several hundred dollars more per year for specially printed forms, but the library staff apparently believes these costs are offset to some extent by the fact that it no longer orders items preprocessed at a cost of $2.05 per item. Among special libraries, perhaps the best-known batch-processing system is at the Washington University School of Medicine Library in St. Louis. The system was begun in 1965 in conjunction with a book catalogue project. The cards were then used to update the magnetic tape record of orders outstanding and orders received, using the university's 1401 computer.

Later changes in the status of particular orders were indicated on copies of the order form, them punched into cards, which again were used to update the magnetic tape file. Some seventeen different lists were printed out from the file at periodic intervals. Very few computerised acquisition of this type have been reported in public libraries. Several that developed from unit record systems have already been noted, but only one that was initiated as a computerised system of the Orange County (California) Public Library. It began as a straight forward book purchasing system in 1966, using an IBM 1460 computer. After converting the system to run ion a 360 Model 30 and then on an RCA Spectra 70 Model 45 computer, the library decided to redesign the system entirely in order to incorporate additional features, including a book catalogue.

Both library staff and a commercial software firm were used to accomplish the design and programming tasks. The new system, termed BIBLIOS (for Book Inventory Building Library Information Oriented System) was implemented in 1969, also on the RCA Spectra 70 computer owned by the county. Development costs were just over $100,000 for the acquisitions portion of the system, and the cost of ordering and receiving a title under the system has been calculated at approximately $ 2.23.

In 1967, Connie Dunlap, developer of the University of Michigan system and at that time head of their acquisitions department, spoke to an ALA Preconference on Library Automation regarding the status of acquisition systems. No no-line systems were then in use, she pointed out, and although several were planned, it appeared likely that most institutions would find such systems too expensive.

By 1975, however, the costs of online storage and the necessary terminal equipment had declined dramatically, and over a dozen such systems were in operation. Perhaps the earliest to be implemented was at Washington State University in 1968, using three IBM 1050s online to an IBM Model 67. Paper-tape readers and punches are attached to the 1050s to provide an alternative means of entry, and as backup to the online system. As purchase order information is entered, each field of information is "tagged" by the terminal operator, and the computer edits each field for valid order number, correct budget information, and so forth.

When the information has been entered, the operator visually edits the resulting typed version and makes any necessary corrections on the spot. A code indicating that the record has been edited is then entered on the record, without which the record cannot be processed. The entry and editing process requires an average of about three minutes per title. The 1050 terminals are also used to input receiving and involve information, to enter accession numbers, and to indicate that can be cleared from the in-process file. Washington State has adopted the Washington University-Yale University process control technique, and as a by-product of the order entry procedure a book card is created for insertion in IBM 357 card readers to indicate when a book is received and moves through various stages in processing. Because both online and off-line input are possible, the library has made comparative studies of the two methods. The results indicate that operators prefer to work online, and make fewer errors as a result.

Most errors are identified immediately by the computer, or are recognised by the operator, so they can be corrected at once and the most of erroneous information flowing through the system is drastically reduced. The increased efficiency made possible by improved communication between man and machine is thus concretely demonstrated. The use of the terminal was limited to a seven-day period beginning on the 17th of the month, however, and appears to have been merely a means of avoiding the necessity for correcting the paper tapes and re-inputting them.

No searching was done via the terminal, and although the device could print out information from the computer no real interaction appears to have taken place or been intended. The project was funded through the Computer Centre, not the library, and when the funds were cut off in September of 1972 the system was discontinued. Meanwhile, also in 1969 and also in Massachusetts, terminals with visual display screens were being used for the first time in an acquisition system.

The "Book Order and Selection System" (BOSS) of the University of Massachusetts in Amherst uses for such devices online to an IBM 370/145 computer. Design of the system began in 1968, and less than twelve months elapsed before the system was operational. Currently BOSS processes about 90,000 orders per year, maintains the on-order file, provides both receiving and invoicing information, and produces claims for items not received.

The original order information as well as changes are entered via the terminal; since the visual display shows an outline or "mask" of the information to be entered, no special coding forms are required. If a keying error is caught by the computer, the visual display screen immediately indicates it. After the error is corrected and the computer determines that all required information has been entered, a mask for the next order is displayed.

The order outstanding file can be searched on the 2260 by order number, author, title, or Library of Congress card number. The unit cost for acquisition of an item has been calculated at $2.55, which includes that cost of searching and some costs properly assignable to cataloguing. Manual file maintenance has been substantially reduced, and the backlog of processing eliminated.

A smaller system was implemented at Oregon State University in 1970 using a CDC 3300 computer and a CDC 210 (later 211) terminal with a visual display screen as well as a 3 KSR teletype (keyboard) terminal. Dubbed LOLITA, the system was developed over a three-year period for around $90,000, a modest figure compared to most other early online systems. In part this low cost was possible because an existing time-sharing system at the university's computer centre was used, and programming efforts could be concentrated exclusively on the design of LOLITA and an earlier pilot project. No time was needed to design, debug or redesign the operating system software, as was necessary at Washington State University and the University of Chicago."

Acquisitions personnel have been transferred to other duties, bookkeeping loads on the college bookkeeping operation have been reduced, list of new books are more complete and are produced with less labour, and the system provides input to the cataloguing operation which has resulted in some further saving there.

The fund accounting system is sound is now accepted by the state for legal accounting purposes. An interesting feature is as provision for entering orders into the system and "holding" them until funds become available. In a recent fiscal year, the library received enough funds in the last ten days to double monographic purchases fro the year, and despite the shortness of time the library was able to encumber the funds using this capability.

Syracuse and Northwestern Universities both implemented online acquisition systems during 1971 using keyboard terminals in the IBM 2740 series, and both connected to IBM 370 computers. Despite some similarity in equipment, however, the systems have marked differences.

Northwestern's provides input from MARC tapes, converts foreign currency, and writes checks, whereas Syracuse's does not; on the other hand, Syracuse's system automatically issues cancellation notices, checks for duplicate billing and duplicate orders, assigns funds based on the subject matter of the item being ordered, assigns funds based on the subject matter of the item being ordered, produces accession lists and delinquent order lists, and provides a wide variety of other management information, none of which is provide at Northwestern.

Unfortunately, no costs for either system have been published. Perhaps the most sophisticated system presently in operation is Stanford University's BALLOTS. BALLOTS is a combined or "integrated" technical processing system, and includes both acquisition and cataloguing functions.

By 1975, over $2.5 million in grants from the Office of Education, the Council on Library Resources, and the National Endowment for the Humanities had been spent on its development. Design began in 1967, but the first production operations did not occur until 1972, when the first part of the acquisition system was implemented. The first segment provided the capability of searching machine-readable cataloguing data supplied by the Library of Congress, and using it to order and catalogue books.

During the first year only MARC titles could be handled, but by late 1973 other parts of the system had been implemented, and non-MARC titles could also be acquired and catalogued. Serials, standing orders, and approval orders are also now handled by the system, although in contrast to most other acquisition systems fund accounting is not.

The equipment used is a large IBM 360 Model 67 computer, a small PDP 11 computer as an intermediary, and a number of Sanders 804 programmable display terminals; cataloguing and acquisition departments share 11 terminals, and others are located at the reference desks in the main and undergraduate libraries, where library staff assist the public in searching the files.

The searching capabilities of the system are in fact its most elegant feature, with many indexes online and numerous automatic hints and instructions from the computer as a search progresses. There is also a program for training new users of the system via the terminal itself.

For libraries which cannot afford to develop a fully automated system directly they are a useful stepping-stone whereby the final goal can be approached by degrees. In Britain a computer-produced checking-in list has been developed at the City University. Periodical parts expected to arrive during the coming month are listed on a line printer.

As the parts are received in the library they are ticked off on this list, making it a simple matter to inform library users about the arrival or non-arrival of a particular journal issue. This printed checking-in list gives full titles of journals, unlike systems which punch an eighty-column card for each expected part, where title have to be abbreviated. The system is capable of conversion to a fully automated one, which would require only a minimum amount of keypunching to cater for parts which do not behave as expected.

Another semi-automated system has been installed at the Louisville School of Medicine, Louisville, Kentucky. Using only punched-card equipment, check-in cards are prepared for each expected title. These require the manual addition of volume number, part number, and date of receipt to complete the full bibliographical data for each part.

A number of libraries in the United States have reported the installation of fully automated computerised systems. The very simplest level at which entries for bibliographies and catalogues can be prepared by automated methods is that involving the use of a paper-tape typewriter or the IBM Document Writer. These machines are used widely in libraries nowadays and their routine application is seldom reported in the literature.

5
Library Networking

In the present times, the term 'network' is used in place of 'resource sharing' or 'cooperative systems'. It is because of two important reasons: potential improvement of library and information operations by interconnecting individual library systems with the more recently developed facilities for data and information transfer; and the significant role played by the computers, telecommunications and new reprographic techniques. Networking and modernisation are becoming very important in all types of libraries as they enable the users to have access to the resources of many other libraries in addition to their own one. The public libraries are also likely to benefit themselves by participating in networks.

The benefits that accrue from networking of public libraries are:

i) Preparation of union catalogues;

ii) Provision of cataloguing data/catalogue cards for the publications available in the network libraries;

iii) Provision of bibliographies;

iv) Optimum utilisation of rare collections;

v) Cooperative acquisition of documents;

vi) Cooperative exchange and distribution;

vii) Cooperative storage of documents;

viii) Savings, both of technical work and collections; and

ix) Minimises cost of the library services in the long run.

Local Area Networks

The decreasing costs of microcomputers coupled with significant increases in storage capacity, memory, speed, and versatility, are contributing to the increased prevalence of local area networks (LANs). Networked computer systems are installed in virtually every sphere of business, academic, and nonprofit environments.

LAN systems provide communication links within offices and, by connecting LANs, throughout buildings, across campuses, even around the world. Beyond basic communications, LANs provide resource sharing of hardware, software, and information. Reliance on these devices and systems is so great that estimates of the productivity losses caused by LAN operation failures for just one major corporation may exceed three million dollars per year.

On average, one-half business day per month is lost due to LAN failure or service disruption. Whether those lost days occur at a major manufacturing site or small business office, they translate into significant direct economic losses in productivity. When library networks are down, there are direct and indirect costs to the library and its patrons. Library management tasks, as well as technical activities, are halted and patron access to local online catalogues or external network connections stops. All the wonderment of automation ceases, reminding library staff that machines can and do "break." Frequently, automation failures are the result of management failures. There are multiple aspects to management of automation that contribute to the success or failure of automation.

Management of hardware and software, at minimum, requires a completed systems analysis, availability and creation of documentation (including operational procedures), awareness of system limitations, and sensitivity to user requirements. Constant re-evaluation of systems, human and machine, is also necessary in light of ever-changing technology. The complexity of environments supported by automation necessitate a corresponding sophistication of management.

Libraries are an example of an extraordinarily complex environment. The activities of the library: collection, acquisitions, cataloguing and classification, reference, and serials service—ultimately the access and retrieval of information—are complex endeavours.

Providing appropriate automation management, especially LAN management, demands attention to all the complications of the library mission. Automation in libraries must serve technical needs of professionals handling the collection, as well as serve various skill levels and needs of library patrons. This is a two-fold problem, as expectations of librarians are quite different than those of most patrons, in any library setting.

Automation of libraries has been an ongoing process for several decades. Like most other enterprises engaging in automation efforts, libraries have been and still are undergoing changes previously unimagined due entirely to the impact of automation on virtually every information task. Librarians and library staff have contributed to developing protocols for data sharing, machine-readable format, portions of the Internet, and many other aspects of automation.

The need for improved management techniques and managers accelerates as library facilities develop or expand their application of, and reliance on, both computer and networking technology. Speed of technological changes in computing and networking has propelled the proliferation of LANs, as well as hardware and software tools to supervise and monitor most technical aspects of LANs. Technological haste has also contributed to management being handled by people who may not have the technological training associated with computers or networks.

Though librarians are practically and conceptually educated in the management of information, the transition to including computers and networks as tools in this task presents a continuing technological challenge. Fundamental to all automation is the function of management, but LAN management is still a developing art.

Historically, management of LAN systems has fallen to "ad hoc administrators who acquire their skills on the fly, learning to deal with new demands as they arise. As enterprise wide LANs materialize, that approach won't remain viable". "An effective network control centre depends on the acumen of human operators ... and most [organizations] aren't paying nearly enough attention to selecting and training this critical personnel". In fact, "network management is as much a black art as a science". Keeping track of technology is not the same as managing systems. Users, documentation, and planning for the future must be accepted components of network management.

Merely keeping these information tools running is not enough, LANs as resources must be controlled, and growth must be monitored to meet the needs and complexity of the facility. Since computer systems in libraries serve multiple-user populations in a variety of areas—technical services, circulation, reference, serials, administration, and public access catalogues—the systems must be flexible. Their design and maintenance should involve the expertise not only of computer specialists, but also the professional information management skills of the various librarians, as well as someone representing the average library patron. Many existing computer systems may not be providing the level of productivity or efficiency for any of the users that was forecast. Focusing on more concepts and methodologies from library and information science will contribute managerial tools to LANs.

Woodsworth points out that experience with automation in general demonstrates the necessity of information and computing professionals to work together to address the successful implementation of information technology. Information management, rather than just technology management, will contribute to the management of LANs. A team effort to integrate the technical skills of computer specialists with the information management skills of librarians is the most direct solution to a variety of computer system problems.

While some may consider this paramount to opening Pandora's box, there may be no other rational alternative.

Team management of resources does not mean one vote per team member; there is still a leader, a decision maker who works to keep in balance the technological requirements and information accessibility of the system. Team management, however, will contribute to a growth of knowledge as technical skills become less mysterious and information management becomes better understood.

Balancing hardware and software requirements with the need to provide services to a diverse clientele, which includes the providers of the services, is not a small task. Automation's impact on our society has changed the way people communicate, and changed what patrons want or even expect from libraries. New services to entice the public and to serve the library audience are being based on automation. The success of the Blacksburg, Virginia, electronic village, which has a library as a key provider of internet access, is but one outstanding example.

The changing role of libraries in schools into proactive resource and multimedia centres with Internet access is another example. These efforts require the expertise of many people, with many points of view and many visions. The success of future automation efforts demands cooperation, communication, documentation, and collaborative efforts.

LANs are tools primarily used for sharing resources, especially information. LANs rely on being able to communicate among computers to share resources of a central computer, and now via wider area links, to share resources of remote computers. LANs, then, are resource storage and communication tools. Beyond storage, they also tend to become depositories and distribution sites of information in various stages of formation. LANs become limited "information centres," though not in the traditional sense that Lancaster described. With the fast growth of networking technology, little time has been given to establishing "acquisition and storage policies ... and a guaranteed source of access". LANs do not "organize and control ... by cataloguing, classification, indexing and related procedures" per se, as Lancaster suggests are the mark of information centres. To be able to access and share resources, including information, there must be organization.

LANs use a variety of organizational techniques to control and access these resources. The initial organizational feature is the file system within a file server, the primary computer of the network. A file server is divided into volumes that are then divided into directories, which may be divided into subdirectories. The least item in the hierarchy is the file, or document. This structure is common to microcomputers, file cabinets, and various other storage and retrieval systems. The structure is also a primary step in the hierarchical, or even relational, classification of data, or information. The file server's structure may be protected by assigning rights and controlling access based on the requirements and skill levels of users.

Using rights to protect the file server is a common and recommended method to ensure resource integrity as well as user privacy. Rights and access control are attached to each user's account. Rights and access restrictions determine which parts of the file server a user may enter and how resources may be used by that account. Failure to assign sufficient rights for users can make the network unusable. Assigning too many rights can undermine the entire structure of the network.

Therefore, assigning too few or too many rights can create situations that result in total system failure. The assignment of rights, access control, and directory structure design generally falls to a person fulfilling the role of network manager. This person often is not specifically trained in the management of the network software or hardware, or even in the management of information in general. This kind of situation sometimes contributes to an inappropriate LAN organization and structure. Location of software files and related organization is critical to the proper functioning of the server.

Software packages must be in directories that allow user access but do not allow a user to modify the executable code of the software package. Placement of the executable files and temporary user files, as well as ensuring user control over these files, can be critical to the proper performance of the software as well as the network. Accessibility of files within the system, whether in shared directories or in personal directories, should be monitored to ensure maximum user access, file server efficiency, and resource protection.

A library LAN provides access to the shared database(s) that contain the bibliographic records of the collection, the acquisitions trail, the circulation records, an OPAC, and possibly some unrelated support software. Two specific user groups would rely on such a system: the library staff handling the input and management of bibliographic records, and the library patrons who access the system only for retrieval purposes.

A system analysis should be undertaken when the library first considers any form of automation. At that time, and periodically thereafter, all aspects of operations should be completely evaluated, documented, and examined. Prior to making any automation decisions, clearly identify and document the operation, activity, procedures, and rationale for actions. Demographics of all user populations should also be collected and evaluated. Give specific attention to the differences in user population needs.

The information that the library staff requires to create the access system that patrons will employ is not necessarily formatted or designed for use by patrons. Understanding the requirements for various groups will better prepare the library to select or design appropriate automation systems. In preparation for a LAN, characterizing user applications for different populations will aid in granting account rights and access that protect the LAN but permit the various user groups maximum system use. Evaluating the details of how much access various user populations require involves cooperative analysis of the functions of the library.

Basically, everyone in a library has a set of tasks to perform. It is necessary for system designers and managers to understand how and why these tasks are performed in order to address the issue of satisfactory access. Sample initial checklist to a systems analysis:

1. Is there complete and comprehensive documentation for each procedure involved in handling an item? If not, this must be completed first.

2. Are the procedures being followed? If not, why not? What procedures are being followed?

3. Are there unnecessary steps or procedures? Is there a sound reason for each step, and procedure?

4. Are there flowcharts with decision statements for each procedure? If not, these should be created.

If each specialist in the various areas of library functions considers and responds to the above inquiries, it is possible to determine the appropriate level of system rights and software access that each account, under each library activity, will require.

Further, this information will provide a basis for evaluating the amount of traffic that will be handled by the system as well as provide data about how much and what kinds of equipment will be sufficient to support ongoing tasks. Determining allocation of computing resources should be based on a clear understanding of the functions of the library, not just the technical limitations of the moment.

Cost-benefit analysis of existing systems of operation compared to proposed systems should be evaluated. Just a few areas that will affect the cost of the project include network topology, number of file servers and client microcomputers, individual user account size, memory size, software requirements, number of terminals available to patrons versus the number available to the library staff, and type of monitors and keyboards.

In the long run, the allocation of resources must reflect a comprehension of the role of certain tasks and services, thereby giving critical items priority in system access, or in type of computer equipment. At the same time, patrons must be satisfied with their level of access. The patron generally sees the Online Public Access

Catalogue (OPAC), but may have access to a variety of online bibliographic databases as well. The patron side of the LAN is facilitated via workstations or "dumb terminals" that provide limited access to the system.

By necessity patrons have "read only" access to the databases. This limitation of access however should not be permitted to become an issue of concern for the patron. The interface should be comfortable and easy for the patron to use, even if making it so means managing the LAN, or performing other library tasks is more difficult.

In the library, the ultimate end user is neither the library LAN managers nor the librarians but rather the patrons. Though most patrons use the computers for only short periods, it is a time when impressions about the library and library services are formed. Therefore, the quality and ease of use of those computers should be of paramount importance. At the same time, because staff will be spending significant time working at computer stations, these too need to be designed well.

Just as the OPAC interface should be easy to use and visually appealing to the patron, the interface that the staff confronts should be reasonably easy to manipulate with appropriate training. All the components of the system, whether used by patron or staff should be designed to satisfy the user's needs rather than the system manager's convenience. Solid planning and attention to detail can make this a much easier task.

Information management in a LAN is not merely the technical monitoring and control of the electronic devices and interfaces. LANs are more than electronic devices, communications centres, and storage and retrieval entities; they are tools used by people. Studies have shown that foremost to people using information systems of any kind, is accessibility. LAN accessibility is dependent upon many technical factors such as the reliability of batch files and the rights assigned and restrictions imposed upon a user account.

LAN accessibility is also reliant upon peoples' ability to navigate the system. Lack of adequate documentation, both technical and assistance documents, can impede the user. Research has reasonably established that people seek and use resources that are readily accessible.

Access to a LAN can be daunting without documentation or training. Failure to provide adequate documentation could be construed as "gatekeeping" or attempting to protect the system or the system's information resources by excluding those who might require documentation. Lack of documentation prevents LAN managers and librarians from being able to handle system failures, user errors, and upgrades in a timely fashion.

System documentation representing not just technical documents but all the aspects of the system should be created and maintained. This includes documenting such aspects as the linkages from controlling batch files, software locations, user access rights, mapping patterns, drive and directory allocations, classification, and structural schemes. Record keeping to sustain system support and ensure maximum user support is critical to provision of service. Keeping the machines operating with the least disruption to the users is not simply a matter of keeping everything plugged into a power source.

LANs are a matrix of interrelating devices, software interfaces, and user interaction. This makes LAN's vulnerable to technical, electronic, and user error. Tracing failures requires keeping information about all possible sources of error. Documenting the LAN is one step toward improving LAN performance. Resources must be organized in a fashion that accommodates the users; therefore, the system design would reflect the LAN's user organization.

The application of directory conventions, that is, agreeing that certain types of documents reside in specified directories that are accessible to specified members, would permit the creation of work groups that have mutual access to joint work or documents that require sharing. Additionally, it would be advantageous to have file-name conventions, or agreements to how files will be labelled, dated, and identified by the users. None of these would be possible without documentation of the system structure.

Hence, the breadth and scope of the server's directory system can be exploited as an organizational component to improve access while decreasing duplication, space waste, and lost documents. Access to software applications should be documented for new users and even established users. Software groups update their product, frequently requiring that users modify how they interact with the software. In general, documentation produced by software companies is still not adequate for the average user.

LAN service can be seriously damaged by users failing to comply with software instructions and requirements. Hence, LAN administration tends to bear the responsibility for creating and maintaining appropriate user-oriented documents. Further, LAN management may be the only group cognizant of unique twists in the LAN related to specific software. Every detail of operational procedures should be documented and periodically reviewed.

By having clearly defined and documented procedures for everything-from how to file the paperwork in order to add a patron to the patron base, to the steps for restarting the system after a failure-the library is ensuring the safety and efficiency of its operations.

Most difficult in preparing these types of documents is including adequate detail to prevent confusion. Any procedure documents should be reviewed frequently, in fact these should be treated as "living" documents. Over time, procedures will change in response to improvements or modifications to the system. Sample information that should be maintained about the LAN and user accounts:

— batch files: names, locations, connections to other files, last update

— rights assigned, restrictions, time limits, space allocations to accounts (system software can keep track of these)

— upgrade records for all software, repair records, error reports

— records and conventions for the location and access of software records and conventions for the mappings of the server and individual accounts

— records and conventions for drive and directory allocations

— conventions for filenaming

— documentation kept current about how to access specific software, how to restart if there is a failure, how to add or delete users, how to perform backups, how to report errors-all procedures relevant to each user group and written oriented to each user group.

A LAN becomes a complex hybrid of all the users and administrators; without conventions and documentation, it can easily become a Hydra with too many heads to cut off to control. Documentation at all levels of the organizational structures, of the linkages between critical points will ease the management of the system. Beginning and maintaining the documentation becomes a significant task, but one that will be seriously regretted if neglected. A number of worthwhile software packages exist to assist in the management and documentation of LANs.

However, one should not overlook the external documentation requirements of patrons and staff; simple how-to documents for users about each software and interface are essential. Documentation and procedures are critical in coping with some of the limitations of the system. It is particularly important that the software structures that control LAN functions are fully documented, such as the batch files, drivers, and system mappings. Batch files perform series of commands.

By using a single batch file name, a batch file can, for example, change drives or directories, run software packages, or load network drivers. Batch files are meant to automate processes users may need, and thus decrease the number of key strokes users must input. Batch files also allow for modifications to be made to the system in an automated fashion in response to changes in software or in adjunct systems.

Batch files exist on the computer server and on workstations; batch files may exist in any directory, local or remote, and may be executed by other batch files. Documenting what is in a system, as well as where it is and why it exists, is critical to managing any resource. Identification and documentation of the batch files in the system should be considered standard and required of whomever is in charge of the system. Naming conventions should be created and followed throughout the system to assist in preventing file duplication, conflict, and overlap. Records that identify all the links between batch files should be maintained. Files that automate processes and control interfaces must be documented.

Lack of documentation for batch files probably contributes the most to duplication of files and failure to remove older versions of batch files. A directory of commonly shared batch files should be constructed. Batch files that are shared via the server do not generally need to exist on workstations or in individual accounts.

Organizing files that many users may need into shared directories, while complying with appropriate server and software protocols, also saves computer time, access time, and server space. However, complex webs of batch files that connect to other batch files for no purpose other than to link two files via many other names serves no purpose. In fact, having a patchwork of batch files that may conflict with each other if started can cause unnecessary problems for tracing system failures.

In addition, there are unnecessary dangers to removing batch files when many files have been overlaid on other batch files via complex webs that make it impossible to trace all the connections successfully. Therefore, as duplicate, erroneous, or outdated batch files are found, they should be removed. While prior versions of network driver files are often retained for a period of time in case of special needs, these do not belong in active use sites in the system.

Appropriate documentation must be maintained. If all the links are not identified, it could endanger the operation of the system, generate erratic system failure, or lock users out. It could be necessary to rebuild completely a server structure in order to repair this type of problem. Drivers are protocol programs that are created by software manufacturers and communication systems to enable computers to successfully transmit instructions and signals to printers, to terminal screens, to server computers, and so on. The driver designs are sometimes overridden by poorly written batch files, modified inadvertently or purposely. Without documentation, it becomes difficult to determine how the changes came about.

Any modification to protocol and driver programs should be fully documented for future reference and error tracking. Any design modifications that appear "spontaneously" should be reported to the vendors. Mapping allows the user to access files that are not in the directory in which the user is working. Mapping establishes pathways that the system can access for searching without having to leave a specific location to access those other locations.

Mapping identifies the drives A:, C:, H:, and so on, as well as locations in volumes or directories. Mapping is critical to efficient operation and ease of movement within the system. Mapping should be minimized to allow for the minimal access that a user needs. If a server's entire memory structure is mapped, that is, if every possible location is set into the standard user's map, this results in overmapping, or faulty mapping, and it will negatively affect access time.

This type of mapping is not necessary for every user either, since not every user needs or has actual access to all memory locations. Faulty mapping causes the system to examine far more locations for items than necessary and may decrease access time, or even increase the potential for inappropriate accesses.

CDROM networks

CDROMs on stand-alone workstations were introduced to libraries in the middle to late 1980s. They were not widely used in libraries prior to 1989. At that time, only a handful of larger institutions and those universities with engineering programs or sophisticated computer expertise operated CDROM networks. Today, CDROM networks are no longer restricted to these types of institutions. Among libraries at smaller institutions, CDROM networks are still found less frequently because of funding problems and lack of staff expertise.

The purpose of this chapter is to review the evolution of a CDROM network in an undergraduate library-ours-at a college with limited financial and personnel resources, and examine the impact of the network's development on the library's collection, personnel, and services. We will enumerate the factors that went into the decisions and experiences surrounding the evolution of our library's network. A list of helpful titles is appended. King's College is a small undergraduate institution awarding more than half of its baccalaureate degrees in occupational or professional disciplines. The library, containing some 150,000 volumes, is staffed by five librarians and nine support personnel. Three of the five librarians provide reference and instructional services in addition to other duties. Like many smaller colleges in the mid-1980s, there was no clear campuswide computing standard or single plan for introducing new technology. However, the launching of the library's CDROM network helped to break up this technological inertia. In 1992 the library installed a small Token-ring CDROM network consisting of three public workstations. The Novell/CD-NET network provided individuals with access to six H.W. Wilson indexes. The network was expanded in fall 1993 to seven workstations with access to seven databases including the National Newspaper Index.

By fall 1994 the network contained ten public workstations with additional access to the databases available through the campus network. The CDROM network also serves as the centre of a buildingwide network that provides librarians and staff with connections to the campus network and the Internet. As you will see, this network project did not emerge all at once but rather evolved in stages. In 1987 the library installed its first CDROM database on a single IBM personal computer. It was intended to facilitate students' use of the journal collection.

By 1990 the library had four Wilson CDROM indexes on two stand-alone workstations. Since each station contained only two databases and could only support one user, only two people could search simultaneously. The two users were limited to the two databases on their respective stations. Individuals wanting to search a different database had to change workstations. Concerned with the growing number of students who had to wait to use particular indexes, the librarians decided to develop a local area network (LAN) within the library.

We had two goals at this point: to make each database searchable from any workstation, and to mechanize the changing of CDROM discs. Tape-loading databases on the public catalogue was considered but rejected. The software to do this was still in its early stages and the library did not want to be a test site. In addition, there was not enough room on the library's integrated system (Dynix) for the databases, nor were there funds to upgrade or replace the system. Although the library had installed an integrated library system in 1989, personal-computer expertise among the librarians was limited and networking experience was nonexistent.

A recently hired reference librarian with some formal computer training was appointed to serve as the network coordinator. While some previous computer experience is necessary, most network managers are self-taught and ours was no exception. The curriculum included a large amount of reading (manuals and computer magazines-PC Magazine, PC Computing, PC World, Computing World, BYTE, Information Today, Information Technology & Libraries, Netware Technical Journal, LAN Times, and CDROM Professional) and practice (playing around with the software). In preparation for the network, the librarians met with computing centre personnel to review how networks function.

After a discussion of the plans for a campus-wide network, the merits of remaining compatible with the computing centre were obvious. This was reinforced by observations of the support problems other departments experienced when they made equipment and software choices at variance with the computing centre's expertise. Remaining uniform with the computing centre would eliminate needless complications and ensure additional technical support and backup. Networking CDROMs is constrained by the triangle principle.

Three basic elements in the design and operation of a perfect LAN are: speed, low expense, and ease of operation. However, with the current technology it is only possible to have two of the three corners of the triangle. The most likely combinations are to have a network that is cheap and simple, but slow; or to have an expensive network that is fast and easy to operate and use. After site visits to two larger libraries with networks, the serious examination of the networking options began. We decided to implement a fast but easy to operate and use network, building it in stages as funds permitted.

Based on our observations of database and online catalogue users, we knew response time would be important. We also wanted an expandable network that would be easy for the staff to maintain and would be easy for students and faculty to use. The criterion for hardware was that it be compatible with the computing centre and its network. In reality this criterion translated into the same hardware standard as the computing centre-IBM equipment,

Token-ring network typology, and Novell network software. Although less expensive equipment could have been purchased, the potential problems of compatibility, support, and service were considered unacceptable long-term risks-in terms of the financial and human costs.

It would be easier and less expensive to purchase familiar brand-name equipment from well-established vendors that our campus computer staff preferred than it would be to obtain additional personnel to troubleshoot a network built with less expensive equipment from newer firms. In the event of trouble, the equipment's uniformity and compatibility would reduce the number of potential complications and the likelihood of finger-pointing by vendors. With the hardware platform determined, we wanted a software-only solution that would be mounted on off-the-shelf computer equipment, rather than a vendor's prepackaged, turnkey, CDROM network composed of proprietary hardware and software: Although this decision eliminated a number of possible turnkey alternatives, it also reduced the possibility that the network would be artificially dependent on or restricted by a vendor's limitations. Although a turnkey system with its single source for equipment and support is theoretically easier to purchase and maintain, you do pay a premium for the convenience.

Once we had chosen Novell network operating system software, we started to select the software required to connect and operate the CDROMs over the network. Our criteria for CDROM-networking software was that it be relatively simple, flexible, fast, reliable, and able to operate in an IBM and Novell environment. There were two basic CD-networking choices, with several software options: peer-to-peer (Lantastic) or client-server (CD-NET, Opti-Net, SCSI Express). The peer-to-peer method had the qualities of being cheap and easy.

However, it was slow, not too secure, and frequently unreliable. Since our criteria were fast and easy, our only other choice was the client-server method. Fortunately there were a number of good software programs. A review of the trade literature revealed three solid contenders: CD-NET, SCSI Express, and Opti-Net. At the time SCSI Express was rated the fastest, but it had problems with CDs that required the use of Microsoft's CDROM Extensions (MSCDEX).

Since we were not sure which CDROM databases we might be networking in the future, this was a potential problem. CD-NET and Opti-Net were each examined against our criteria of fast and easy. Although both products met the criteria, CD-NET offered a Network Loadable Module (NLM) version (which would work tightly with Novell) and a built-in menu interface. In addition CD-NET was faster than Opti-Net and had been chosen by PC Magazine as an Editor's Choice. In addition to the published sources, an Internet discussion group (CDROM-LAN, "Use of CDROM Products in LAN Environments" <CDROM-LAN@idbsu. idbsu.edu>) proved to be a great source of practical information and useful advice from networking veterans.

CDROM-LAN is dedicated to the use of CDROM products in LAN environments and to the problems of networking various products. The list is owned and moderated by Dan Lester, Network Information Coordinator, Boise State University Library, Boise, Idaho. Vendors and their support services were frequent sources of information. The information they supplied and the questions they asked us served as a type of "reality check" on our proposed plans.

In planning the network the decision was made to take a multiyear view and design a multipurpose, buildingwide network rather than just a ten station CDROM public network for reference. This would provide flexibility for future growth within the building and facilitate the development of a campus network without having to redevelop sections of the installed network. The idea was also in our minds that the library's existing integrated system would eventually be replaced by an automated system that was designed to take advantage of network technology.

The decision to remain uniform with the computing centre and to build a fast and relatively easy to use and operate network meant that the network would be expensive and would have to be built in sections as funds permitted. Building the network in stages proved to be a good financial, learning, and human resources strategy. Besides being easier to budget for, it made the project much more manageable and helped to reduce the risks involved. With the network coordinator in the lead, existing personnel were used to research, design, and install the network. Individuals gained a better understanding of networking than they would have gotten with a turnkey system.

With our own personnel involved, the project seemed less of a technological threat or wonder. Because we didn't bring in outside help, the measured growth also kept the project humanly possible for existing staff. The controlled installation provided time for learning, permitted the exploration of options, and allowed us to take in stride the surprises that came from unexamined assumptions. Although the network cable had been pulled during the winter by personnel from the college's physical plant and the equipment and software ordered in the late spring, nothing arrived in the sequence expected or needed.

After all the equipment arrived and some initial learning experiences with the CDROM drives and the Novell software, the network was fully operational within six working days. With just three days before fall classes began, the librarians and staff were introduced to the network.

In thinking about the network and what to put on it, we decided early in the planning stages to stay with and expand the selection of H.W. Wilson databases currently offered for a variety of reasons: we were already familiar with the company and the product; the databases were easy for undergraduates to search and students were comfortable with the software interface; the databases were relatively simple to explain or demonstrate; the uniformity of the interface made it easy for students to move from one index to another; and the indexes provided access to a large number of the journals held by the library. Wilson's commitment to provide abstracts was an added attraction.

As a company, H.W. Wilson was responsive to our needs and the licensing arrangements were very reasonable. The various configuration options also were comprehensive and flexible. Our subsequent experience with other database vendors has reaffirmed our original choice. A primary consideration for adding items to the network was the database's ability to return users to the network menu. Once users had their information, they frequently just walked away, rather than exiting from the program. This meant that anyone wanting to use that station had to figure out what index they were in, determine where they were in the program, exit it, and return to the main menu before they could start their search.

With a campus network this would mean that ports could be needlessly tied up, if users did not correctly exit the database. Software without a time-out feature, which automatically returns to a DOS prompt (network menu) after a period of inactivity, was deemed unacceptable. Although some people said that undergraduates should be able to figure these things-out, we felt differently. Ideally individuals should be able to do these things; however, based on our experience, the fewer obstacles users of all ages have to deal with, the better.

An individual's lack of computer or software expertise should not be a handicap to using this network. Several databases that are "technically networkable" are not networkable in our definition. We realized that the cost and licensing agreements of some desirable databases would probably keep them off our network for a while. There were also some databases that would have been nice to have but were not necessary in an undergraduate environment. "Networkable" also does not mean it should be on a network. There have been no major problems with the network. On occasion the token-ring cable connections worked loose, just enough to cause a workstation to lock up. Now the connections are kept out of harm's way and checked regularly. The other problem we encountered was due to a power outage.

A campus-wide electrical outage tripped a fuse in the CDROM-drive tower. We did not discover the tower fans were not working until three weeks later, when the CDROM drives started to overheat and malfunction. The network used the same makes and models of computing equipment; unfortunately, it did not stay that way for long. Our printers were the first to break this uniformity. Because of the openness of the reference area (thus the need for quiet printing), we relied on our previous experience and chose Hewlett Packard Think Jet printers when we built the network. However, the cartridges for ink-jet printers were expensive. The cost was considered a trade-off because they were easy to use and care for. Unfortunately, sometimes good products are discontinued by manufacturers.

When it came time to expand the network, a good replacement printer was not readily apparent. Four new printers were ordered sight unseen on the basis of their technology and word-of-mouth recommendations. This was a mistake. The new dot-matrix printers were as quiet as expected, but not as quiet as the ink-jet printers. But the real problem was the paper feed, which tended to jam frequently and was difficult to clear. We should have tested a machine before we purchased four printers. In the end, the greatest source of network aggravation for the reference librarians were and are the printers and their maintenance.

Although efforts are made to check the cartridges or ribbons and stock them with paper, the printers inevitably "run out" when reference activity is busiest. Although the network has been relatively trouble-free, the amount of time required for system-related maintenance has been more than expected. Keeping the network at peak performance is facilitated by regular hardware and software maintenance. The intent is to prevent problems before they develop. On a regular basis the printers are inspected (ink, print-heads, sprockets, oil gears, etc.).

Dust is a problem, so filters on the CDROM drives and the CDROM lenses are cleaned once a semester. Keeping the dust off the monitors and out of keyboards keeps them attractive and functional. The inside of the server and workstations are vacuumed whenever they are opened up. In addition to hardware maintenance, software upkeep is important. Network error files are checked and the DOS "CHKDSK" procedure is run regularly on the workstations. The -CHKDSK- command analyzes the directories, files, and file allocation table on the disk; it produces a disk and memory status report.

The network traffic, cache buffers, packets, and memory are monitored frequently for signs of trouble. Status reports on the network's "health" are run regularly. The TRACE.LOG file on the Wilson Disc program keeps track of the commands, the search terms, and the databases used during search sessions. These TRACE.LOG files provide statistics and a profile of database use. This information not only tells us which Wilson databases are being used, but how often and in what ways. The statistics make it possible to track growth and changes in network activity and searching behaviour from year to year.

Upgrades and enhancements in hardware and software frequently contain some kind of surprise or new learning experience. We have found that some software that works before a new release does not always work after a new release. In the process it becomes apparent that assumptions about what is required or how something works cannot be made based on previous experience. Likewise, it is not uncommon for a database update to contain an intermittent 'problem', which locks up a workstation or two. In such cases, it takes a while to determine if the problem is network or software-related. When the vendors are contacted, they frequently are aware of the problem and are willing to mail out a replacement disc.

According to Timothy Dugdale, a reference librarian/computer specialist at Georgia State University, LAN maintenance varies according to several factors: (1) the number of individuals who are able to assist with it; (2) the reliability and stability of your system and equipment, particularly the amount of memory available; and (3) the number of other functions, such as word processing or electronic mail (e-mail), that also run on the CDROM network. A related factor is the number of personnel who can train or assist individuals in the use of the network. Dugdale reports that in his situation, with a split position between reference and the network, 70 percent of his time is devoted to computers. Time is also taken up by training staff, and apprising them of software updates and changes in the setup. The size of the network and the degree of hardware and software standardization also influence how much time is devoted to LAN maintenance.

In our situation, one reference librarian splits her time between the network and reference, with initially 60 to 70 percent of her time devoted to network related maintenance or troubleshooting. The actual time that can be devoted to the network is limited to about three hours each afternoon. This librarian is scheduled to work four hours at the reference desk each evening.

Currently, no other personnel are trained to assist with the network. Since the network is fairly stable, only a small amount of time is devoted to dealing with problems per se. The largest amount of time is spent dealing with upgrades, software changes, and anomalies in upgrades. Communication among library personnel is important.

Conveying information about network-related changes is an integral part of network administration. This is particularly true if the changes may affect users. Because of its complexities, it is critical to document the state of the network.

It is important to keep the manuals, documentation, and information about the hardware configuration and software in a central and easily accessible location. Knowing the details and keeping track of them for emergencies is vital but easily overlooked. At the present time we are developing more complete documentation. In addition to the configuration information and the telephone numbers of the various technical support personnel, the documentation contains descriptions of likely problems and the steps necessary to diagnose and correct them. In writing the documentation we are trying to anticipate the assumptions of personnel more familiar with networking, such as those who have a working knowledge of DOS. Two manuals are being developed: a procedures manual for the network coordinator (with corollary Netware materials) and a troubleshooting/emergency manual for use by others, when the network coordinator is not available. Cooperation with the computing centre provides us with backup only.

We consider the network a critical operation, because if it is down it causes public service problems. Though we have a good relationship with the computing centre and they are willing to help, they are often too busy to deal with our problems right away. They are also not familiar with CDROM networks. For these reasons it is important to have good documentation and to keep problems in check. Currently, if the network coordinator is unavailable to deal with network problems, there is some difficulty in solving them in a timely manner. We have not yet discarded most of our print indexes in favour of the CDROM medium.

Even if we have no network, students will still have access to the information; it just will not be as easy to access as they are accustomed. However, financial considerations and practicality may dictate that we reduce this duplication. When looking at a technological advancement like a CDROM network, it is easy to lose sight of the fact that it is only a tool to facilitate the use of information and remove impediments for those who use libraries and their resources. As a tool it really does not have a life all of its own, only the life we give it.

Like any success there is a tendency to build on it, figuring that more of a good thing is better. This is not always so, at least not right away. The ramifications and implications sometime need to be digested and the lessons studied before proceeding further. Previously, students were reluctant to use journals, preferring to find what they needed in books rather than consult paper indexes.

With the introduction of journal indexes on CDROM, students are more willing to use newspapers and journals and, with the network, are regularly searching multiple indexes. However, students remain reluctant to go back to older print indexes when necessary. Students' use of the networked indexes has greatly reduced the number of paper indexes to be reshelved. While use of the CDROMs has reduced the number of index volumes to be reshelved, it has greatly increased the number of journal and newspaper items (print and microfilm) to be reshelved. Use of the newspaper and journal collections has increased an estimated 379 percent between 1983 and 1992. In 1983 an average of 420 items (issues/volumes/reels of microfilm) were reshelved per week.

By 1991 the influence of the CDROM indexes on stand-alone stations was evident; an average of 1,562 items per week were reshelved. Upon implementation of the network, journal use increased again. In 1992 an average of 2,011 items per week were reshelved, a 28.7 percent increase over 1991. Along with the increase in the number of items reshelved, there was a 35 percent increase in the number of titles used. In 1991, 386 titles were used at least once. In 1992, 524 titles were used at least once. While more titles were being used, some of the most heavily used titles in 1983 were still among the most used in 1991 and 1992. The top 25 titles, 5 percent of the titles, accounted for 56 percent of the use in 1992. While the list of the most heavily used titles has not changed dramatically, the volume of activity has changed. The descent from the heaviest to the least used title was more gradual and less precipitous in 1992 than it was in 1991. Just as there was stability at the top, there was also stability at the bottom of the list. The number of seldom used titles did not vary much-12 percent in 1991 and 11 percent in 1992. The addition of a single database to the network can have a dramatic influence on journal use. The library has subscribed to General Science Index in paper since 1983 but did not install it on the network until 1992.

Networking General Science Index resulted in a 22 percent rise in the number of science titles used and significantly more use of those titles that had been previously utilized. To more accurately gauge the increase in journal use, interlibrary loan activity must also be considered. While faculty interlibrary loans for journal articles remained relatively stable, only 6.8 percent growth, student interlibrary loans for journal articles increased 86 percent in 1992 compared with 1991. Although the computerized indexes allow students to search several years of journal articles, it is frustrating to users who equate access with ownership. With the rise in journal use came complaints about the number of journals in the library. The contrast-between the satisfaction of having quick access to the journal citations and the frustration of not having similar access to all the articles found-is unsettling for both students and faculty.

Other libraries with CDROM indexes report similar phenomena, increased journal use along with complaints about the number of journal titles available. Heightened expectations as to what technology will do for them during the research process may also contribute to unrealistic expectations. Many individuals equate improved technological access with instant physical possession of the article. Technology makes their work easier, but it does not eliminate the most important work involved in the research process: the interaction of researchers and their materials. The introduction of stand-alone, CDROM indexes in the library had a dramatic qualitative and quantitative impact on the way students researched.

Moving from the stand-alone station to a network had a further dramatic quantitative impact. Because of the easy access CDROM indexes provide to periodicals and newspaper articles, students were far more likely to see them as viable sources of information. Before CDs, students might have been willing to check a volume or two of a printed index. They were far more interested in finding a book on their subject. With CDs, the students checked several years of one or more indexes more quickly and easily than they could have checked two years of the print sources.

As a result, students were finding their way to substantial numbers of journal and newspaper articles. Just as the automation of the catalogue produced increased book use, computerization of the indexes produced increased periodical use. This transformation is not only the result of ease of access and use, real and significant as it is, but also because of the "glamour" of using a computerized database rather than the old-fashioned print database.

Faculty, conscious of the mandate to develop the computer and information skills of students, give research assignments that encourage and specifically require students to use certain CDROM databases, thereby accomplishing several pedagogical goals simultaneously. However, faculty and librarians express frustration at students' reluctance to search print sources when computerized versions are not available or not appropriate. The "learned helplessness" and lack of intellectual initiative of some students may be at least partially explained by the presence of the computer.

The network permits users to move from one database to another without physically relocating, thus allowing them to quickly and easily massage relevant materials from several sources, and giving them much larger quantities of citations than the previous stand-alone stations. A problem is that many students tend to confuse quantity with quality. Thus, it becomes even more important for individuals to have the intellectual tools necessary to analyse information sources. Doing research has become simultaneously easier and more complicated. It promises to become more so in the foreseeable future, and we have to find ways to address this issue.

Students use the research strategies they believe will give them the greatest benefits with the least cost in time or effort, and electronic resources are perceived as the most effective way of accomplishing this objective. When students used printed indexes, the time and effort needed to read and write the citations acted as an automatic filtering system. Students evaluated and selected citations using their own criteria as they read them and before they wrote them down. That physical filtering system is no longer operational in the network environment. In some respects the network makes it easier for students to work together or ask for assistance. When a computer is involved, some students find it easier to ask for assistance from those around them, just like they do in the computer labs. It is not uncommon to find students huddled over a computer discussing the contents of a screen display and then returning to their separate computers.

A concern of the reference librarians is the accuracy of either the information or the strategies that students are sharing with each other. Students teaching each other ineffective strategies or passing on bad information is not in anyone's best interest. In a satisfaction survey, first-year students report that the CDROM databases are their favourite service, with reference services ranked fourth.

By students' junior and senior years, the CDROM databases have slipped to second place with references services ranked first. It appears that undergraduates at first gravitate toward machines and technology; but as they progress with their education, they come to appreciate the librarians' expertise. How should reference and other service points be staffed in the CDROM-network environment? There are two levels of need for undergraduates using CDROM technology: (1) the need for technical expertise to physically access the data. This is fairly simple and straightforward compared to (2) the need for information skills to intellectually access the information. This is far more complicated and profound. The first need merely requires some instruction and experience in manipulating the hardware and software. Although a great deal of time may be needed, it can be accomplished rather easily-either individually or in groups-by support staff with basic credentials. The second need of achieving intellectual access to the data is an educational need.

Students need to learn how to think, understand how the database is constructed, and understand how the literature is structured in the discipline. While this also can be achieved in individual or group settings, it requires a higher level of expertise and credentials on the part of the instructor. The acquisition of these skills and knowledge is cumulative, subtle, and crucial. Although this need has always been there, it is writ large when students are working with computerized databases probably because of the software's accounting functions. The ability to store and print the kinds of searches students do tells us directly what we could only suspect when students were using print sources—that their ability to think is critical to their ability to research effectively.

Networking the stand-alone CDROM databases provides a "multiplier" effect: it magnifies the impact of this realization. We know now that when students use terms such as "education" to search ERIC or "business" to search Wilson Business Abstracts, they are not approaching the databases intelligently. A surprising number of students start out using "big" words (e.g., education) to search specific topics (e.g., dropouts). However, when students are struck by the sheer volume or the total lack of citations, they frequently generate a series of reference questions to narrow their searches.

Although students may be quite content with their CDROM searches, an examination of their strategies indicates a real need for more and better computer research instruction. Although a connection exists between the technical manipulation of the database and the intellectual access of the data, the distinction between these two levels of learning may require us to take a radical new look at both the kind of staff needed to best serve the needs of students in an undergraduate environment and the kind of instruction needed. We really need a library classroom for teaching.

The lack of a networked instructional facility limits the type and effectiveness of the network training and instruction the librarians can provide. A training facility with hands-on capabilities would help librarians to teach students the most effective ways to utilize the databases and the network. Point-of-use instruction, in any form, only goes so far. From an administrative standpoint, the creation of the network was a project the library did not want to avoid.

The library is trying to shape its future rather than have it shaped by others. The situation on campus was such that the library's network sparked the computing centre's interest, and spurred the discussion and development of other network-related projects on campus. As a result, the library's CDROM network provided something to put on the fledgling campus network. The project has fostered better understanding and good relations between the computing centre and the library. As the campus network develops, these relationships have proven to be mutually beneficial. A recognition of common interests can be advanced through cooperation.

Library networking in India

Networks offer provision of more number of materials, that is, comprehensively, at less cost and quickly. With rapid advancements in the various technologies such as telecommunications, satellite communications, microprocessors, computers, etc., several networks are either presently functional or in the formative stage in India. They can be grouped into:

i) *General networks:* NICNET, INDONET, VIKRAM.

ii) *Subject networks:* VIDYANET, BTISNET, SIRNET INFLIBNET, ERNET.

iii) *Specialised/business networks:* BANKNET, COALNET, RAILNET, TOURNET, SAILNET.

iv) *Geographical networks:* CALIBNET, DELNET, HYLIBNET, PUNENET, BONET, etc.

NICNET is a Government of India network aimed at providing information to support planning, decision-making and monitoring Government schemes and programmes. It links all the districts and states with the headquarters at New Delhi. INDONET is a commercial computer network developed by the Computer

Maintenance Corporation Ltd. (CMC), New Delhi. It is expected to have about 100 centres in several parts of the country like Calcutta, Bombay, Madras, Bangalore, Ahmedabad, Bangalore, Pune, Hyderabad, etc.

VIKRAM is a packet switched public data network being developed by the Department of Telecommunications, Government of India. The network's main centre is located in Delhi and would link to 8 switching modes. While NICNET is meant solely for the use of Government departments, INDONET and VIKRAM are public networks. SIRET is a computer communication network of CSIR aimed at linking about 40 CSIR laboratories spread throughout India. BTISNET, set up by the Department of Biotechnology, Government of India, is a specialised network linking the information centres in genetic engineering, cell culture, biology, etc. DESINET, developed by the DESIDOC for the DRDO units, covers the defence scientific and research information, and connects all the DRDO laboratories, scattered throughout India. ERNET is a network meant for the academic and research community. It links 5 IITs, IISc, NCST and DOE.

INFLIBNET (Information and Library Network), being developed by the UGC, will link the institutions of higher learning covering all disciplines, R& D institutions and other national organisations like CSIR, WAR, DRDO, ICSSR, etc. VIDYANET links several research institutions and laboratories, universities and higher education institutions, research centres of industrial and other commercial organisations. CALIBNET (Calcutta Library Network), DELNET (Delhi Library Network), HYLIBNET (Hyderabad Library Network), PUNENET (Pune Libraries Network) and BONET (Bombay Libraries Networks) are the library networks linking the library and information centres located in their respective geographical regions. CALIBNET is a metropolitan network linking 38 libraries in the Calcutta metropolitan area. The libraries or the institutions linked in this network are either scientific research institutions like Bose Institute, Saha Institute of Nuclear Physics or the higher learning institutions like Jadhavpur University, etc. DELNET links All-India Institute of Medical Sciences, DESIDOC, DST, India International Centre, IIPA, INSDOC, JNU, NPL and NASSDOC.

In none of the networks mentioned including the geographical area networks, not even a single public library has been included. In fact, no sincere and worthwhile efforts have been made in India for public library networking. Recognition of the importance of resource sharing among the public libraries can be traced as far back as to 1919. Shri Suri Venkata Narsimha Sastry, a pioneer in the library movement in Andhra Pradesh, had emphasised the importance of resource sharing among the public libraries at the VI Annual Conference of the Granthalaya Sangham held at Madras in 1919. No library can be entirely self-sufficient and selfreliant.

Libraries in any region have necessarily to develop interdependence and depend on each other. In the matter of acquisition of a collection, it may be appropriate for a library to concentrate on one or more disciplines or areas of knowledge by building up a strong and comprehensive collection supported by some books generally recognised required in other areas. Occasionally when need arises one could draw on the book stock of another library strong in another field. Such an arrangement results in available resources being utilised more economically and a larger book stock being used by readers in the region. All the libraries within a state should form part of a network extending from the community library of the village through intermediary levels to the district and to the state central library. The state network should eventually connect with the national level. The main players in the area of library automation in recent years have been the special libraries of the country.

These libraries/documentation centres are in the R & D institutions under the CSIR, Indian Council for Medical Research (ICMR), Indian Council for Agricultural Research (ICAR), or the Defence Research and Development Organization (DRDO). Notably libraries belonging to the private sector and public sector industrial R & D organizations such as BHEL R & D and Steel Authority of India (SAIL), and the international organizations such as International Crops Research Institute for the Semi-Arid Tropics (ICRISAT) have also made useful contributions. In fact such libraries have provided the leadership and have become training grounds for other libraries. Considerable impetus to the use of new information technologies in special libraries has been provided by the support that the Dept. of Scientific and Industrial Research (DSIR) has extended to the Sectoral Information Centres established in some of the CSIR laboratories under the auspices of the National Information System for Science and Technology (NISSAT).

NISSAT has also funded several training programmes and software development projects which have played an important role in improving awareness of new technologies and their potential, and in transfer of skills and software to different special libraries in the country. Understandably, the emphasis in most special libraries has been on database development and on information retrieval services.

With the exception of a few university libraries such as IIT, Kanpur and Hyderabad University, the university sector has not been very active. Unlike in the UK or US, academic libraries in the country are not in the forefront of developments and innovations in the application of new information technologies. So far as public libraries are concerned the situation has not changed at all. There is no evidence of any activity nor of any planning for the introduction of new technologies in the public library system of the country.

Several factors have favoured the adoption of new technologies in special libraries. Although most of these are publicly funded, they function relatively autonomously and so decision making is easier. Secondly, special libraries are under pressure to deliver more efficient services and to provide better and wider access to information. The easy and wide availability of personal computers has undoubtedly contributed to special libraries being able to automate their libraries and to their building of specialized databases. The one factor that has probably made the greatest contribution to automation in special libraries in India is the free availability of Unesco's Micro CDS/ISIS and the relative case with which it is possible to build specialized databases using CDS/ISIS.

Unlike special libraries, academic libraries in India function in a relatively less autonomous environment; they have to compete for scarce resources; they are by comparison small units within a large setup; graduate students far outnumber post graduate students, faculty and research staff and as a pressure group graduate students do not have a great stake in improved library services; and in general these libraries do not seem to be under pressure to improve their services as much as are special libraries. However, the UGC in 1988 took the initiative to plan for a country, wide academic library and information network called and this is referred to later in this paper. This initiative has the potential to make a significant impact on operational efficiencies and user services in libraries in general and academic libraries in particular.

The last few years have seen some important and useful initiatives in the development of library automation software. Some special libraries notably at BHEL R & D, SAIL, ICRISAT, INSDOC, NIC, Defence Scientific Information and Documentation Centre (DESIDOC), IIT Kanpur have successfully developed software for library automation.

Understandably these centres have concentrated on developing applications which are important in their specific environments, and where the pay off in terms of better control, new services, or more efficient operations was seen as important. Book and serials acquisitions, computer assisted cataloguing, union catalogue, SDI and current awareness provision are some of the applications developed.

In addition to efforts at the above mentioned centres, CMC Ltd., a public sector computer company has built an integrated software package called MAITRAYEE suitable for a library network. This package will be applied in CALIBNET, a network of libraries in Calcutta. More recently, DESIDOC has built an integrated application using Micro CDS/ISIS as the software platform'. This is a welcome development because a properly built application using a public-domain software package like CDS/ISIS and the free distribution of such a package could go a long way in enabling small libraries in the country to reap the benefits of automation.

The use of a public-domain software and common standards for databases, bibliographic description, indexing and classification can go a long way in enabling better sharing of resources among libraries in India. This is a need which is becoming more and more important as time goes by, thanks to the erosion of the purchasing power of libraries and fall in the value of the rupee vis-a-vis hard currencies. CDS/ISIS has also been used as the platform for the development of useful utilities. One such example is the development at ICRISAT of a general purpose program for the production of SDI outputs based on stored user profiles for use with any CDS/ISIS database'.

Similarly, ICRISAT coordinated a project on behalf of International Agricultural Research Centres (IARCs) of the world to produce a Union Catalogue of Serials. This is also available as a CDS/ISIS database. The database on diskette is available with a built-in software to enable libraries to automatically generate inter-library loan or photocopy requests based on the database. The IARC Union Catalogue as a CDS/ISIS application has been distributed to more than 1200 agricultural research centres worldwide. Although not documented in the literature, some libraries have used CDS/ISIS to develop a stand-alone serials control system.

The last few years has seen the availability of commercially developed software for library automation.

LIBSYS, and TULIPS among the better known commercial packages have been developed both for the DOS and UNIX platforms and are therefore available not only on microcomputers but also on minicomputers and mainframe and in LAN environments.

One measure of the maturity of these packages is that they are written as applications under well known DBMS packages, e.g., Oracle, Ingres. Most of these packages are offered as integrated library management packages. There are differences, however, in the features of these packages as compared to similar packages such as GEAC or VTLS developed in the west. Firstly, none of these packages, with the exception of the CMC package, MAITRAYEE, fully support MARC records. This need may not be felt at the moment in India.

However, when large libraries such as university libraries begin to retrospectively convert their catalogues into machine-readable form, the need to access MARC records on CDROM or other media to restructure such records for use in local systems will undoubtedly be acutely felt.

Similarly, the need to prepare for cooperative and shared cataloguing of Indian publications and for accessing current cataloguing information on external networks will make it essential for locally or commercially developed software to be capable of using MARC records. Another difference between integrated packages developed in India and those of the west is that our packages have attempted to be more than library automation software.

For instance, they have attempted also to he information retrieval systems. Some of them allow entry of information on serial articles, chapters from books and other analytics. They also provide SDI capabilities. Such a facility on the face of it is good but the packages in question have not always adhered to internationally accepted standards for such types of documents.

Also, it is naive to think that libraries, however big they may be, will on their own be able to provide comprehensive information retrieval and dissemination services in respect of periodical and specialized literature of the world from their databases. Access to external databases and information retrieval systems would still be required. It would be interesting to find out to what extent., the information retrieval system capabilities of commercially available Indian packages are in fact being used.

Packages in the West are increasingly emphasizing the incorporation of end-user friendly interfaces, and the provision of online public access catalogues (OPACS). Indian packages, however, are still oriented mainly to use by librarians and information specialists and not by the occasional end-user student, teacher, researcher etc. The question of OPACS in India at the moment is an academic one considering that the computing and teleprocessing power required to enable the provision of OPACS is considerable and not yet available to libraries in India.

Considerable research is ongoing in the US and UK on the design of friendly interfaces including the use of artificial intelligence methods and Graphic User Interfaces (GUI). Developers of library automation software in India will hopefully take note of such developments in their software development work. Integrated systems in the west recognize the centrality of the cataloguing record in library operations.

Automation of acquisitions, cataloguing, circulation, reference and information retrieval functions are dependent on the capture of and access to bibliographic records. The information infrastructure of the west is indeed well suited to ensuring that libraries of all types have wide and easy access to cataloguing data. Library utilities and networks ensure that comprehensive access is possible to cataloguing data.

Data networks ensure that access to such data is reliable and cheap. The MARC record produced not only by the national library but cooperatively by several others is the kingpin in the whole process. Libraries in the west have a long history and tradition of centralised, cooperative and shared cataloguing, and adherence to common standards in classification, cataloguing, and indexing.

Professional manpower in the west is expensive. The larger of the libraries in the west have dedicated minicomputers or mainframes for library automation.

Smaller libraries including special libraries have access to computing power and auxiliary storage capacity either on mainframes of their parent bodies or on their own PC-based local area network (LAN). Integrated library management software in the west is designed to take full advantage of the infrastructure there and the whole emphasis in a library that acquires and uses an integrated software package is firstly the cost-effectiveness with which a publication can be acquired, processed and made accessible to users including access on an OPAC, and secondly the speed with which both the bibliographic record and document is possible to be shared by other libraries.

In India, on the other hand, key elements of the infrastructure that make for the effective application of an integrated library management software package are missing. For instance, we do not have library utilities and so publications acquired by libraries are catalogued several times over, whether we use an integrated software package or not. We do not as yet have anything like an Indian MARC that libraries can subscribe to or access on-line to obtain cataloguing data on Indian publications including those in Indian languages. Thirdly, unlike in the west, few libraries can afford to own mainframes or minicomputers dedicated to library automation.

Libraries in India simply do not have a culture of shared and cooperative cataloguing. Objectives of using integrated library management software packages in India at the moment are not the same as in the west. It seems to me that the one reason why a library goes in for an integrated library management software is so that it can avoid buying different software packages for different applications.

Again, within-the-library integration of functions is not often possible because the different functional units of a library-acquisitions, cataloguing, reference, circulation-normally do not have concurrent, online access to the databases and authority files that constitute an integrated application. Such access is possible only if a library has several terminals to a mainframe or minicomputer or has a dedicated LAN of its own. Even where a library has access to a mainframe or minicomputer, the disk space that is available for library applications is simply inadequate for a proper integrated application. This is because the library has to compete with other departments for the limited computing and related resources.

Only when libraries improve the quality and efficiency of their services will their bargaining power for more resources improve. Even small improvements can go a long way in convincing the managements of the parent organizations of the need for more investment in training and new equipment. It seems to me that libraries in India will need to concentrate on tasks that will have a direct bearing on user services rather than on increased operational efficiency. Like in manufacturing industry, so in the information industry, the capital expenditure on building the appropriate infrastructure in a developing country falls to the government of the country. This infrastructure in the form of better communications networks, facilities for database development, easier access to hardware and software, etc., is now slowly being built in India.

The recent liberalization of India's investment and economic policies will no doubt provide a further impetus for private sector investment in information technology and its applications. Effective utilization of this infrastructure is the responsibility of individual libraries of all types. This means that libraries in India should give the highest priority to improving their services and ensuring easier and wider access to documents and information for their users. The only way libraries in India can cope with the rising costs of informational material and increased demands from users is by better coordination, cooperation and sharing of resources with libraries having similar interests.

The networking of libraries and the application of new technologies for this must obviously get high priority. A vital prerequisite for networking is agreement and conformity to common standards for library processes. More importantly, there is need for a greater commitment to the sharing of both bibliographic records as well as physical documents and copies thereof. Our record in the sharing of resources has been poor to say the least. Part of the problem is the lack of initiative on the part of librarians and partly the lack of policy support to encourage libraries to share their resources with others. Technology alone cannot help bring about the required changes.

Attitudes, practices and policies need to change if libraries in India are to truly, benefit themselves and their community of users by the application of new technologies. The questions, we need to ask ourselves are: Is the western model of library automation and networking relevant to us in our present state of development? If so, to what extent? What are we as professionals doing to enable benefits of automation and application of new technologies to flow not only to libraries but to users of all kinds. We would like to distinguish between infirastructural networks and application networks. The former are those that provide the hardware, software, protocols, and freeways for the free flow of information.

Application networks are those which are set up by or for a specific community (librarians, bankers, etc.) using the infrastructure to serve well defined end-uses.

The last few years have seen considerable thinking and investment in the development of infrastructural networks. Public packet-switched data network: The Department of Telecommunications has established this year, a nationwide public packet-switched data network

(PSDN) called I-NET. I-NET follows from successful experiments with packets-witching technology in the last 3 or 4 years. Initially I-NET will have nodes in 8 cities connected through high speed (9600 and 64000 bytes per second) links. I-NET supports CCITT standard protocols/ interfaces: X.3, X.28, X.29, X.25 and X.75. I-NET is accessible using dedicated or leased lines for asynchronous (X.28) or synchronous (X.25) connection with standard modems/drivers. I-NET is ideal for users whose data traffic volumes do not justify a dedicated network. Database mounted on I-NET hosts are an obvious application of interest to the library community.

Similarly, electronic mail is possible on I-NET. Further, I-NET provides international connectivity to important data networks outside the country through the GPSS (Gateway Packet Switched Service) of the VSNL, India's overseas communications service at Bombay, Madras and Delhi. PADS (Packet Assemblers/ Disassemblers) at these cities ensure access at 300-2400 bps to the gateway and to external networks. I-NET and the GPSS have ushered in an era of relatively less expensive and reliable computer communications in the country and it is now up to the library and academic community to take advantage of these facilities.

Library networks using a combination of dedicated lines and dial-up access connections using the infrastructure of I-NET are a distinct possibility and one can look to the future of library networking in India with hope.

NICNET: A unique infrastructural network with a history that goes back to the 1970's is the National Informatics Centre's (NIC) network called NICNET. NICNET is unique in that it uses almost exclusively, satellite-based communication using low cost roof-top micro-earth stations to connect 450 district headquarters and 32 state and union territory capitals with a central hub at Delhi.

Another unique feature of NICNET is that it uses 500 Very Small Aperture Terminals (VSATs), each of which is connected to a specific outbound and inbound channel on the satellite's transponder. Data transmitted by a VSAT is received and relayed via the satellite (INSAT 1 D) to another VSAT, all of which are addressable. Both individual and group addressing of VSATs is possible.

VSATs have been used to connect computers, terminals, telexes, or other devices to other computers/ devices via the satellite. Because of the technology used, even remote corners of the country are possible to be connected without recourse to telephone lines, multiplexers, modems, etc. NICNET has large mainfirames at four cities in the country and superminicomputers at the state capitals and union territories, all linked via the VSATs and satellite.

NICNET is designed primarily to be a government information network. Its objectives are to promote the collection, storage, analysis, transmission, and exchange of data at the districts, state headquarters and the central ministries and departments at New Delhi for use in planning, management, and monitoring of projects and government sponsored programmes under the five-year plans of the country. The potentials of a network such as NICNET are indeed quite wide. For instance it has been used during emergencies caused by natural calamities. Similarly, it has been used to obtain problem-solving help and information in health and agriculture related areas.

Although NICNET is principally meant for use by Government departments, it does have the potential for use by the library and information community. It is possible to mount databases on one or more of the mainframes of NICNET for online access by users in govt. The Indian MEDLARS Centre (IMC) of the NIC in fact has mounted the MEDLINE database on one of NIC's minicomputers at Delhi and this is remotely searchable using dial-up access from NICNET terminals in the country.

In addition to the MEDLINE database, the IMC provides dial-up access to CDROM databases of the US National Library of Medicine, and to Biological Abstracts and the science Citation Index. An example of how NICNET has been used to mount an application network is seen in the Biotechnology Information System (BTIS) of the country.

This network initiated in 1986 under the auspices of the Department of Biotechnology of the Govt. of India, operates through nine centres called Distributed Information Centres (DICs), affiliated to University departments or research centre under the CSIR or ICMR and specializing in an area of biotechnology. The DICs are charged with the responsibility to develop bibliographic and nonbibliographic databases in their areas of specialization and to provide computer-based access to these to users of such information in the country.

Further, the DICs are expected to provide access information elsewhere in the world through collaborative and cooperative programmes including the exchange of data, databases, and mutual access to such information.

Each of the DICs is a NICNET node and hence all the DICs are interconnected for mutual access to databases and E-mail via NICNET, Further, each of the DICs may possess specialized databases on CDROM which are possible to be remotely searched from NICNET nodes in the country. The DICs also provide remote access to specialized software useful in biotechnology research and development. Since NICNET was designed primarily for governmental use, the extent to which it will be available for library networking and for access to public databases is not yet clear.

Once traffic on NICNET becomes heavy, it may not be able to service the needs of the library community and information users among the general public as effectively as one would desire. There is no doubt however that an important network such as NICNET will keep abreast of new technologies in satellite-based communication and therefore the library community in the Governmental sector should stake their claim to use NICNET wherever possible.

INDONET: INDONET is a commercial distributed computer network to provide access to the considerable computing and software resources of the CMC Ltd., a public sector company in India. The objective is to provide computing power and software to users who cannot afford or fully justify, investment in dedicated hardware and expensive, specialized business and scientific software.

INDONET has three IBM mainframes at Calcutta, Bombay and Madras and smaller computers at Delhi and Hyderahad. The network uses dedicated lines operating at 2400 to 4800 tips. It has plans to use roof-top antennas and packet switching for data routing, within the nodes of the network. Intra-city access to INDONET computers via line-of-sight packet radio is also being investigated. The Bombay node of INDONET is connected to VSNL's GPSS enabling computer-to-computer abroad. INDONET also has plans to mount public databases on one or more of its computers. However, the costs of using INDONET will probably preclude its use by the library and information community to any appreciable degree, especially since cheaper alternatives have become available.

The last three or four years have seen considerable activity in the planning for and building of library and information networks. Three major efforts to network libraries in country are briefly described below. An attempt has also been made to raise questions believed to be important for the future of library networking in India.

INFLIBNET: INFLIBNET is envisaged as a computer-communication network linking libraries in universities and colleges in the country and libraries in institutions affiliated to the CSIR ICMR, ICAR, DRDO and Govt. department. When full fledged it is envisaged that INFLIBNET will network 184 universities and 23 institutions deemed to be universities, 7200 colleges and over 200 libraries affiliated to other organizations. INFLIBNET is envisaged as a multi-service network and will provide catalogue-based services, access to databases and document supply services, and facilities for computer mediated communications such as E. Mail, conferencing, bulletin board, etc.

INFLIBNET is designed to operate at four different levels, viz., national, regional, sectoral and local. The National Centre will coordinate the activities and services of the network and provide the policy frame for the network. Regional centres in north, east, west and south of the country will be established in designated university libraries in the different regions. These will maintain regional union catalogues sectoral centres will be at specialized institutions, e.g. CSIR laboratories, and these will create and maintain specialized databases in specific disciplines or missions. End-users will be serviced, at the local level, i.e. at the colleges, R & D centres, university libraries, etc. About 400 local nodes are proposed to be setup initially.

In addition, INFLIBNET proposes the establishment of 100 document resource centres in different universities and R & D centres. Theses centres will be the focal points in a country-wide document delivery service. The network will use both satellite-based and terrestrial communication channels for connectivity. The system will have 400 ground terminals at 150 university libraries, 50 autonomous colleges and 200 other centres. Intra-city links will be provided via local area networks.

INFLIBNET is expected to evolve standards based on national and international practices for uniform adoption throughout the network. INFLIBNET as conceived is undoubtedly a bold initiative that the UGC has taken. The magnitude of the effort envisaged can be seen by the expenditures that are estimated. A capital expenditure of Rs. 10300.82 lakhs (Rs. 1030 million) and a recurring annual expenditure of Rs. 4767.63 lakhs (Rs.467 million) is the estimated need.

Further, it is recommended that the whole expenditure on capital goods and services required and working capital be provided by the Central Government. It is vitally important for the future of library and information networking in India that INFLIBNET succeeds in its mission to improve interactions among academic and research libraries in the country for the efficient and effective sharing of resources, databases, information, document delivery and other services for the benefit of the library, student, teaching and research communities in the country as a whole.

There has not been enough debate and discussion about the conceptual and physical design features of INFLIBNET among the important stake holders in INFLIBNET, viz., the library community of the country. The following comments and observations are offered as a contribution to the discussion from the perspective of this author. INFLIBNET has followed a typically top-down approach to network planning. A few specialists comprising senior librarians, systems analysts, administrators and telematics professionals met in Delhi over a period of three months in 1988 to formulate the INFLIBNET plan. Such an approach obviously could not have taken into detailed account ground realities in a large country like India.

However, given the need to make quick headway into networking, a top-down approach was probably the best way to make an initial plan, which at best can be thought of as a macro-plan. Refinement of the plan and its implementation, however, would need to take into account the realities of the situation in different parts of the country.

More importantly, commitment to the plan not only from the librarians but also from the top-managements of the different institutions to be involved in the network needs to be obtained. Unfortunately, there does not seem to have been any attempt at micro-planning required at the different institutions so that they could in turn take up suitable activities within their own organizations. Although the plan is more than three years old, not much has been done to build awareness among librarians and to get their input into ways of implementing different components of the network.

As of now university and other librarians do not seem to be clear about their roles and the kinds of investments in equipment and software, training and staff skills they would need in order to become full-fledged participants of the network. Part of the problem with INFLIBNET is its ambitiousness.

The investments envisaged seem to be far more than what the UGC or Govt. of India can provide during the Eighth Five-Year Plan. This has apparently necessitated rethinking on the outlined activity plans. The sheer size of the plan and fie ability/willingness of the Govt. to commit resources needed, lead one to ask if it would not have been wiser to start small and build incrementally in the interest of the sustain ability of the whole project and providing proof of the workability of ideas and methods envisaged in the plan. It is probably pertinent at this point of time to look at the experience of the United States in library networking. Butler writing as far back as 1975 on the state of networking in the US identified three factors that aid or hinder library network development.

The factors listed below were seen to be predominant in the success of the networks in the US.

i) A network's development time in planning is inversely proportional to the number of skilled, experienced library planners involved, but the minimum number is two.

ii) Network development is inversely proportional to the time required to produce the first network product, i.e., the longer the network group is required to support development without production of a valuable output, the less likely it is that the network will survive.

iii) Network development is directly proportional to the level of funding and centralized administrative management. That is, money is significant, and there must be a strong central administration which means decision making power and management which includes planning, development, and marketing the network's functions.

INFLIBNET combines in itself both the functions of a library utility as well as that of a consortium of libraries. Some members of the network will probably have to provide utility services in addition to serving their local clientele. This could lead to inefficiencies on both fronts due to equipment, staff or managerial difficulties.

An alternative would have been to set up a commercial or quasi-commercial agency which would specialize in providing utility-based services, leaving the libraries to concentrate on their main business, viz., of acquiring and processing documents, and servicing these, and more importantly to engage in cooperative acquisitions, resource sharing within the consortium, and generally cooperating with each other to maximise resources and services in the consortium. Such an approach would help strengthen links that already exist between libraries of a region or sub-region or discipline and the successful of these would be models for other consortia.

Coordinating a well defined group of libraries with shared interests is probably more feasible and manageable than coordinating a heterogeneous group of libraries. INFLIBNET envisages a hierarchical model for the computer-based communication paths in the network. For instance, a college library will be linked to the university library which in rum will be linked to the Regional Centre and Sectoral Information Centres. Multilateral communication is possible but only via the central hub in New Delhi, since the whole network is envisaged as a star configuration, except in the large cities where libraries are to be linked by a terrestrial local area network.

Multilateral communication in most cases will be only for message transfer and not for database access. Such an approach would probably be adequate to begin with but as more and more libraries become computer-proficient, libraries will begin to look for more autonomy in computer use, database development and access to external databases. Such a phenomenon in fact has occurred in the west and this is well described by Hildreth. It is important to consider how we might cope with such a situation.

DELNET: DELNET is one of two experiments that are now ongoing in the country to network libraries in big metropolitan cities. These experiments may provide guidelines for the city-wide sub-networks envisaged in the INFLIBNET project. DELNET will network thirty five libraries in the Delhi area. A packet-switched network is envisaged with each cluster of libraries being serviced by a packet-switching exchange. Participating libraries have begun creating databases of their monograph and serials holdings using CDS/ISIS.

Records are in conformity with the Common Communications Format (CCF). A union catalogue of serials has been created and is available at one of the libraries in the network. All databases created cooperatively are expected to reside on a central computer system and dial-up access will be provided to all participating libraries. In addition, the network will have e-mail, file transfer and bulletin board facilities.

CALIBNET: CALIBNET will network 38 science and technology libraries in the Calcutta Metropolitan area. The plan is for the introduction of automated systems in the participating libraries before networking them. Each of the libraries is expected to automate their book acquisitions, cataloguing, serials control, fund accounting and circulation control. It is not clear, however, if all the libraries will use the same software package, viz. MAITRAYEE developed by CMC Ltd. The network centre will provide online access to the networks' union catalogues. In addition, the network centre will provide current-awareness services including SDI. Libraries participating in CALIBNET will use AACR-2 bibliographic description. The software, MAITRAYEE supports MARC records and will also enable records to be imported/ exported via the CCF format. CALIBNET will be linked to DELNET via dial-up access and to external networks via the GPSS.

6
Automated Databases

Despite a lack of certainty, the ways in which automation affects organizational structures is an important topic, for LIS must consider not only how to put technology to the best use, but also how to change structures to maximize the benefits to their users. Having introduced automated procedures, organizations appear to go through a series of phases in its use: first comes the automation of the routine work, such as circulation control, for example. This then frees staff to deal with other aspects of the service that were less well handled because of the demands of the routine, and at this stage LIS can begin to examine the possibilities for an extension of the service provided. Once this is under way, LIS managers can examine the possibilities for changes to the organizational structure and workflow, a process that may involve creating new supervisory levels and moving staff from one service area to another.

There are differing views over how this can be translated into an organizational "picture." It may result in an increase in the number of middle managers supervising a reduced number of nonprofessional staff, or in flatter hierarchies in which more professional work is carried out by paraprofessionals, with fewer professionals being used to deal with those tasks outside the competencies of the paraprofessionals. In addition, the professionals may move away from technical services, such as cataloguing and classification, and take up an increased intermediary role between information resources

While automation obviously has a major role in reducing the routine work of LIS staff, it also provides numerous other opportunities further "up stream" in the flow from information creator to information user. This in turn has major implications for staffing and professional education: automation can mean one-third fewer staff and a reduced number of work activities, enabling professional staff to move to "front of house" activities in direct contact with patrons. A different set of skills is then required of the professional, namely, the ability to communicate with LIS patrons, to understand their information needs, and to use a range of resources to meet those needs.

If there is a lesson to be learned from the application of automation in other organizations, it is that automating the routine work is only the start of a change process that will ultimately affect the entire organization. Automation can be introduced as part of a strategic plan based on a user-centred philosophy of information provision, rather than on an ad hoc basis, thus minimizing disruption and the adverse effects on staff. Change is unsettling for everyone, and it seems that change caused by automation is particularly unsettling, with a wide range of concerns being expressed. Planning from the start is a way to reduce that friction and to deal with staff concerns; another is by involving staff in the entire process from design to implementation, and many methodologies now exist to incorporate staff participation. The need to change is made all the more urgent by the rise of competitors in information provision who use the self-same technology, often on a commercial basis, and the development of networked information resources via the internet, which, in theory at least, can be accessed by anyone with the appropriate equipment without the need for an intermediary service.

If LIS do not restructure to gain the maximum benefit from automation, including the provision of online information resources, they run the risk of being sidelined by newer offerings. The value added by LIS has been in cataloguing, to provide a uniform record of a document, and in classification, to provide a subject arrangement and finding tool. Information needs were met primarily by the collection, augmented as required by interlibrary lending. Not surprisingly, this approach, though valid for the concept of a document collection, meant that emphasis was placed on the skills of the cataloguer and classifier.

With the growth of electronic information resources that may be located anywhere in the world and that do not have to be physically present in the LIS building, the philosophy is now one of access to information, rather than custody of documents: the LIS becomes a window onto information that can be retrieved as required. It has become a clich to speak of "just in time" information provision replacing "just in case" information storage. However, this conflicts with the traditional notions of the collection and organization of material through cataloguing and classification. These professional skills become less central to the service (especially with growth of shared cataloguing systems), and are replaced by at least a basic technical knowledge of computer systems and (more importantly still) by knowledge and understanding of the networked information resources, a task made difficult by the rapidly changing nature of these resources.

The LIS professional must know these resources as well as he or she knows (or once knew) printed reference sources and must be able to use them in the service of the patron, with the added complication that electronic resources, though theoretically more current, are also less stable than printed resources.

The added value here is understanding of the structure of networked resources and the ability to evaluate them in the light of the patron's needs. LIS managers, therefore, must be aware of the potential for structural change in their services and how to cope with it, just as their counterparts in the commercial sector have recognized the need for new workflows and structures. Simply replacing manual routines with automated ones will not extract the maximum benefit from automation.

The possibilities using the parallel of organizations in other sectors are flatter hierarchies in which there are fewer professional staff in middle grades and a higher degree of semiprofessional work carried out by paraprofessional staff, and/or more flexible structures that adapt to the rapidly changing information environment within which LIS operate and that is now populated with many other providers. Providing access to information means increased face-to-face contact with patrons and, as was suggested earlier, this is facilitated by automation.

Old structures based on processing the flow of documents are no longer relevant, and this means that LIS managers must reexamine the existing divisions into technical services, public services, and so on. At its most extreme, changing structures may involve merging with another unit: this has become commonplace in the United Kingdom (UK), where many university libraries have merged with the university's computer centre to form a new information services department, often with the former librarian in charge of a very different service built around access through technology.

Another example is that of Tilburg University in the Netherlands, where a specific plan has been launched to create a "modern information and study centre" that will provide facilities to optimise the searching process in that explosively growing amount of information. For this, knowledge navigation systems have to be developed that are easy to use for researchers, teachers, and students. This will also require an integration of librarian applications with other computer applications that are important for the primary process.

Managers must also be aware, however, that the impact of automation will differ for the various grades of personnel within the service. It is important to note that, in an essentially conservative profession, many of these changes will be resisted to a greater or lesser degree. For some staffing levels at least, automation is a source of increased job satisfaction: Waters has found that clerical staff report improved flexibility and creativity in the work done, and Lynch and Verdin report higher levels of job satisfaction among reference personnel than among those working in any other area. Similarly, the majority of library support staff experience increased job satisfaction following automation and feel that they are more effective. However, LIS staff are no more immune to concerns over automation than any other service: personnel are concerned about job losses, the effect on social relationships at work, and health and safety.

In a study of Canadian libraries, Dakshinamurti found significant numbers of people expressing concern over loss of interpersonal communication and feelings about insecurity and insignificance, while a survey of UK public libraries found suggestions that the introduction of automation had created more work for some staff, because the system's effectiveness made it possible to carry out tasks not previously considered feasible.

LIS managers must therefore be capable of introducing and managing change successfully, using participative decision making, communication skills, and understanding. There is a need to appreciate that restructuring does not just happen. It must be a conscious decision that is incorporated into a strategic plan for the LIS: only this way can maximum benefit be derived with minimum adverse effect on personnel and service quality.

An excellent example of this process, along with instances of restructuring and changing workflow, is afforded by Pennsylvania State University Library, which developed a strategic plan built around its move to shared cataloguing. As a case study, it exemplifies a great deal of what can and should be done. The entire operation was, first of all, based on an explicit plan that included reorganization, redesign of the workflow involved in cataloguing procedures, and a resulting change in the roles of personnel. Penn State therefore introduced two new sections: bibliographic processing, for copy cataloguing and pre-order searching; and cataloguing, to which section all professional and paraprofessional cataloguers were moved from previously separate sections.

All acquisitions became part of a unified workflow, with separation of basic clerical routines from those materials that need professional or paraprofessional judgment. The new bibliographic processing section was able to deal with 97 percent of all titles using shared cataloguing. The remaining 3 percent of complex cataloguing problems, often in foreign languages, were referred to the cataloguing section and its professionals or paraprofessionals. Paraprofessionals were used to supervise clerical staff, representing a major change in their job functions; while, in addition to developing subject headings and maintaining authority files, the professionals were brought out of the "back room" into liaison with public services, thus placing them in more direct contact with library patrons. This was facilitated by a reduction in the staffing levels needed for professional cataloguing and the absorption of these posts into other areas of the library. The reduction in overall staffing numbers, combined with an increase in the number of titles processed annually, was achieved by natural attrition, though it is not clear which posts were lost in this way. Also part of the plan was the concept of speedy service to patrons, here taking the form of rapid processing of new material rather than a concern for perfect cataloguing, but we should note that the majority of patrons were satisfied with the new system. It had become an effective finding tool, which was their main criterion for judging the library: patrons have little appreciation of the minutiae of cataloguing and classification if it means a delay in obtaining new material. Nor is this an isolated instance of improvement: it has been found in other libraries, though there was also evidence that the cataloguers took the opposite view and gradually reimposed the earlier standards of cataloguing. There must be a note of caution, however: while Penn State and a few others may stand as examples of what can be done, it seems that they are, for the moment, relatively unusual: "The responding libraries indicated overwhelmingly that technical services and public services divisions will not be added to anyone's endangered species list very soon". Why this should be so is not entirely clear, though conservatism must be a major factor, as we saw with the move back toward perfect cataloguing at the expense of processing speed.

There is also the risk that cataloguers are allowing their concern for professional levels of processing to displace the concept of service to users. Their immediate interest is in the organization of a collection of documents, but the demand is for access to and exploitation of the information those documents contain. This genuine concern for the maintenance of professional standards is entirely understandable, and a result of decades of education and training that emphasized knowledge and understanding of the cataloguing codes and classification schemes required to organize collections of documents. Such knowledge and understanding is, however, a requirement of the older philosophy of collection maintenance and organization; it is not the basis for a service providing access to, and mediation of, information in numerous formats, including electronic. This type of service requires personnel capable of acting as intermediaries between information and patron, intermediaries who are familiar, with technology and possess communication skills, and this means a change in the already crowded curriculum designed to produce LIS professionals.

Cataloguing and classification, as curriculum subjects, will disappear in the immediate future, but they have to take their place alongside newer topics, such as networked information resources and communication skills. Such changes have, of course, already been introduced into many schools of library and information studies, but it will take time for the new generation of graduates to move through the ranks of the profession to a point where they will have an effect on structures. In the meantime, existing LIS managers must grasp the nettle, and many have done so. The need to concentrate on access, with all that implies for structures and the deployment of staffing, is particularly acute when we consider the growth of electronic information resources exemplified by the Internet.

While these resources are accessible to the user with the relevant equipment, they can be intimidating and difficult to use effectively. As the virtual library concept develops, the question of the organization of documents obviously becomes less pressing, being replaced by the need for knowledge of changing resources, which are more varied in nature, less permanent, and often of more varied quality. Thus, the information professional needs not only an ability to find information in the vast web of the Internet, but also the skills to judge its provenance: Where does it originate? What are the credentials of the provider? What procedures are in place to ensure currency and accuracy? These are not necessarily qualities the typical net surfer will acquire, giving the intermediary an even more important place in the information chain, especially since questions are raised from time to time about the overall quality, accuracy, and currency of resources provided over a network for which there is no central controlling body.

LIS must be able to provide these resources in the full knowledge that they are less amenable to the application of cataloguing and classification rules. It is impossible to fix these electronic resources in time: the best that can be done is to know how to use them to the best advantage of the patron, but the knowledge of what is there and how to retrieve it will exist largely in the heads of LIS staff, rather than on machine readable catalogue records. Some LIS are maintaining "databases" of Internet addresses and World Wide Web Uniform Resource Locations (URLs) or incorporating them into Web browser booklists, but this is a far cry from applying AACR2.

LIS consider ways in which these electronic resources can be listed in some form that is accessible by patrons, and the possibility exists for Online Public Access Catalogues (OPACs) to contain built-in links to Internet gopher, ftp, and Web sites. This would suggest that LIS will have to assign some form of indexing to these sites, so that patrons can retrieve them with standard subject searches of OPAC, along with references to documents in the LIS collection. While there is no suggestion that Internet resources and the like will replace printed material in the immediate future, it is the case that patrons will expect LIS to provide access to them.

The University of Akron is a heavily wired campus, having recently passed the 100-mile mark in installed fiber optic cable. In computing terms, it is also a diverse campus. At least three types of e-mail systems are well established; computing platforms are extremely varied, extending from terminal-based mainframe systems through microcomputer-based desktop systems and on to high-powered computational and graphics workstations.

The library has a decade of local systems experience, and has recently installed its second generation online system as part of its move into the OhioLINK project-a project linking library catalogues and services of all public higher education institutions in the state of Ohio.

In the midst of this information-rich campus, there was until recently a large unmet need for a campus-wide information service (CWIS). As the computer centre addressed this need and set a goal of installing a CWIS, its network operations office first asked what the goals of such a project would be.

With any automation project, the first thing to do is to define the project goals. In setting up a campus-wide information service, one must first ask the question: What do we want such a service to do? The first answer sounds simple: We want it to provide certain types of information campus-wide, and indeed worldwide, on a minimal budget, with no increases in staffing, across multiple computer platforms. We want it to be easy to use and easy to maintain. We want it to be able to handle potentially huge amounts of data with minimal overhead. We want the system to be a combined effort of a lot of people across campus. If people from many offices mount and maintain information on the CWIS, then the workload is distributed; the need for new personnel is minimized. Again, the first organizational principle for any automation project is to clearly define the project goals.

At The University of Akron, the CWIS task force agreed to mount all types of information: press releases, student registration and advising information, library hours, and book store information to name a few. It was decided to maintain only text-based information. This decision was based on the fact that more than 500 text-only terminals were still in use by people needing access to the CWIS.

In addition, being primarily commuters, many students would be accessing the service using low-speed, dial-in connections that support only text-based information. The decision to limit the service to text-based information was clearly a compromise between an ideal and the various hardware realities on campus. This compromise was reached only after an honest, global look at the project's hardware environment. Such an examination is an important early step in the planning process for any automation project.

A close look at the project's information environment is equally vital. Concerning the potential information for a CWIS project, it will often be found that some information (such as student records) cannot be released to everyone. If this type of information is to be provided, a more complex system capable of authenticating the user is required. The files necessary for authentication can increase the system's requirements for size, budget, and maintenance. Authenticating users of one system by passing them through another system on which they have an authorized account can sometimes be a solution to this problem. But such a solution can add its own layers of complexity and overhead. This problem of user authentication applies to many campus information projects, including user-initiated library loans and document requests as well as remote access to proprietary bibliographic databases and Internet services. Various methods to authenticate users are becoming generally available.

The Kerberos system from Project Athena at the Massachusetts Institute of Technology allows for an individual's single password to be used for authentication on any number of cooperating information services. Kerberos passwords are encrypted before being sent across the network, adding to the security of the overall system. The use of smart-card systems allows for an additional level of security.

Users must not only be in possession of a valid user account and password, but also a credit card-sized microprocessor that displays a coded sequence of numbers specific to that user's account. Even if the user account and password are discovered by someone else, they are, of no use without the corresponding smart card. The planning for such an authentication system clearly must be campus-wide in scope; the technology can be used to control access to a variety of resources and services from food services to library databases. Other questions about the type of data to be provided by an automation project also help determine the complexity of the resulting system. For example, if any of the system's information is to be provided by the user, the system will have to be interactive, hence necessarily more complex, and maybe more difficult for the users to learn. If the service is to be accessible to the general public, certain information, like proprietary bibliographic databases, may have legally restricted access; mechanisms will need to be available to accomplish this restriction.

Mechanisms like concurrent user metering and network address filtering can require higher maintenance, as they add complexities above and beyond the authentication technologies mentioned previously. Public relations departments are a natural source of organizational information, and they may consider the electronic dissemination of their information as a logical next step to the printed version.

At The University of Akron, the public relations department has been actively involved in the CWIS planning from the beginning, and now their normal routine includes posting all university news releases on the CWIS. Data that is maintained by an institutional research department can represent a great source of information for a CWIS.

Many organizations depend upon such a centralized facility for organization-wide information management. Examples of such information include: personnel data for an online directory; student records and enrolment data; course descriptions, room assignments, class meeting times, and required textbooks; and calendars of campus events. Much of this data may be stored in database management systems in the central computing department, allowing information to be extracted and formatted by software programs into effective reports. Organizations that allow the campus's departmental staff direct access to data will be able to provide this information quickly for the CWIS. Those that depend upon the central computing department for such extraction, formatting, and reporting services may find that other work has higher priority and the time required to get the information into the CWIS may be painfully long.

At this early juncture in a CWIS project, defining the scope of information and determining its initial organization, the library can serve the campus well. Experienced in researching and finding information, in understanding and addressing the global information needs of its campus-wide constituency, in organizing information logically for a wide range of consumers, and in using automated systems all the while-the library staff is poised like no other to build the structure of a CWIS most successfully. Indeed, if structure and politics permit it, the CWIS manager might best be a lead librarian who is accomplished in these skills. Building a CWIS provides a good opportunity for building a partnership with the computer centre.

The CWIS system administrator most likely should come from the computer centre. And, for the CWIS to be successful, the manager and system administrator need to have a close working relationship. Not providing the information required by the campus is a sure ingredient for the failure of any automation project. Users of a CWIS are interested in finding specific information for specific needs. If the service does not fulfil those needs, they will stop using it. The analysis of what information people need and how that information will be obtained is as critical an aspect in establishing a CWIS as it is for any information management project.

Determining the information to be provided also requires consideration of where the information will reside. Less effort will be required if most of the information is centrally managed; however, this may not be the case. Many publications are not produced on campus and will require additional effort to be made available. Some organizations use off-campus printing services; student newspapers, for example, often are printed by commercial printing firms. This practice can be a source of problems since these services sometimes are not prepared to provide electronic copies of their publications.

Getting electronic copies of these publications may often entail an additional cost and additional processing, like manual retyping or scanning of the publication, to prepare it for use on the CWIS. A world of information is available via the Internet. If any of this information is included, access issues will need to be considered. Matters of network security and Internet etiquette have never been more important.

At The University of Akron, the computer centre and the library each chose, under the portions of the CWIS that each manages, to provide access to many Internet resources. Providing access to some resources on the Internet requires the use of the remote-access service known as "telnet," which connects the user's machine to a remote machine linked to the Internet. When not properly controlled within the CWIS, telnet's power to establish remote connections can be abused. Such abuse can occur most easily if the system provides the user an open telnet prompt, that is, the prompt: "telnet> " waiting for the user to input a destination machine address. Such an open prompt allows the user the potential to connect to any other machine on the Internet, opening an avenue for potential hackers, who are bent on compromising remote systems.

Such a situation is the network manager's nightmare, but it has a good chance of becoming a reality when a CWIS is set up-especially if access to the CWIS is provided at unsupervised public workstations in a library or computer lab. Even if the local system manager is careful to eliminate any open telnet access from the local machine, it is impossible to eliminate such access from other sites to which users may connect from the local site.

No matter what decisions are made about the type and amount of information to be provided, no information management project will be successful without the support of the organization's administration. Getting the top academic and administrative officers to support the project is critical to its success. Lack of support from the administration can result in the absence of key information.

Many organizations have information scattered across multiple departments, and often the departments that control the most important information are also the busiest. Some of these may not see the benefit of spending their limited resources to make their information available to a wider constituency that they do not necessarily recognize.

In fact, some may even consider making their information more widely available as a "loss of control" issue and refuse to participate. Only a convinced administration can provide the leadership to pull all parts of the organization together to accomplish this task. Once the departments see that the administration wants this service to succeed and that its success depends on everyone's participation, it becomes much easier for them to find the necessary resources to place their information on the service.

The supervisors of the Information Providers (IP's), the employees in various departments throughout the campus who maintain their departmental information on the CWIS, will need to be aware of the efforts these people are making to provide a valuable resource to the organization. Too often this type of activity remains invisible to the management and, therefore, unrecognized. Making certain that the IPs' efforts are recognized will certainly motivate them to continue to participate. Not providing sufficient support for the IPs is a sure route to failure. IPs need training, timely assistance, motivation, and rewards. Without such support, few of them will contribute effectively and promptly to the service.

For most organizations, there is no CWIS without IPs. The success of a CWIS is in these people's hands. The service manager must be ready and able to provide the support they need, or face the almost inevitable failure of the service. Often this failure is not the service manager's fault, but the lack of commitment by management. Service managers who are spread too thinly will not be able to provide the necessary support. This fact applies to any sort of information management project, not just a CWIS. To this point, we have examined the general requirements for a CWIS, which are the requirements for any successful automation project. They include:

1. defining the project goals;
2. defining the scope of information to be managed, which includes an examination of the project's information environment;
3. examining the project's hardware environment;
4. examining the issues of information access and licensing, system security, and user authentication; and

5. gaining management's support for the project.

The CWIS manager is the person who organizes meetings, heads the planning task force, communicates with various offices, maintains the intellectual integrity of the system, and manages the data on the system. The CWIS system administrator is the person who manages the software and hardware that actually make the system run. In some organizations the CWIS manager will also be the CWIS system administrator. Given an exceptional person, this situation can be ideal in terms of control and personnel costs. Unfortunately, the talents required to perform these two jobs will rarely be found in a single individual.

For most organizations, a partnership between the CWIS system administrator and the CWIS manager will be the most suitable arrangement. Again, a computer centre system administrator and a librarian system manager can be an ideal combination. If the task of providing and maintaining information is distributed to departments throughout the campus, then the manager and the system administrator can share in providing the necessary training in addition to monitoring the use of the service.

In some larger organizations, additional IP trainers may be necessary and can be supervised by the CWIS manager. Having more than one person capable of providing training and monitoring the service allows for continuous management of the CWIS during vacations and illness. A CWIS is grown, not built. The key to a CWIS is information-information that is not static. If the service is not continuously enhanced, updated, and reviewed, it will cease to be of use to the campus. A CWIS is never done. In fact, the physical installation of the service is only a minor part of the overall project. The need for continuous information maintenance must be addressed at the beginning of the project.

For some managers this continuous maintenance requirement can be new and potentially discomforting. The manager must be able to work with a broad range of IPs, keep them interested and trained, and ensure that the information being provided is of use to the campus. For some organizations this work can be a full-time job. Often, establishing a CWIS is viewed as a computer project, and a computer specialist will be put in charge of seeing that the service is installed, tested, and documented. Unfortunately, this is only a fraction of what is required to make a CWIS work.

The rest of the job involves coordinating IPs from many different departments, motivating them to continue to participate, and looking for new and interesting information that would be of use to the organization. If their experience has been limited to processing known information to answer specific, routine questions about matters like enrolment and student retention rates, computer specialists may be ill-suited for this part of the job. In fact, some will have no interest in performing these duties, and the service will suffer from their involvement.

The CWIS manager should have experience with electronic information services, but does not need to be a programmer or systems administrator. The more important skills required are the ability to motivate a diverse group of people and the ability to coordinate a wide-ranging project that includes many types of information.

The librarian, trained to be an information organizer, is the professional who can make the distribution system attractive to users by organizing it logically. So, he or she would be a natural choice as the CWIS manager. Even the best manager needs sufficient time and resources to operate the service. If the CWIS is not seen as a living, growing thing, there may be an administrative tendency to place unrealistic completion dates on the activities of the people involved.

The worst mistake a superior can make is to assign the manager additional projects just as the CWIS is installed and becomes available. It is at this point that the manager needs to be the most aggressive and spend the most time recruiting and training IPs from all across the campus. Additional assignments at this time limit the time the manager can spend keeping the service current and the IPs motivated.

Information starts to become stale; IPs stop adding new information; users become dissatisfied with the service and management cannot figure out why. Managing a CWIS can be a full-time job for organizations with even a few hundred users-a fact that must be faced at the start of the project. One of the most important aspects of starting a CWIS is establishing policies and procedures that will be acceptable to the campus community. One of the best ways to accomplish this campus-wide acceptance is to include a cross section of the campus in the planning process.

The creation of a CWIS task force made up of people from various departments provides a means to bring together different viewpoints and knowledge of the information that can be made available. Just as administrative support for the CWIS is essential, reaching out into the organization for input and support is critical. Providing a way for departments to assist in the design and specification of the service gives them ownership of the project. These people become the frontline representatives of the service and can be used to stimulate interest throughout the rest of the organization. Without this type of support, the task facing the system manager will be monumental. Key design decisions, such as the appearance of the point of entry to the service, should be worked out by the CWIS task force.

CWIS experts agree that providing a stable point of entry for CWIS users is essential. Users can become disoriented when the point of entry changes, even if the changes are relatively minor and infrequent. In order to accomplish the necessary stability, a great deal of thought must be given to the design of the point of entry, the first screen. A task force with knowledge of the information to be made available and how this information will be used can design a point of entry that will remain useful for a long time. Onc resource that must be included in the task force is librarians, people who are trained and practised in organizing information in intuitive and meaningful ways. Their input-will ensure, that the structure of information will be useful to the campus community.

At The University of Akron, the initial CWIS task force included five librarians: a combination of reference librarians, subject specialists, and public service managers. The task force may be established only to build the foundation of the CWIS and then dissolved, or it may be an ongoing group that reviews the service periodically and continues to provide input to the service manager. At The University of Akron, the CWIS policies and procedures were established by the CWIS task force.

The task force wrote the first-level menu and decided that it must remain stable. The menu designs for the next level of menus were assigned to specific departments throughout campus. The task force also agreed on the need to maintain the currency of the data on the system. Feeling that it would be best to automate the process of maintaining data currency, the system administrator wrote a program that checks each file on the system for currency and warns the contributing IP by e-mail when the file is about to expire. The task force agreed to begin each file placed on the system with a header that specifies creation date, expiration date, contact person, and file title-all of which could be read by this currency-checker program. In this manner, data on the system is guaranteed to be current. The job of providing and maintaining a large amount of information on a CWIS can be daunting.

For most organizations no single person is capable of doing this job. Distributing the responsibility for providing information is essential. The most efficient method of providing and maintaining this information is to allow the departments that "own" the information to be responsible. For example, in most organizations the purchasing department maintains the purchasing policies and procedures, and in turn can make these available on the CWIS. Changes to the policies or procedures can be updated as they are approved, making them available immediately. The purchasing department may eventually come to see the CWIS as the primary method of delivering information and promote its use throughout the organization.

Distributing the responsibility for departmental information among the departments themselves is an effective and efficient means of getting a large amount of information on the service. This process also distributes the maintenance task. Departments that have a sense of ownership for their information will also be more comfortable with this arrangement. This practice, of course, means training and coordinating a large group of IPs.

Training people to be IPs is a critical aspect of distributing the job of providing and maintaining information on the service-but it is not a simple matter. People chosen to be IPs for the departments can have widely varying capabilities and experience. Additionally, in many organizations, the hardware and software being used by various departments can be considerably different. Both of these aspects can complicate the job of training. One IP, for example, may transfer files across campus using the file transfer protocol (ftp) on the campus administrative network with one set of menus and commands, while another may use dial-in lines and a communication program. One may use a DOS machine, one a Macintosh, and another a Unix workstation. The manager must be able to train IPs in each of these environments.

Under such circumstances, individualized training may be the most effective way to prepare new IPs for the task. Individualized training can take place in the person's office, using familiar hardware and software. Practices and procedures learned this way will be more easily remembered. More time can be spent with people who have little computer experience, whereas more material can be covered with those that have more experience.

At The University of Akron, Gopher software was selected to run the CWIS. So, IPs are trained on how to produce and manipulate ASCII text files. Even though ASCII may not be the file format that they normally use, most learn readily to import and export ASCII text files to and from their word-processing software. They also must be trained how to write brief caption files that serve to build Gopher menus and how to transfer ASCII files across the campus network to the CWIS server, where the information ultimately resides.

One way to keep IPs up-to-date and interested in the CWIS is to hold IP gatherings. These gatherings allow IPs to exchange experiences and discuss problems with others performing basically the same function; they can also be used as a forum for discussing policies and any compliance problems. Pertinent information-from that which indicates the number of user accesses to what information each IP has placed on the service-can be distributed. Possibly, awards for the most-accessed information can be made. These meetings should be more like pep rallies than lectures or evaluations.

Most beginning training should concentrate on the basics of information formatting and information placement on the CWIS server. Some IPs will grow beyond these basics and desire more advanced access to the CWIS server. Some of the advanced capabilities IPs may wish to use include: the ability to link to other information available on the Internet, to build indexes of information for keyword searching, and to create interactive forms to collect information from users. Training must be available for these people to allow them to continue to develop their skills as IPs.

Many IPs will need direct access to the CWIS server so that they may manipulate their information. Such training can be performed in a group, since the people receiving this type of training are already comfortable with the use of their own hardware and software. The functions and features available on the CWIS server will evolve over time. As new functions and features become available, IPs will need to be trained on their use. Most system administrators will want to operate a separate test service in order to test new functions without affecting the production service. Advanced IPs should be given access to this test service to assist the administrator in determining which new functions and features are of value to the organization. Most CWIS systems today are based on client-server architecture. This architecture provides high functionality by utilizing the capabilities of the desktop microcomputer systems that are pervasive today. In some cases, CWIS clients use multiuser, mainframe-type systems; however, these clients usually take advantage of only a portion of the capabilities of the microcomputer-based clients.

We chose the Gopher software developed at The University of Minnesota to run the CWIS for five reasons:

1) the client software is available for a wide range of computer systems, including IBM's VM/CMS operating system;

2) putting information on the Gopher server is comparatively simple for IPs with little computer experience;

3) there are thousands of Gopher servers worldwide from which our server could provide access to information outside our university;

4) both the client and server software are available at no cost to educational and nonprofit organizations; and

5) the Gopher software manages textual information, and because of infrastructure limitations, the CWIS had already been limited to textual information only.

CWIS users need access to a client system (workstation) equipped with the necessary application and network software. Systems with the necessary capabilities are available today for a few thousand dollars. A basic workstation consists of

1) a system unit with a microprocessor, memory sized for the operating system and applications being used, hard disk, and a network interface;
2) a monitor, preferably colour, sized for the needs of the user;
3) a keyboard and pointing device-mouse or trackball;
4) operating system software appropriate to the computer system being used;
5) network software appropriate to the network configuration; and
6) the CWIS client software.

Simple VT-100 terminals can access a CWIS running Gopher software if they can reach a computer system like an IBM VM or a Digital Ultrix system that is running the appropriate Gopher client software. A CWIS server system will also be necessary. Most CWIS server software operates with the Unix operating system. A wide variety of server systems that offer the Unix operating system are available at prices starting under $10,000.

The University of Akron purchased a Digital DEC Alpha 3000/300LX with 32 megabytes of memory, built-in Ethernet adaptor, a 16-inch colour monitor, 2 gigabytes of disk storage, a CDROM drive, and the OSF/1 operating system at an educational discount price of under $7,000. Unix systems come with support for Transmission Control Protocol/Internet Protocol (TCP/IP) networking. Most CWIS systems utilize TCP/IP software.

However, it may be necessary to enhance the organization's infrastructure to support TCP/IP. This enhancement could entail adding TCP/IP software to client workstations, LAN servers, or WAN routers. Network managers will need to learn to configure and maintain the TCP/IP software. There may also be a broad range of hardware capabilities across the organization.

A CWIS system that requires a great deal of resources, color graphics displays for example, may bypass users with older and less capable workstations. Other infrastructure considerations are also important. Users accessing the service remotely by telephone connections will have much slower transfer speeds, making services that transmit large amounts of information, like graphics, intolerably slow. Many campus networks may not be up to the task of providing this type of service.

At The University of Akron, buildings are interconnected by a fiber-optic backbone. Telephone wiring is used to provide 10 megabits per second (Ethernet) connections to individual workstations within buildings. This infrastructure provides a campus network capable of delivering large amounts of information in reasonable lengths of time. Determining your users' skills and hardware capabilities is challenging and important. Consideration of the amount of training (and retraining) of users is essential.

Most organizations will have users with a broad range of experience and capabilities. Some will have limited computer experience, or experience limited to different systems. Some will visit the CWIS infrequently, but they must be able to remember the necessary steps to access the service and navigate the information they find there. They may not be interested in investing a great deal of time to learn to use the service. These people must be able to access and use the service with a minimum of instruction or they will not use it. The service must be easy and consistent and provide hints and prompts to help the user along wherever possible.

The Gopher software has a fairly effective built-in help system, although it may not be initially apparent to the user. A basic design rule for menu-driven systems is to make every menu selection work as soon as it appears. Putting up menu selections for services that are not yet available can frustrate users.

While building an empty framework for the CWIS menu structure may be a valuable paper exercise during the design stage, mounting that empty framework on the system can be disastrous. Once users see a system with lots of blank boxes indicating "nothing available," they will likely never return. We have mentioned the dangers of including data that requires the most sophisticated hardware. At the other extreme, allowing existing hardware capabilities to limit the type of information provided can serve to limit the system's growth and potential.

There is a tendency to build services for the lowest common denominator. For many organizations, this denominator will be character terminals, or "dumb terminals." Indeed, at The University of Akron, the CWIS was limited to text-only information because of the broad installed base of text-only terminals. If the information actually needed by the organization requires greater capabilities, following this tendency to the lowest common denominator will be a mistake. An example would be not taking into account that a great many existing documents use multiple fonts and styles, have embedded graphics, and may even utilize color.

The process of converting such information for the much simpler character terminal means losing all of the effort, and in some cases the actual content, that has been put into these documents. It is clearly a difficult decision to chose a hardware and software environment for a CWIS that at once does not tie it to old technology, does not limit the service only to owners of high-end platforms, does not shut out important data formats, and does not require extensive training and overhead.

We were faced with these conflicting issues-trying to accommodate the lowest common denominator while at the same time trying not to shut ourselves out of the future entirely. Our decision was to take a middle line in selecting the Gopher software. The Gopher system supports our broad installed base of VT100 and IBM 3270 terminals and does not limit the service to those with high-end workstations. It supports advanced capabilities, such as information linking, keyword indexing, and interactive forms.

Although it does not provide graphics and multimedia, information on a Gopher server can be read with the more sophisticated World Wide Web browsers like Mosaic, which do run on high-end workstations. Additionally, the Gopher system requires a minimal amount of training to make IPs productive. Our campus is in the process of moving from terminals to desktop systems capable of graphics and multimedia. We have installed a World Wide Web server, which operates in parallel with our Gopher server.

Many of the original CWIS task force members are learning to use Web browsers like Mosaic and Netscape. We see a natural evolution from terminal-based Gopher software, to Gopher clients that run on workstations, and on to Web browsers with advanced graphics and multimedia capabilities. This evolution will continue as more powerful CWIS systems become available and workstations become more capable. Not providing workstations with adequate power for CWIS users can result in a shrunken user base. Some CWIS client software packages require substantial workstations in order to perform acceptably. For example, CWIS clients that support graphics, as do Mosaic and Netscape, require a much faster processor in the workstation as well as additional network bandwidth. When attempting to run such clients, workstations with limited capabilities will be unacceptably slow.

If the workstations are not up to the task, users will be disappointed in the service and soon stop trying to use it. Once this happens, it will be difficult to regain these people as users, even when they have workstations capable of performing well. Trying to run the service on an underpowered server can be another ingredient for failure. Just as important as having client workstations capable of doing the job, the server system must be able to perform with acceptable responsiveness. Today, server systems capable of servicing a large number of concurrent users are relatively inexpensive. Despite this fact, too often an existing system that does not have sufficient spare capacity to perform properly is pressed into providing the service. Slow response time will alienate users and result in the loss of users that will be hard to regain once the server system is upgraded. The small investment required for a first-rate server will yield a large return as the number of users and amount of information on the service both grow.

Competition in the production of these types of systems is fierce, and many vendors are now producing systems with attractive price-performance ratios. Before estimating the cost of developing a CWIS, analyse the existing capabilities. If most potential CWIS users have access to systems that will allow the use of the selected CWIS software, the major cost of upgrading a large number of user systems can be avoided.

If server hardware with sufficient power and storage is available for the selected CWIS software, the total cost will be that much smaller. The campus infrastructure, its data network, must be reviewed to ensure its capacity to handle the additional traffic created by a CWIS. This analysis should be performed after the analysis of the information to be provided, and after the initial selection (but before the purchase) of the appropriate CWIS software for the job. If the existing computing capabilities of the organization are allowed to drive all of the decisions as to information content on the CWIS, the long-term viability of the service may be jeopardized.

The cost of enhancing systems and infrastructure may be worth the investment if the CWIS is to be of value to the entire organization. The largest continuing cost of the CWIS will be for staff if a full-time manager or administrator is needed. Hardware and software upgrades will be incremental and not substantial if the client and server systems have been chosen correctly; however, annual server hardware and software maintenance costs combined can total up to 24 percent of the purchase price. The proliferation of new electronic databases and search engines is delivering a host of new choices for librarians and system administrators. The problems presented by these choices are particularly difficult ones for small- and medium-sized academic libraries. Many indexes are available in a wide variety of formats so that the choices to be made have become much more complex.

More and more libraries are cancelling paper indexes in order to subscribe to an electronic version. When an index is made available in electronic version, the print version gets very little use as a rule. Cancellation of paper indexes was almost unheard of in libraries even a few years ago for a number of reasons. Academic librarians were suitably nervous about accreditation for various programs where subscriptions to certain indexes were required.

Today, when students and faculty are given appropriate access to the electronic version, paper indexes are not required for accreditation by most accrediting bodies. One small academic library in the San Antonio area made a dramatic change in its collection by dropping many journal and index subscriptions and allocating the money to a full-text CDROM system. This system is very popular with the students, but it is a single-user workstation and would not be a workable solution for a larger library, unless the dozens of CDROMs containing the full-text journal images were networked.

When extra funds are difficult to come by, as they are in most small libraries, current budgets must be reallocated in order to fund different materials. One way to consider allocating the budget is to institute electronic indexes on a trial basis and then study the use made of the electronic index and the paper index by the students. If twice as much use is made of electronic indexes as paper ones, the funds might be allocated such that twice as much of the index budget goes to electronic indexes as to paper indexes. A similar argument might be made for budgeting of full-text materials in online and in paper format. Until recently, small college librarians were also wary of the inherent unreliability of computers and computer networks. Card catalogues and paper indexes never "go down" and so were much more trustworthy than computer-based resources.

When electronic access is unavailable for long periods and at unpredictable times, good reference service requires a backup. This predicament kept many libraries subscribing to paper indexes along with the electronic counterparts. There is no substitute for reliability and if downtime is excessive and unplanned, the computer system needs closer examination. Appropriate downtime for maintenance and upgrades can be anticipated as part of normal operations, and the library should plan to be closed for major upgrades. In some cases, nights and weekends may be the time of choice for shutdowns on the grounds that fewer users will be adversely affected. Proper maintenance is most helpful in ensuring reliability, and upgrades are a necessary part of computer maintenance. When these caveats are followed, the improved reliability of current computer technology makes uncontrolled downtime less of a risk. Most electronic databases are not available for purchase as paper indexes are. Access to them is totally available or totally unavailable unlike paper indexes, which, once purchased, are owned by the library and are not returned if the subscription is cancelled.

Some librarians want to have physical materials to show for their expenditures, and these services provide nothing that can be retained. In most cases, nothing is left to store if a cancellation is made. However, CDROMs offer much better searching and take up very little space. They can, however, only be searched by one person at a time while multivolume paper indexes can be shared by several patrons. This limitation of CDROMs can be corrected, at a cost, by multiple subscriptions or by computer network access. It is time to make intelligent collection development choices and select appropriate formats rather than simply duplicate resources. It has been our experience that if the network is unavailable, people do not use the paper indexes. They ask when the network will be in service and return to do their research then. We also find that people prefer to use an electronic index even if it is not appropriate to their needs, rather than a paper index that is appropriate. For example, many of our users, in researching topics for religious studies, will use the computerized *Humanities Index* on our network instead of choosing the paper *Catholic Periodical Index* or *Religion Index. Humanities Index* is an excellent resource, but the other titles clearly give better subject coverage.

We need to compensate for these poor choices in our bibliographic instruction program by demonstrating how an online index, while easier to use, is not always the best choice for the user. In order to take advantage of electronic resources, the library must have in place a reliable method of doing so and a budgetary plan for purchasing the electronic resources as well as the hardware needed.

Many of the indexes used in libraries have become widely available in many different formats, so a library that makes them available electronically must consider dropping the paper subscription when enough computer access is available. Often, however, the cancellation of print indexes will not cover the price of a substitute computer index, so other funds must be made available.

Many libraries have simply reassigned funds from existing book and journal budgets, while others have attempted to increase their budgets using the need for electronic resources as justification. Again, usage is the key and collecting usage statistics is very important for justifying budget requests. When an index strongly supports one or more disciplines that are important at a college, and it is used heavily by students, it should be purchased.

Online or CDROM indexes save time and can produce better results; librarians must make decisions about funding based on concrete evidence of needs and usage. Keeping usage statistics online and sampling the use of paper indexes will provide the necessary information to help make decisions and justify budget requests. Many academic administrators assume that money can be saved by accessing electronic resources, rather than by purchasing printed materials. This is usually a false assumption. First, equivalent electronic resources are generally far more expensive than their print counterparts. Second, the vast majority of recorded information is not yet available electronically. This is true for full-text book and journal resources, although computerized access to full-text materials is increasing rapidly. Traditional paper publishing is not withering away; on the contrary, it seems to flourish. Further, due to the fear by publishers of copyright infringement as well as other problems, much of this newly published material will not be available in electronic format in the near future. Several hundred years of published materials are also unavailable in electronic format. Electronic publishing is not going to eliminate the need for printed textual material, although it will reduce the need for searching through individual volumes of paper indexes.

Once the decision is made to purchase a particular resource in electronic format, consideration turns to the variety of formats available. For some databases, there is only one choice, but this is becoming the exception rather than the rule: should the database be locally mounted or made available by searching a remote site? Locally mounted databases require more local expertise as well as more local resources, such as hard disk space and processor power. Alternatively, remote resources are subject to high connect charges and sometimes to connection problems. These problems are exacerbated when indexes are accessed over the Internet.

The best resources may become very difficult to access and use when Internet traffic is heavy. One would never wish to depend solely on Internet access for a heavily used resource. Library management may need to consider using a local area network and having a predictably heavily used index mounted on its own system. Any sort of remote access should be verified for costs, reliability, and accessibility over a period of time.

Remote access is probably most useful for lesser used indexes though it may also be the best answer for all electronic access in small libraries without the expertise or money to build and maintain a large in-house computer system for local database access. There are a variety of remote database options available at the present time, including UnCover from CARL for journal indexing and the FirstSearch database service from OCLC. Telnet access on the Internet is currently free to UnCover, and the number and variety of periodicals covered is very large, though the searching capabilities are somewhat limited.

There is also no actual indexing done on this database since it uses only the article title, author, journal title, and abstract terms as access points. Custom gateways are available for a fee. Ebsco offers a competing online product, Casius, which presents much the same information as UnCover, *i.e.*, keyword searching of journal tables of contents. It is more expensive but offers better searching capabilities. Access to FirstSearch is available either by purchasing blocks of a specified number of searches or through individual passwords that allow unlimited searching for a year. FirstSearch allows access to a collection of databases, which are generally well indexed as opposed to only allowing keyword searching of journals' tables of contents.

A distinct advantage of FirstSearch over other collections of individual databases is the common search interface, which is fairly user-friendly. However, it can be much more expensive than the other alternatives. Dialogue is an important source of online databases with a common search interface; however, the pricing structure of this service places it out of reach of most libraries for end-user searching. Usually, this service has been reserved for library-mediated searching, often with part or all the charges being borne by the individual user. Library service plans should include a standard for when mediated searching is preferred and when end-user searching is preferred. Mediated searching is usually used for expensive search services. Flat fees for unlimited searching of databases are more easily budgeted for by libraries than for end-user searching.

For most libraries, the best option for heavily used databases is local access, assuming the library and its parent institute are able and willing to invest the money necessary to build and maintain the supporting infrastructure. In this case, the choice of databases can be made in the library and by using traditional collection development guidelines: which users does the library support and what are their needs? In colleges, both circulation and use of current indexes are usually good guidelines. However, evaluate current use with caution since some indexes are difficult to use in paper format and thus are used less; they may be much easier to use in electronic format. There are also databases available that have no paper counterpart; they exist only in electronic form.

Local access to databases can be divided into access via tape-load or CDROM. Tape-loads of data on the disk drives of local public access catalogues have the advantage of giving a common interface for all databases, which is a considerable blessing. End-user training time is vastly simplified, reducing the workload for librarians. Tape-loads also have the advantage of being searchable in one pass; CDROM databases are often split into more than one disk and, in many cases, multiple disks cannot be searched at the same time.

The online catalogue computer must have vastly increased disk space to hold multiple tape-loaded databases as well as increased power to process complex searches and return the answer in a reasonable time. As a rule, CDROM access time is slower than that for accessing data stored on a hard disk—although the time spent on either search will vary depending on the processing power of the computer, the complexity of the search, the size of the database, and other variables. The blessing of the common search interface of the public catalogue can be a limitation.

Often the CDROM search software is carefully matched to the database, thus providing powerful search capabilities. Many online public catalogues, however, offer only author, title, subject, and keyword access, plus the boolean operators "and," "or," and perhaps "not." The specialized search software of CDROMs often allows much more intricate search capability. For instance, one may wish to limit the search by year of publication, and then search material only in particular journal titles, or search only thesaurus terms.

CDROM search software is generally well suited to the database it is paired with. Often, OPAC search software leaves much to be desired when it is used for searching journal indexes, because of its more limited searching options. If a decision is made to purchase CDROM databases, a variety of choices must be faced. For example, will the CDROMs be placed on stand-alone work stations or will they be networked? Here the trade-offs are cost and access.

Networks are more costly, but they allow several patrons to search at once. While the trend in the industry seems to be toward unlimited access for networked databases, there are some publishers who base charges on the number of simultaneous users on a network, the number of workstations attached, or the total number of possible users of the database. Such restrictions can place a severe burden on the network administrator who must remain within the contract requirements and within the budget available. It is preferable to decide which indexes will be most needed in the library, and then consider purchasing the CDROM product that is common to most of them. This will mean a single, main computer interface and will reduce end-user training time and librarians' training workload.

Many indexes are now being introduced that have no paper equivalent; so if the library is considering replacing a particular paper index, close equivalents should be considered. Typical near equivalents often contain much more information than the printed index. When purchasing indexes of any type, librarians must consider their library's journal holdings and the holdings of nearby libraries, if users are able to access them. Even with high-speed fax machines and overnight document delivery, local holdings are still most convenient for users. Other factors to consider in choosing a CDROM search product include ease of use for end users, memory requirements at the workstation, network installation and security requirements, the possibility of adding local holdings statements to the data, and the stability of the software. Search interfaces that are difficult for end users to grasp make a heavy workload for librarians.

Software installation requirements can be a big problem, particularly for CDROM networking. Many CDROM systems allow users to exit to DOS, which can create a problem in networks. Others may require the capability to write temporary files to a particular network directory; some must be installed in the root directory; some require that particular software be installed on the workstation, such as a DOS "share" program or DOS extensions.

Some are unstable in a network environment and "freeze up" periodically for no apparent reason. One of the biggest problems for CDROM networking is having enough available memory in each workstation to run the search engine. Some interfaces require only a minimal amount of conventional memory, while others require large amounts.

Though workstations may have several megabytes of expanded and/or extended memory, DOS programs are still restricted by the first 640K of memory. Even with appropriate memory management, this can be a problem when the operating system and all the network drivers are loaded. Slow access time for CDROMs can sometimes be remedied by copying the database to a hard disk on the network server, if the producer allows this and if there is a large enough disk drive available. Copying the database consumes time and processor resources while it is being accomplished, but it provides some of the advantages of a tape-load onto an OPAC, and typically at lower costs.

When the library makes good indexing available in electronic format, it is much easier for the researcher to collect a large bibliography of useful citations. This increases the use of and requests for full-text materials.

There are a number of ways to satisfy these needs in addition to the traditional methods of journal subscriptions in paper, microfilm or microfiche, or interlibrary loan. Some vendors such as University Microfilms International (UMI), Ebsco, and Infotrac are introducing ASCII full-text searchable journal and newspaper articles. Again, the library will often have a choice of whether to use remote, tape-load, or CDROM access for this.

Most of the same considerations apply to this as to the decision on purchasing indexes in the three formats. One drawback to these full-text databases is that most graphics, such as charts, graphs, and pictures are often absent. Searching a full-text database requires end-user training so users do not waste time and become frustrated browsing through hundreds of items that are only peripherally related to their searches.

Full-text journal article access is also available in another slightly different format on CDROM from at least one vendor, UMI, through its ProQuest product. This access includes a traditional index to the articles on CDROM with links to "photos" or graphic images of the full text on another set of CDROMs. In this case, the full text is not searchable since it is present only in graphic format; however, all graphics are included in the product. Full-text access, however, tends to be fairly expensive regardless of format or vendor.

The price for overnight document delivery during a test run of CARL and FirstSearch averaged $10412 per article. Document-delivery services are an expensive option for fast delivery of full-text material. The table-of-contents services mentioned above, including those from FirstSearch, Ebsco, and CARL, all promise quick delivery of full-text journal articles. Sometimes these can be delivered within an hour by fax, while most promise same day or overnight delivery. All copyright fees are paid by the vendor and are included in the charge to the buyer of the service. If remote access to databases by end users is seen as a separate step from document delivery, the ease of end-user searching, speed of access, and availability of appropriate journals in the database could be evaluated most strongly, with delivery capabilities as a secondary consideration.

If document delivery is a primary process following end-user searching on locally held databases, then cost, reliability, and speed of delivery should be considered more strongly as factors in the decision-making process of choosing a document-delivery vendor.

There are many factors that must be developed in the library plan for service and must be considered when final decisions are made regarding the purchase of indexes as well as full-text materials in various formats. The first five factors listed below are specific to choosing indexes, however, and the remainder apply to both indexes and full-text materials.

Collection development considerations:

— Number of titles indexed
— Number of years covered
— Library holdings of titles indexed
— Indexing coverage (full or selective)
— Indexing quality
— Library holdings of other local libraries
— Curriculum subjects focus
— Number of undergraduate students in the subject area
— Number of graduate students in the subject area
— Number of faculty doing research in the subject area

— Number of research-intensive assignments in the subject area

User needs:

— Scholarly research or casual use

— Ease of use

— Speed of access

— Availability to concurrent users

— Training needs of users

— Anticipated level of use (heavy or light)

— Anticipated level of downtime or unavailability

Cost considerations:

— Training needs of librarians

— Hardware needs

— Space needs

— Personnel needs (reference assistance, system maintenance, system administration, and so on)

— Supply needs (shelving, filing, paper, ink or toner, and so on)

— Cost to the library

— Cost to the user

— Security requirements

There is no one correct answer to the problems of database and document access for every library and every user. Each library must be evaluated according to the goals it sets for itself and the needs of its users. The factors discussed above should be considered for each database, balanced against the advantages and disadvantages in different types of access. Each access decision that is made has repercussions on every other decision. It is necessary for librarians and system administrators to evaluate current access decisions against those made previously, in terms of new choices that may make a different mix of products a superior solution.

Technologies for cataloguing

Many mid-sized and larger libraries have relied heavily on the major bibliographic utilities, but there are other choices. Here we describes them and the trade-offs involved using them. In cataloguing departments across the country, many librarians are facing a critical decision-is the utilization of CDROMs (CDs) and the Internet to find MARC records as part of the day-to-day operation feasible? Are cataloguers already taking advantage of this new technology? If not, why not? What impact, if any, does this technology have on workload? Can it be used by technical services librarians to help perform their work more efficiently?

To answer these and other questions related to the utilization of developing technologies, a survey was developed and mailed to 204 libraries. The participating libraries were categorized by holdings: under 100,000 volumes, 100,000499,000 volumes, 500,000-999,000 volumes, and over one million volumes; and by professional cataloguer staff size: less than 1,1 1-2, 3-5, 6-9, and 10 or more.

It is interesting to ascertain whether cataloguers are using "old" technology, before determining whether they are using "new" technology,. When asked whether they currently use a bibliographic utility such as Online Computer Library Centre (OCLC) for cataloguing, 96 per cent reported that they do. Not surprisingly, an overwhelming majority (84 per cent) of those cataloguers who responded yes to the above question, listed OCLC as their bibliographic utility. Other bibliographic utilities named were: Western Library Network (WLN) (6 per cent), Bibliofile (2 per cent), Research Library Information Network (RLIN) (2 per cent) and Southeastern Library Network (SOLINET) (1 per cent). Seven per cent of the respondents did not identify a bibliographic utility. Bibliographic utilities are chiefly used by those libraries that fall into the 100,000-499,000 volumes group and by those libraries with at least six professional staff members. The main alternative source of cataloguing information used by cataloguers is the National Union Catalogue (NUC), though several did say they use the Internet.

There are several CDROM cataloguing support systems available today, including Bibliofile, CAT CD450, CDMARC Names, CDMARC Subjects, Precision One, and SuperCat. Some of the CDROM software can be used in combination with a bibliographic utility or they can stand on their own. Knowing what some of the advantages of each system are may make the decision to use one or another easier. Bibliofile contains the Library of Congress Machine Readable Cataloguing (LC MARC) database plus extensive indexes. It allows for copying to floppy or hard disks, enabling the creation of a locally maintainable database. Records may be modified, and there are multiple search access points. Barcode readers can be attached for direct input of circulation information. Updates are monthly. OCLC's CAT CD450 combines offline cataloguing with batch processing. It does not replace the online connection and current online catalogue, but it can stand on its own. CAT CD450 is not compatible with other software, and a library must be an OCLC subscriber to purchase it.

Full-record editing and cataloguing tasks, such as catalogue cards, labels, and exporting can be done offline. Catalogue cards can be produced locally. Bibliographic records can be batch exported in OCLC-MARC format to a local system. CAT CD450 consists of seven cataloguing collections: recent books cataloguing collection, older books and most-used nonbook collection, law cataloguing collection, medical cataloguing collection, music cataloguing collection, Hispanic cataloguing collection, and LC authorities collection.

The LC Authorities Collection is the complete file of the Library of Congress Name and Subject Authority records. Its source is the OCLC Online Union Catalogue. The CDs are updated quarterly and are cumulative. They may be purchased as a set or separately. Precision One contains LC MARC records. The titles are prechosen and are representative of the titles most frequently held by school and public libraries.

The CDs are updated monthly. SuperCat contains the LC MARC Record database of English bibliographic records (foreign records on an additional disc is optional). It can stand alone as an ongoing cataloguing workstation or as a retrospective conversion utility with the LC MARC records database as a source of cataloguing records. The most important advantage of CDROM catalogue systems is that "the Library of Congress (LC file of the MARC

(Machine Readable Cataloguing) bibliographic records forms the base for all the compact disc (CD) cataloguing support systems currently being marketed". Cataloguers can continue to add records to their local online database or card catalogue that meet the same national cataloguing standards as the online bibliographic utilities. Some available software, such as CAT CD450 and SuperCat, can emulate online bibliographic utility functions; for example, original cataloguing, editing records, preparing statistical reports, and printing cards, labels, and pockets. Other software is helpful with retrospective conversion projects.

All of the CDROM systems that have been mentioned can be used for retrospective conversion. Several respondents cited this as the reason their CDROM software was purchased. CDROM cataloguing support systems have the same advantages of CDROM technology in general, large memory storage capacity on one disc and multiple search access points. A good illustration of this is *The Cataloguer's Desktop,* which is available from the Library of Congress. On one disc can be found all the following: Library of Congress Rule Interpretations, Subject Cataloguing Manual: Subject Headings, Subject Cataloguing Manual: Classification, USMARC Concise Formats, USMARC Authority Format, plus all of the USMARC Code Lists.

When asked if they use their bibliographic utility in conjunction with a CDROM cataloguing system for cataloguing new material or retrospective conversion projects, 87 per cent of the respondents said they did not. They relied on their bibliographic utilities to perform standard cataloguing functions. Of those who do, the CAT CD450 or the CDMARC Names and CDMARC Subjects are the most popular systems.

The majority of those who currently use a CDROM system, do so for cataloguing both current materials and retrospective conversion. Only six respondents (6 per cent) use it for card and label production, while the greater number use their bibliographic utility. For what reasons are libraries not using these systems? While there were several libraries that cited their workloads or their staffs as too small to warrant the expenditure, the two most common reasons were "too expensive" and "not necessary."

While a prohibitive cost factor may have been true when the cataloguing CDROM products were first on the market, that is not the case today. According to Dolly Chao, CDROM software has some of the same one-time costs, such as hardware purchase (unless leased), telecommunications installation charges, and training; in addition, recurring costs that are associated with both a bibliographic utility or a CDROM-based cataloguing system include hardware maintenance, software maintenance and updates, and telecommunications charges.

While the question of necessity will, of course, be different for each situation, CDROMs have proven themselves to be useful to cataloguers in several ways: retrospective projects, for both general and special projects; doing cataloguing work offline; and exporting records to a local system. Nearly half of the cataloguing departments have approximately 2-4 terminals for cataloguing purposes. As one might suspect, those libraries with professional staffs of 10 or more and with collections in excess of one million volumes, which generally presuppose larger budgets, fell into the 5+ terminals category. Most of the respondents using a

CDROM product for cataloguing were not trained by the CDROM software company, but those who were trained by the company representative felt the training overall was adequate.

The majority of professionals rated their computer skills as competent prior to the purchase of CDROM software. Those who use CDROM software felt that it did ease the departments' workload, although a small number felt that it had no impact on the workload at all. Fourteen out of the 16 respondents who use CDROM software said they would recommend the CDROM systems they were using to other librarians.

The internet is a "network of networks". It is the backbone that connects smaller networks such as BITNET and enables these networks to communicate with each other by means of a standard language or "protocol". The benefits to a catalogue librarian of accessing remote catalogues through the Internet include the opportunity to verify a citation or to find an appropriate subject heading or to see how someone else classified a particular item. For a catalogue librarian, these two fundamental applications on the Internet are a benefit:

1) Remote log-in—telnet/gophers/mosaic—accessing national and international OPACS (Online Public Access Computer Systems), databases, and online informational services.

2) File transfer protocol (ftp)—the transfer of documents, software, or images.

While almost all respondents (96 per cent) said they were familiar with Internet, the percentage dropped to 89 per cent for those with access to Internet and to 69 per cent for those with access from their terminals. For those without access from their terminals, either the reference department or the campus computer centre was the nearest access point.

Several respondents said they would be getting access, and in some cases direct access, in the near future. Thirty-seven per cent of the Internet users received training for the Internet in their library. Twenty-five per cent of Internet users got training from the campus computer centre, and 19 per cent attended a library workshop for instruction. Thirty-seven per cent of Internet users are self-taught. For 23 respondents, their training was a combination of two or more kinds of training. All but one had a combination of in-house (from colleagues) and self-taught instruction.

Respondents were equally split between campus computer centre and library workshop sessions as an additional means of Internet instruction. When asked how they would rate their Internet skills, 20 per cent of responders said poor, 55 per cent said fair, and 8 per cent said very good. Since 75 per cent of the respondents rate their Internet user skills as poor to fair, additional training would appear to be needed. Two possible sources of training sessions are library schools and library conferences. Occasionally, there can also be an online Internet user instruction course. These are usually posted on discussion groups.

In-service Internet workshops taught by personnel from the on-campus computer centre can easily be geared toward various skill levels and can be repeated more frequently throughout the academic year. One source of training that should not be overlooked is in-house training, which makes use of colleagues' training, learned skills, and tricks. When asked if they have subscribed to Autocat (a library cataloguing and authorities online discussion group), 64 per cent said they did. Of that group, 61 per cent indicated they used it to request help with a problem, 64 per cent used it to reply to a problem, and 88 per cent just read messages. Besides accessing

Autocat, other cataloguing uses cited for the Internet included: browsing through remote card catalogues, accessing the Library of Congress, sending electronic mail (e-mail) to cataloguing colleagues, accessing online discussion groups other than Autocat and ftp/telnet/gopher. CDROM cataloguing software products are slowly garnering the attention of cataloguers form small, medium, and large academic libraries. Several of the respondents indicated that they had a system under consideration.

The software has already proven to be advantageous to libraries who are engaging in short-term or long-term retrospective conversion projects. It can also work with or independently of a bibliographic utility. Between cataloguing and reference work, cataloguing staffs may be a bit overwhelmed by their present workload. Particularly affected are those cataloguing in small to medium-sized libraries where the prospects of additional staff may be unlikely.

As networking opens every library's Online Public Access Catalogue (OPAC) to users anywhere, it is also important to pay careful attention to cataloguing so that the local database reflects generally accepted rules and procedures and is consistent with other catalogues found through networking. Since 1902, libraries have been able to order catalogue cards from the Library of Congress (LC) Card Distribution Service. In addition to supplying cataloguing copy in card format this service provided a built-in authority structure for names and subject headings. Although the cards saved time and effort in deriving cataloguing information, only main entry cards were supplied, so subject headings, added entries, and call numbers had to be typed on each card. In 1968, the Machine Readable Cataloguing (MARC) format was developed for automated systems. The Library of Congress developed the MARC format correctly believing that a common record structure and format would facilitate the exchange of bibliographic information electronically between libraries, groups of libraries, and systems, thus it made the cataloguing process more cost-effective. Studies have shown that staffing costs are from 85 per cent to 90 per cent of technical services budgets. An automated system can allow a smaller staff to process materials faster at a lower cost, a real boon to libraries in this age of cost cutting and staff reductions.

The term "bibliographic utility" identifies cooperatively based online systems or networks whose origins were in the sharing of cataloguing data. At present, the three major bibliographic utilities in North America are Online Computer Library Centre (OCLC), Western Library Network (WLN), and Research Libraries Information Network (RLIN). All use mainframes or clusters of minicomputers to support online cataloguing by their participating libraries. OCLC was chartered in 1967 and went online in 1971. Each database comprises millions of records, composed of the full extent, or at least a major portion of the LC MARC records, as well as other records in the MARC format contributed by participating libraries. For a fee, libraries can download needed records, sometimes directly to their local systems, thus reducing the amount of time professional staff have to spend in original cataloguing.

Nowadays, the utilities have broadened their offerings to provide access to authority records, support for original cataloguing, online editing capabilities, catalogue card and shelf list production, subscriptions to magnetic tapes of any library's online cataloguing, and electronic messaging for interlibrary loan.

Whether a library is planning to purchase its first automated system or is planning a migration to a more advanced system, a study should be done to determine what operations will be automated and what the system should be able to do. Automated systems are either commercially developed turnkey integrated systems, or locally developed or single function stand-alone computers. Richard Boss believes a turnkey system is more cost-effective because the price includes all hardware, software, training, installation, and ongoing support. The best way to judge a system is to visit a library where the preferred system is in operation.

The flow of work and the movement of items through technical services will be affected by automation and the tasks that staff perform will change. The optimum way to redesign workflow in an automated system is to use the management concept of re-engineering—a complete restructuring of technical services operations. Hammer and Champy define re-engineering as "the fundamental rethinking and radical redesign of business processes to achieve dramatic improvements in critical, contemporary measures of performance, such as cost, quality, service, and speed".

To re-engineer means that the library administration and staff need to be willing to look at what they do with a fresh eye rather than continuing "business as usual." Accomplishing a radical restructuring of workflow assumes employees have the creativity, vision, and training to take on new challenges. Another important element of reengineering is that once a process is set up it must undergo continuous reevaluation and adjustment.

Every institution wants the best cataloguing available at a reasonable price. There are ways to arrange a workflow that can result in actual money saved. At the same time, the obvious ways to save money may result in inconveniences or inefficiencies in the workflow—each institution needs to balance these needs against each other. Technical services will require a radical transformation to survive in an automated environment. Some automated libraries may decide they no longer need a separate cataloguing department, and all operations that work with the bibliographic record become part of a continuous workflow.

Outsourcing is a term now appearing frequently in library literature, especially when cataloguing costs and staff reductions are discussed. Outsourcing means that a library contracts out its cataloguing and receives items ready for the shelves. It is not a new concept, and libraries have used LC-printed cards since the beginning of the century. For many years short-staffed school libraries and small public libraries have relied on catalogue cards supplied by vendors or have received items already catalogued from a regional centre.

Libraries should give outsourcing serious consideration because it can free professional time for the arduous and important work of maintaining the online catalogue, and the higher challenges of the new online environment. Cataloguers should be freed from performing routine tasks so their high-level organizational skills can be applied to making the online systems a success. Outsourcing all of a library's cataloguing is a radical step for academic libraries, however. Wright State University Library claims to be the first in the country to outsource all of its cataloguing, including original and member copy. Outsourcing also enabled us to increase substantially the quantity of material catalogued while simultaneously reducing costs. A decision to outsource library cataloguing will require careful planning, including a well-thought-out, precise cataloguing profile (editing requirements) for the cataloguing vendor. This is a good time to evaluate whether the amount of local editing can be reduced and still provide records that meet the access needs of the user.

Outsourcing plans must also include attention to quality control and database maintenance. Another form of re-engineering is having cataloguers work from home using a modem to connect to the library's electronic system. Transferring books and other materials from library to home can be a major obstacle to this process but some libraries photocopy the title page and contents, and make notes for the at home cataloguer. This new management concept may not reduce costs since it requires purchase and maintenance of off-site equipment, but it does allow valuable professionals, whose life situation requires them to be at home, the possibility to continue working. Re-engineering of the cataloguing process assumes that no one model will work for all situations. When a library manager is ready to design a more efficient workflow the questions on the following pages should be considered.

Library literature emphasizes access to the bibliographic record and the physical item as the two most important goals for technical services. The chief reason for automating cataloguing is to get records into an online catalogue as quickly as possible by facilitating copyediting and physical processing of library materials. A second important goal is to cut processing costs. Properly managed automation can cut costs by eliminating redundant tasks and reducing professional staff costs. Staff reductions occur if vacant positions are not filled or staff are reassigned to public service areas. Some libraries will have other urgent reasons for adjusting workflow. Is workflow design the job of management and professional staff or should paraprofessionals also be part of the design process? For a successful outcome, all staff should participate and so attain a sense of ownership of the new procedures. Redesigning is not easy and requires careful planning. It is important that all involved understand the goals and are committed to make the re-engineering work. With good planning, personnel should not feel threatened, but look on this as an exciting opportunity to make their work more rewarding.

Optimum workflow design should eliminate repetitive searches of the bibliographic utility since it is costly to search more than once for the same item. For libraries that do in-house cataloguing, as well as some original, two suggestions are:

— Search, then download records from the bibliographic utility directly into the local system to be edited; or,

— After the initial OCLC search, load records into OCLC's Cataloguing Micro Enhancer (CAT ME Plus).

Later these records can be updated and produced free of charge in non-prime time and added to the library's database.

Libraries that outsource cataloguing will save money on utility searches because they may only have to search once, at the time of ordering.

Copy cataloguing means using LC MARC records or another network library's cataloguing copy, if available. When acceptable copy is found during acquisitions searching, library materials can be pre-catalogued before the items are received in the building.

The cataloguing copy can be edited to local specifications and a call number assigned. Authority work can be done and labels and shelf list cards can be generated and filed with the order forms. If the pre-cataloguing records are released to the OPAC, the status would indicate "on order." In those libraries that are not outsourcing, materials received in the library can be barcoded and the ownership mark and security tapes applied immediately. Or, this physical processing step can be done after the item is checked against the OPAC record. If no further editing is required, the status is updated, the label is applied, and the item goes on to circulation.

A second search can be done after materials arrive in the library if a Cataloguing in Publication (CIP) record was found during the acquisitions search. Most of the time a full record will be available by the time materials are received. Libraries using the Dewey Decimal Classification or libraries that do extensive editing of network-supplied records are more likely to want the item to be in hand for cataloguing. Some records will not have a suggested Dewey number, or the suggested number will need to be adjusted to fit into a library's collection. Some Dewey libraries have special schemes for certain sections of the collection.

Original cataloguing is the creation of a record from scratch, a costly and time-consuming process. OCLC users find records for up to 95 per cent of their acquisitions, and a similar rate is probable for other utilities. There will always be some items for which copy cannot be found or for which there are unacceptable records.

Original cataloguing must be supplied for these items and it is nearly always done by a professional librarian. Short-staffed libraries may put a provisional record in the OPAC and allow items to circulate, or they may prefer to store items like this for a period of time and do another search of the bibliographic utility in the hope that a record will have been added in the interim. To best serve users, the first option is preferable. The value of materials diminishes the longer they are held from circulation; keyword searching in an OPAC will enable users to retrieve these items. Also, putting items on the circulating shelves is the cheapest storage and costly materials are not kept from users who need them. If the second option is chosen, a place must be found to store items waiting for original cataloguing. If items are to be placed in storage, the library plan should state for how long a time they should be stored before doing another database search. There are other sources to search for records not found in the utility.

If the library owns national catalogues, such as National Union Catalogue (NUC), British Museum Catalogue (BM), and Bibliotheque Nationale (BN), they can be searched for older books or foreign language books, or other online library catalogues can be accessed through the Internet.

As data obtained from electronic networks and other electronic information sources become more common, libraries will have to decide whether to catalogue this information. Library managers will need to keep abreast of new cataloguing rules for electronic information and other new formats. Copyediting can be done directly on the utility or a library can download records to be edited on the local system.

Since it is expensive to provide a terminal for each cataloguer, sometimes librarians edit printouts of the bibliographic record and a staff person inputs necessary changes at a central terminal. If local system terminals are less expensive to purchase and maintain than utility terminals, a library might decide to have cataloguers edit records on the local system. If access is your primary goal, consider downloading records directly to the OPAC as the materials are ordered. Status can indicate "on order" or "in processing." The ability to add records to the online catalogue at any time is another benefit of automation. There will need to be a way for users to request "on order" or "in processing" items, if the library decides to allow items to circulate before they are fully processed.

Some libraries will still prefer to wait to release records to the OPAC until the materials are completely processed and ready for the user. In this case, materials should move quickly through the workflow and the cataloguing backlog should be minimal. If there is satisfactory copy available, or if pre-cataloguing has occurred, those items can continue in a fast-track workflow. Decide what items are priority cataloguing-usually the newly received items or RUSH orders.

Items needing original cataloguing, nonprint items, foreign language materials, and special collection materials are often processed separately. Staff with foreign language skills and subject expertise may have such items assigned to them. Making these decisions depends upon the number of staff available at different levels (students, clericals, technicians, paraprofessionals, professionals) and the level of difficulty of the task. Sometimes lower-level staff are more receptive to automation and quickly learn to manipulate records efficiently. Librarians can devote time to bibliographic work and other professional activities, if they delegate routine cataloguing tasks such as bibliographic utility searches, data entry, and checking authority files to paraprofessionals.

The quality versus quantity dilemma is difficult for librarians trained in traditional cataloguing methods. But more and more, libraries are reducing the amount of editing of LC or member copy. However, library administrators will need to examine past practice and the extent of scholarly research the library supports, before making a decision to limit the amount of copyediting.

Each library needs to decide what local fields are essential. Can your library continue to do detailed editing of each record, such as deleting other libraries' call numbers, and still maintain production goals? It may be necessary to accept other cataloguers work, even if not perfect. It is really essential to update records from one set of cataloguing rules to another? Consider whether some record, even if not perfect, is better than no record. If your decision is to edit each record to meet local standards, then you must also decide whether this is professional or paraprofessional work.

Authority control in cataloguing means establishing uniform headings in a consistent structure for names, subjects, and series. Consistent headings are essential in a card environment, so that like items can be filed together in an alphabetical scheme; and they are important in an online environment as well. To achieve authority control, libraries have traditionally kept separate files for each kind of heading. With the advent of online systems, many libraries now have their authority files built into their systems to facilitate authority work. Full authority work means checking every record against files for name, subject, and series. This is a labour-intensive, time-consuming operation, even when files are available on the system.

Keeping three separate files up-to-date requires constant attention. Some libraries are cutting back in authority-control work because it seems less important with an online database and the availability of keyword searching. Some librarians have questioned the effort put into authority work and wonder if it really benefits the user.

Smaller libraries, or any library suffering severe staff reductions, will want to consider dropping some, if not all, authority-control work. Series authority work especially seems less necessary in an automated library. Larger research libraries will likely continue authority work, but should consider maintaining files on the same system used for cataloguing if not already doing so. Files can be either local and specific to the individual library, or they can be external and generalized.

Some systems allow both. If the decision is to continue authority work, consider the following points when planning how it will fit into the workflow:

— How much authority work is necessary for your library?

— When will authority work be done? Some large libraries have a separate authority-control unit, or an authority specialist, and checking is done pre- or post-cataloguing. In an automated system cataloguers can also check authority files as they catalogue items.

— Who will do the work, librarians or staff? Library staff have been trained to search authority files in many libraries. If cataloguing is outsourced, professionals have more time for authority work.

The shelf list is another tradition now being questioned. Some automated libraries continue to order shelf list cards from the bibliographic utility, adding barcode(s) so that the shelf list can be used for inventorying the collection. Other libraries have decided that the shelf list can be managed online—especially if the automated system can provide call number browsing capability in order to display records in call number order. In this case a printout of records in call number order can be used for inventory purposes. Other reasons for closing a shelf list are the need to control floor space that the shelf list files take up and the time it takes to maintain a manual file. If the decision is to close the shelf list, good database management is essential. A shelf list should not be closed until an inventory has been taken so that the library's database is an accurate record of library holdings.

Libraries need to have a database maintenance unit or a librarian who is responsible for quality checks, correcting errors, and deleting records for items no longer in the collection. This unit may also revise records when additional copies or volumes are added. Some quality checks must be built into the workflow. There should be at least spot-checking of records going into the online catalogue. Checking every record slows the release of records, and in some libraries delays patron access to new materials.

Copy cataloguing done by paraprofessionals should be closely supervised and all work checked until the supervisor is satisfied with the quality of work. Often one librarian does the majority of checking so that common errors can be flagged. In some departments a casual over-the-shoulder occasional checking may be all that is needed. Or, professionals can check each others' work. When rule updates are published, or copy cataloguers have questions, or a pattern of errors is occurring, consider holding a group problem-solving session to help in maintaining the cataloguing quality.

Sometimes libraries have a backlog of items awaiting processing before they can be released for circulation. The size of the backlog will depend upon factors such as:

— A large number of items received in a short period of time, usually due to a budget release that required large purchases in a limited time frame;

— A shortage of staff;

— Too much time spent editing cataloguing copy;

— An inefficient workflow.

One school of thought says there is nothing wrong with a manageable backlog, especially for times when there is a lull in the number of items being received. However, once a review appears people will want the item, a good reason to expedite material out of the backlog. In some academic disciplines, relevancy and currency have a limited time span of their own; so new material must be available before that time span is shortened significantly. To keep a backlog under control, items should be moving continually into the cataloguing workflow. If records were downloaded into the OPAC from time of ordering, they can be updated as materials leave the backlog area. For libraries that store items needing original cataloguing, they can be left for a short period—perhaps three to six months—while periodic searches are made in the database for a usable record. After an agreed upon time, they should be sent to cataloguers for original cataloguing if no record has been found.

Libraries produce a workflow chart that shows how materials flow through technical services from receiving to circulation, including stops to apply ownership marks, security tapes, barcodes, labels, and book covers. A flow chart can be useful in evaluating a library's workflow and when training staff for their particular tasks. A workflow cannot remain static in this electronic era. There should be a continuous process of assessment and adjustment as new equipment updates and enhancements are added to library systems. Libraries should be prepared to make necessary changes in order to use expensive equipment to its full extent. Establishing a small task group to meet and review workflow periodically is one way to do continuous evaluation.

Library managers must provide for adequate staff training in the new skills required to work in an automated environment. Training will be necessary in the following situations:

— Upon the installation of a new automated system or when system upgrades are installed;

— When new employees are hired or when library staff has been reassigned to cataloguing from other library departments.

All staff need to know how their jobs fit into the overall workflow and the importance of doing their best to help meet cataloguing goals. Persons new to cataloguing will need training in bibliographic utility searching and the MARC record. They will also need to learn how to manipulate data in the editing process.

Training should take place as close as possible to the date when a new system is installed. Steps in the training process include identifying who needs specific training and who will provide the training. As paraprofessionals take on more of the cataloguing process, librarians take on more of a training role. When a new system is installed, those who are trained first can serve as trainers for others. Training manuals should be available from the vendor, but most libraries supplement the vendor materials with locally developed guides to introduce new equipment and new techniques.

Contact other libraries using the same system to see if they have training materials you can use. To train cataloguing staff:

— Provide practice on a test database with hands-on exercises at the computer terminal. This can reduce stress if fear of automation is rampant.

— Keep in mind how adults learn. A good training program should include a variety of training techniques. Working under close supervision, followed by a period of independent practice and experimentation, with a librarian near at hand to answer questions, is probably the most effective means of training; it is also the most costly.

— Be open to suggestions for additional training or for new ways to do a task.

Responsibility for training does not stop when everyone seems to have gained confidence in the use of the new system. Training must be scheduled when there is a new release or an upgrade is installed or a new procedure is being initiated. Staff can be kept informed of recent developments by circulating print memos, in-house newsletters, or e-mail. The importance of structured training cannot be overemphasized. Some larger libraries have a training coordinator who is available to provide training on request.

Computer technology in the library requires staff to spend more time in front of a computer screen—nearly the entire day in the cataloguing unit. An unpleasant work environment and poorly designed individual workstations can affect productivity. Physical discomfort can lead to carelessness and errors.

There are many sources to consult for information on ergonomics, or the relation between a worker and the work environment. Dyer and Morris, and Dainoff and Dainoff discuss staff complaints about lighting, back and other physical pain, stress, and noise. They offer many suggestions to library managers on ways to alleviate staff discomfort.

Staff will have a sense of "ownership" if they participate in designing their workspace. It is good if they can visit well-designed offices in a nearby office building or on campus, or try out chairs and desks at an office furniture outlet. A scale drawing of the newly designed workspace should be displayed for several weeks, so that staff can check that workstations are in logical positions.

Managers must not become so involved in technology that they ignore the effect of stress concerns on previously good working relationships. Expect more conflicts among the staff and listen carefully as concerns are expressed.

Good communication between management and staff is essential to avoid conflict and keep the workflow moving. The advent of automation and the need to contain cost have changed library technical processing, leading to new management concerns. Another important factor to considers that new information technologies have made users impatient for quick access to library materials. A cataloguing process that does not have rapid access as its roles as its goal will not be serving its users adequately.

Automated bibliographic databases

Automated bibliographic databases, such as Online Computer Library Centre (OCLC), Research Libraries Information Network (RLIN), UTLAS International (now CATSS), and Western Libraries Network (WLN) revolutionized the process of cataloguing and created an entirely different approach to the management of cataloguing. Workflows changed dramatically in an effort to take advantage of the benefits of using computerized cataloguing. Staffing requirements and levels of responsibilities were also changed dramatically in order to allow cataloguers more time for original cataloguing and research and to allow support staff a greater sense of accomplishment and creativity in their positions.

The additional sources for automated cataloguing that are more cost-efficient for smaller libraries that cannot afford the major bibliographic utilities may be of questionable value for larger research libraries. CDMARC Bibliographic allows a cataloguer to access the Library of Congress catalogue via CDROM. Commercial companies can supply libraries with other CDROM products, such as Bibliofile from Bro-Dart.

Approval vendors like Blackwell North America send acquisitions librarians a disk or tape, which is a compilation of bibliographic records corresponding to the approval titles sent to the library as a part of the approval plan profile. Large academic libraries will need to consider carefully the usefulness of the above-mentioned catalogue record sources before starting to use them in conjunction with their holdings. For a community whose researchers range from a post-doctoral professor requiring publications in several languages to a beginning freshman writing an English class essay, the catalogue department head must be aware of these demographics in order to meet as many research needs as possible, while taking into consideration time, staff, and cost. A high level of quality control and subject specialization must be built into the bibliographic database, which is the research library catalogue.

As a result of this technological activity, cataloguing department heads must learn how to manage and control automated cataloguing tools and resources. If this control is not applied and proper management not engaged in, the inevitable result will be ever-increasing costs. The increasing costs of technical services, and in particular cataloguing, have brought some academic cataloguing departments to a point of financial exigency, which has prompted library administrators to look closely at the cataloguing operation.

The catalogue department head has an obligation to use this technology wisely and costeffectively in order to stay in control of the process of catalogue production and maintenance, or they will see that process transferred to outside providers.

Many research libraries are finding it necessary to reduce collection development costs by cancelling serial subscriptions and allocating less monies to monographic acquisitions. In order to stretch shrinking budgets further and possibly transfer money back into the acquisition of materials, libraries are beginning to explore the avenues for cost containment in the technical services area. Before the cataloguing manager can effectively evaluate methods for reductions in costs, however, a cost study of the current operation must be done. It is necessary to know how much is spent currently to catalogue and process materials before decisions can be made concerning where and how to reduce or contain those expenditures. In large academic and research libraries, one of the most significant expenditures is automation.

These costs must be accounted for when determining overall operating costs. The equipment used for the processing of materials and the costs for maintaining this equipment have been decreasing recently due to the reduction in costs for computers, but equipment and maintenance are still expensive. In addition to the equipment, the costs levied by the bibliographic utilities for copy cataloguing as well as the costs and/or cost reductions for original cataloguing must be identified.

Telecommunications costs must be factored into any study of automated cataloguing operations expenses. Cost studies can be simple or elaborate, depending on the amount of time and detail used for the analysis. A simple approach is to divide the annual operating costs for the department by the annual cataloguing production, determining a quick-and-dirty estimate of the average cost of cataloguing one item. Much better costing methods exist in the literature of technical services and should be consulted before embarking on this project.

The Technical Services Costs Committee of the Association for Library Collections and Technical Services (ALCTS) has published an easy-to-use, accurate guide to costing. Another excellent guide for costing methods can be found in Morris's article relating a study done at Iowa State University in Ames. The formula outlined in the article is detailed but extremely accurate in its results. Based on the separate tasks involved in performing each technical service function and the amount of time required to perform each task, Morris's method can yield, highly accurate and scientific calculations for the exact costs of acquiring and cataloguing an item. One of the critical managerial decisions concerning cost containment and automated cataloguing systems involves deciding how to use the machine resources effectively. One of the most expensive tools used for cataloguing is the bibliographic utility.

There are varying charges that include membership dues as well as system usage for cataloguing tasks. Some utilities give credits to libraries for contributions to the system and thus offset those charges. The catalogue department manager needs to be aware of both charges and credits generated by his or her department since he or she is responsible for providing good catalogue copy within an automated services budget. Currently, only an item-by-item accounting of the monthly billing will yield this information.

However, OCLC is testing a cataloguing service concept that would set a single monthly subscription price for a library's cataloguing needs and, if successful, would eliminate the need for item-by-item accounting. Many libraries routinely enhance and upgrade records found in the bibliographic databases both as a professional service and, if allowed, in order to receive the price breaks for providing this information. By making these enhancements, cataloguers are providing quality cataloguing for both their own library patrons and other cataloguers using the database. Some research libraries use one set of vendor tapes to download records directly onto their local databases and then another set to send information on their holdings to the bibliographic utilities.

For a small fee, the utilities will then use the tapes to attach each library's holdings to the utility's online bibliographic records. This method eliminates some of the costs of searching for and updating utility records. Many federal document depository libraries use tape records from vendors, such as MARCive, to download bibliographic information onto the library's online catalogue. The library can then purchase a tape from

MARCive, which can be sent to a bibliographic utility such as OCLC. The utility will then attach the library's holdings code to the appropriate record for interlibrary loan purposes. OCLC released another vendor tape-load service, called PromptCat, in 1995.

Approval plan vendors who join PromptCat will provide OCLC with a list of the approval plan items being sent to a particular library. OCLC will provide the appropriate record, download it electronically to the library's database, and attach the library's holdings to the downloaded record. Only time and experience with vendor tape-load and OCLC services will provide definitive answers as to the desirability of these vendor databases to the large academic library.

Some vendors cannot provide sufficient cataloguing information to comply with the quality standards needed by larger research libraries, while other vendors will provide the quality of cataloguing specified by an individual library through profiling. Additionally, some vendors will provide both authority records and MARC-based bibliographic records while others have no authority control and do not use bibliographic records compatible with MARC-based systems.

Most importantly, before adopting any of these cost-containment measures, the department head must assess costs and effects on both cataloguing quality and workflow. Cooperative cataloguing was from the beginning one of the enormous benefits of automated cataloguing.

Through the use of the bibliographic utilities and other bibliographic databases like Bibliofile, cataloguing records become available to the local library for downloading and editing. However, like almost everything else in automation, this is both a help and a hindrance to the catalogue department manager.

The manager must be careful that the appropriate balance between not checking anything (and therefore sacrificing quality) and checking everything (and therefore sacrificing time and money savings) is maintained. Too many catalogue departments actually reinvent the bibliographic record with each item being catalogued. The ten most popular bibliographic records in OCLC were updated by individual libraries over 1,000 times per record. Assuming that many of these changes were cosmetic in an effort to achieve the "perfect" record, updating all automated bibliographic records could be very expensive and perhaps not necessary. The amount of time spent in carefully checking all information in the record may far outweigh the benefits that might be gained through this practice. However, the assumption that extensive editing is not necessary and only adds to the costs of cataloguing cannot automatically be made in all libraries. Attention to the needs of the user of the research library may dictate that catalogue records be edited and enhanced (to provide better access and information for research) more frequently than the catalogue records for the smaller library. In either type of library, the automatic perusal of every record for catching all errors is usually not necessary and very costly.

The only way the cataloguer can assess the costs and benefits of extensive editing is to study thoroughly the needs of the library patrons. The catalogue manager must be aware of the unique needs of the individual library patron to be able to make an informed judgment as to when and where it is essential to edit records to conform to local practices and policies. The large research library may find an extensive amount of enhancing, editing, and updating of records is essential, if the catalogue is to serve as an effective research tool for all patrons.

Large academic libraries are now experimenting with contents listings for almost all their collections and with back- of-the- book indexes, in an effort to provide more access to the information found within the item. In many cases, the omission of optional elements of descriptive information requires that an individual library update the record to include the missing data. Cost-effectiveness considerations will always lead the department head to decide that editing of records for the general good of the catalogue and the individual library are to be encouraged, while editing simply to achieve a "perfect" record is to be discouraged.

In any automated catalogue system, searching and editing costs should be factors in cost containment. Whereas the bibliographic utilities have charges attached to searching for, editing, and downloading an appropriate record into the local catalogue, the CDROM databases bought from commercial vendors will not carry these costs. However, trade-offs may need to be made.

The CDROM may have fewer records matching the needs of the library, which creates a need for more in-house original cataloguing. It may also be necessary to cope with reduced automated resource sharing capabilities through interlibrary loan due to the lack of a connection to a bibliographic utility's interlibrary loan union listing file. These trade-offs are not feasible for the large research libraries, who must depend on each other for interlibrary loan support for their scholars and for copy cataloguing of a major percentage of their new acquisitions. Without access to interlibrary loan, libraries would never be capable of supplying all the information needed by their patrons and, without access to a large bibliographic database for cataloguing purposes, large libraries would not be able to sustain the enormous costs of original cataloguing.

However, since no one source is capable of providing access to all the information needed by a large research library, there is a blending of bibliographic utilities, bibliographic CDROM software for cataloguing, tape-loads, and other electronic sources for finding cataloguing information and attaching holdings to interlibrary loan databases.

In some automated cataloguing operations, paper workforms are still passed from one catalogue station to another or from the acquisitions department to the catalogue department. A workflow that allows an automated record to be used by each person in the process is much more cost-effective and efficient.

Many libraries have changed their automated cataloguing procedures to use the system more effectively and to reduce the incidence of paperwork related to acquiring and cataloguing materials. In many research libraries, searching for and down-loading an appropriate record for cataloguing is done at the "point of order" in the acquisitions process. Order information is attached to an appropriate bibliographic record or, if a record is not found, to a provisional record provided by acquisitions personnel.

Any subsequent changes made by the appropriate people in the catalogue department are made online in the local system. Only original cataloguing is done online through the utility. No paper copies are needed and, except for original cataloguing, no further searching or editing is done through the bibliographic utility. Commercial vendor tapes of bibliographic records have not always changed the way in which research library cataloguing departments handle materials, primarily due to the need for stringent quality control.

When federal depository libraries purchase MARCive tapes of government publications, some download the tape information, send the materials to the documents staff for processing, and catalogue the material from both the processing information and the tape information. Other depository libraries use the MARCive information for the download, but route all materials through the catalogue department, for final cataloguing and processing. Several approval book plan jobbers, such as Blackwell North America, provide tapes or disks of records corresponding to their approval book shipments to libraries. OCLC's PromptCat also provides approval book records to libraries.

Catalogue managers must make several decisions in advance concerning the usage of these record sources to ensure that the library is using them effectively and that quality is maintained. As a result, some catalogue departments have changed workflows and job responsibilities for staff. Some large research libraries have defined certain types of records as acceptable quality and items with these designated records are catalogued at the point of acquisitions check-in and order confirmation. For example, a record that is catalogued by the Library of Congress, using the most recent cataloguing rules and full-level descriptive entries, would be catalogued in acquisitions and the item would not be sent to cataloguing.

In this workflow scenario, all decisions concerning authority work, cross-references, and the definition of a quality record must be made before the items arrive in the library. Some research libraries will choose to let the problems with authority control be caught by a quality-control unit after the item has been catalogued. Other libraries will not be able to perform quality control at the end of the cataloguing process and will find that it is necessary to maintain the original workflow, requiring all items to be catalogued in the catalogue department. Each library must decide which scenario provides the desired balance of efficiency of workflow and effective quality control. The demise of many of the paper files found in the catalogue department precipitated a crisis in shelf listing practices in those research libraries that discontinued card shelf listing.

Granted, the call number search can be utilized as a shelf list checkpoint and author numbers can be aligned properly through this checkpoint; but, in many cases, the local system does not allow for recording the other shelf list information commonly found on the card file. As a result, catalogue department heads have to ascertain what can be recorded on the local system, where it can be recorded, and if the information is essential enough for the library to warrant recording. Of equal import is the question of the adequacy of an automated system that will not accommodate information on individual items previously kept on the shelf list cards.

Adherence to standards, such as Anglo-American cataloguing rules and machine-readable bibliographic input standards, are required when inputting any data into an international bibliographic database, such as OCLC.

Local automated systems also require standards for database quality if the system is to be usable and consistent. In a large research library, these standards become very important in order to blend the varying types of materials found in the research library and the varying levels of researchers using the collection. At the same time, the department head must determine the level, of quality control to apply and how to achieve the desired quality with a minimum of workflow disruption and production slowdowns. The volume of materials coming through the large library catalogue department does not regularly permit exacting checking of every record, unless the library is willing to fund correspondingly large staffing levels.

In today's tightening budgets, a large staff for cataloguing purposes is neither realistic nor feasible. Therefore, other measures of achieving quality catalogues are necessary. Many catalogue departments use a system of quality control that may involve a senior cataloguer proofing and evaluating junior cataloguers as a part of the routine. This method is effective for catching errors and determining situations where individual retraining or revision of the training program is needed; but it is very costly in terms of staff time and reduced production levels.

Some libraries have a system of periodic review of staff work in order to maintain quality and accuracy through correction and retraining when necessary. This alleviates the problems of costly staff time and production levels, but it is less effective for catching errors than the other method, which checks every record.

Still others have established a routine of error checks within a database maintenance unit, which oversees the quality of the bibliographic records in the library's catalogue.

This method reduces the costs of staff time and production levels and is very effective for trapping errors, but it does not address the need for individual retraining since no individuals are identified. Also, this method may not be possible for some libraries due to the lack of cataloguing-error trapping and reporting available on the library's system. When choosing a method of quality control, the catalogue manager must first determine realistically the level of precision needed to achieve the desired level of catalogue accuracy.

After determining a realistic level of accuracy, the manager must then determine the method that is the most effective while being the least costly in terms of staff time and production levels. Some catalogue departments specify critical errors and noncritical errors and exercise levels of quality control based on these criteria.

A noncritical error is an error that does not affect access to the bibliographic record. This error would be caught and corrected but would not be considered serious enough to warrant retraining for the individual committing the error. A critical error would be an error that seriously violates cataloguing standards or renders the record inaccessible. This error would not only be corrected but would be considered reason for the cataloguer to be retrained in the area where the error was committed. If more than one cataloguer is committing the same critical error, a revision of the training program may be desirable. In any case and by whatever means the department proposes to establish a quality-control mechanism, it is essential to the success of the machine catalogue that quality control be established.

Computerization has created a problem when trying to determine paraprofessional and professional duties. Copy cataloguing by paraprofessionals has been hailed as the future of the catalogue department and the harbinger of the demise of the professional cataloguer. We have learned since the decade of the 1980s that the truth lies somewhere on the continuum between the two extremes. The catalogue manager must find the appropriate division of duties for the department's staff. Paraprofessional staff, like professional librarians, need to feel a sense of accomplishment and pride in the work that they are assigned. Many of these staff persons have several years of experience in cataloguing materials and need to be placed in a position that utilizes this experience and expertise. Copy cataloguing can be challenging if the appropriate personnel are matched with the proper level of needed knowledge.

Professional cataloguers in today's world need to be far more than original cataloguers. The knowledge base for a cataloguer now includes database management, personnel management, and research expertise. Internet defines four areas in which the professional cataloguer must be knowledgeable:

1) standards, which include descriptive cataloguing standards, machine cataloguing standards, and media standards;
2) management;
3) research for planning and decision making; and
4) computing.

In today's automated cataloguing departments, continual training and staff development is essential. This training and development can be obtained either through commercial avenues or through in-house training and development programs. A library's choice of commercial or in-house training may depend on the degree of relevance to the library's specific training needs and/or the cost of the training and its impact on the budget. Research libraries with large cataloguing staffs frequently find that the expertise to supply in-house training exists and is more cost-effective than commercial training.

Several types of commercial training for automated cataloguing can be utilized by a library; however, the most commonly used by the large library are those offered by the bibliographic networks. Network distributors for the bibliographic utilities will normally provide the initial training for the utility's cataloguing system. These sessions are designed to train librarians who are new to the use of the utilities either through affiliation with a new member library or through recent entry into the catalogue office of a member library. Some networks also offer for-a-fee training in other aspects of automation and/or automated cataloguing.

For example, the Southeastern Library Network (SOLINET) offers several training tracks, one of which is a cataloguing track aimed at both professional and paraprofessional staff. Upon successful completion of the "track," the staff member receives a certificate of "track completion" (SOLINET). SOLINET also offers single sessions on many cataloguing and noncataloguing topics. The use of these training opportunities by a large library may not be the most cost-effective method of training.

If the library is a new member library and there is no resident expertise within the catalogue department, then the initial training offered by the network is relevant and worth serious consideration. Most large academic libraries, however, are already members of one of the major networks and the training by the network is relevant only to the new employee, thus making in-house new cataloguer training a more desirable choice. On the other hand, if the network training is being offered to demonstrate new techniques and/or system changes such as format integration, then the use of the network training is timely and convenient for developing the necessary expertise in the library.

Independent consultants also provide cataloguing training on a contractual basis for libraries in addition to networks. A department that has limited staff and training time might consider bringing one of these expert cataloguers into the department for some period of time to provide updated information and training for the staff. In the case of training for a new program being initiated by the library, e.g., cooperative cataloguing program, consultants brought into the library are a better choice than sending staff to the program offices for training.

In many cases, almost all of the staff can be trained at one time by the consultant, making for faster and more accurate learning. Assuming there is staff and time for in-house training, there are several options for providing this activity.

Catalogue departments need to compile a manual in support of on-the-job training programs for new cataloguers, whether they are new to the profession or just new to the library. The amount of time spent to ensure a consistent and complete manual and developing the program is well spent, especially in light of a constantly changing automated environment. A well-developed program and a well-written manual will include a multitude of technical information necessary to perform the job effectively, but they will also include a multitude of necessary philosophical and library-specific information to show why the job is being performed.

An excellent example of a training program is being developed by the ALCTS Cataloguing and Classification Section (CCS) Committee on Education, Training, and Recruitment for Cataloguing, and it can be found in ALCTS Newsletter. The training manual should always include the policies and procedures manual of the department as a component. This one tool represents a major portion of the knowledge needed by any new staff member in the department. It will not replace but will enhance the myriad of automated system, bibliographic utility, CDROM product, and other documentation that is also needed in order to fully train and develop catalogue department staff.

The professional literature has long upheld the concept of the cataloguer spending brief periods of time in the public services area of the library in order to better understand the needs of the library patrons for access to and familiarity with the idiosyncracies of the automated catalogue. Giving personnel the opportunity to work in other library departments will further develop their skills and knowledge.

Spending brief periods of time within the acquisitions or the collections departments will allow staff to further understand the selection and acquisition process and, if some of the cataloguing is done in acquisitions, will enhance understanding of the cataloguing process at the point of order. Some time spent in the systems office of a library can also enhance the knowledge and skill of the catalogue staff in the area of computerization.

Cataloguing should have two overriding priorities: the first of these is quality control for the catalogue and all associated databases. Quality includes adherence to standard that may be dictated by cataloguing community or may dictated by the machine on which cataloguing is accomplished. The successful manager must be aware of those quality standards and know how to apply them with a minimum of workflow disruptions and production bottlenecks. The second priority for the cataloguer is responding to the needs of the community for which the bibliographic database is provided: staff, faculty, and institution. The successful manager has a clear definition of what constitutes acceptable levels of quality and usefulness for he database.

7
Serials Automation

The term 'automation' refers to the application of machinery to perform work that would otherwise be done by human beings. The use of photocopiers, facsimile machines, and typewriters in libraries could technically fall under the library automation. However, library automation is generally understood to refer to the use of computers, computer networks, or CDROM.

Application of computer technology to library functions is generally considered to have begun during the 1960s or 1970s. The major automation trends affecting serials may be briefly recapitulated as follows. During the 1960s a number of systems were developed in-house, first in a batch mode and later online. In the 1970s these systems were further developed and not infrequently adopted or modified by other libraries. The 1980s witnessed integrated systems, off-the-shelf software, OPACs, and stand-alone systems run on microcomputers. The major trends of the 1990s are system migration, the client/server model, the Internet, the WWW, and electronic journals.

The earliest computerized serials systems were developed in-house, often by an academic library collaborating with a university computing center. Vendor-supplied systems were not available on the market, so libraries wishing to automate serials had no other option.

The first computerized serials control system was developed at the University of California at San Diego library in the early 1960s. Prepunched cards corresponding to serials issues were processed at the university computing center. This system produced lists of serials holdings, received items, nonreceived items, claims, and expired subscriptions as well as binding lists. Certain functions were likely to be automated with each other, such as check-in and claiming, binding and holdings information, and routing and renewal. Moreover, the earliest automated serial systems were rather crude by contemporary standards.

The *Kansas Union List of Serials,* issued in 1965, was reportedly the first computer-produced, multiple-institution serials holding list. It listed 22,000 serial titles held by eight academic libraries. During the 1970s computer technology was used to produce the *Pennsylvania Union List of Serials* and the *Minnesota Union List of Serials* as well as similar lists at the University of California at Los Angeles (UCLA), Stanford, and the University of California at Berkeley. By 1968 an online serials control system was operating at Laval University in Quebec, Canada. Undoubtedly the most famous in-house serials system was PHILSOM (Periodical Holdings in the Library of the School of Medicine), developed by the School of Medicine Library at the University of Washington (in St. Louis) and originally implemented in 1962.

William Saffady lists the San Francisco Public Library and the UCLA Biomedical Library, as well as the libraries at the University of Arizona, the University of Massachusetts, and the University of Washington, as others that implemented their own custom-designed online serials control systems during the early decades of library automation. Several of the successful systems were adopted for use, often with modifications, in other libraries. For example, the Lister Hill Library of the Health Sciences at the University of Alabama at Birmingham adopted a modified form of the PHILSOM system in the late 1960s and in the mid-1970s implemented a modified version of the UCLA Biomedical Library serials control system.

The late 1960s and early 1970s saw the development of the four major North American bibliographic utilities: OCLC Online Computer Library Center (OCLC), Western Library Network (WLN), Research Libraries Information Network (RLIN), and University of Toronto Library Automation System (UTLAS, now called ISM Library Information Services). Their initial purpose was to support the automation of the cataloguing function, but they now offer a wide variety of services, including retrospective conversion, authority control, archiving electronic journals, and so forth.

The widespread acceptance during the 1970s of the MARC record (machine readable cataloguing), including the MARC-S (machine readable cataloguing serials format), was a major boost to library automation. The Cooperative Online Serials Program (CONSER) project to create machine readable bibliographic records for serials, became operational in 1973. During the 1970s many of the in-house serial systems of the 1960s were upgraded and converted to online. However, the decade's major library automation efforts focused on circulation, which, along with cataloguing, was one of the first two functions to-be automated.

According to Saffady, circulation lent itself well to automation because of its labour-intensive nature and because its resemblance to inventory control was easily understood by computer specialists with little knowledge of library operations. Although there is no reason why serial volumes can not be bar coded and circulated, circulation automation was clearly oriented toward monographs. In the 1980s, vendors began offering a variety of serials automation options to libraries, so that in-house development was no longer a necessity or even a desirable option. Heitshu reports the number of vendors marketing automated serials control systems increased from 4 in 1980 to 60 in 1986. Early in the decade serial subscription agents began offering access to their databases on a time-sharing basis.

The Online Public Access Catalogues (OPACs) and integrated systems—both of which often treated serials as a stepchild were developed in 1980. An integrated system uses a single database to perform such basic library functions as cataloguing, circulation, acquisitions, and serials control. The same bibliographical record is linked to separate records for ordering, payment, routing, etc. Using of the same record for multiple functions is cost-effective and reduces the probability of inputting errors. When all modules are fully functioning, an integrated system allows exchange of information among the various modules so that received serials issues or new serial titles on order can be displayed in the OPAC. Unfortunately, serials control was all too often among the weakest modules or the last to be fully developed. Many of the initial OPACs did not include serials holdings information.

However, serials presented an automation challenge because of their ongoing nature, frequent title changes, and the number of exceptions involved in serials work. Heitshu stresses that academic libraries now had a choice between the serials module of an integrated system or a stand-alone serials control system, such as B. H. Blackwell's PERLINE. During the 1980s a number of microcomputer-based serials control systems for small and medium-sized libraries entered the market. Saffady mentions CHECKMATE, marketed by the Cooperative Library Agency for Systems and Services, and the SC350 Serials Control System, developed by OCLC, as examples.

During the same decade, many libraries began using off-the-shelf word processing or database management software run on microcomputers for a variety of serials management or control functions, such as creating print-format serials holdings lists, budget control, assigning titles to subjects and departments, and organizing data for cancellation projects. Some commercial binderies began marketing their automated binding systems to libraries. The 1980s witnessed the rise of so-called turnkey vendors, who provided libraries a complete automation system, including hardware, software, installation, staff training, and ongoing maintenance. The term's derivation refers to the library ability to metaphorically "turn a key" and receive an automated system-just as one can turn a key and drive an automobile off a dealer's lot.

The 1990s represent the fourth decade of library automation, yet in 1995 Chiou-sen Dora Chen wrote,

"Finally in the 1990s, the time has come for serials automation. A major trend of the mid—to late- 1990s is the shift to client/server integrated systems, although Jeff Barry, Jose-Marie Griffiths, and Gerald Lundeen wrote in April 1995 that the term *client/server* had become a "buzzword" whose precise meaning is ambiguous.

In the 1990s the vendor market remained somewhat volatile. In 1994 Trisha Davis and James Huesmann wrote, "In the past year, several serials control systems have been phased out of production, others have been replaced or updated by dramatically different versions, and new systems have been introduced. It is a dynamic, growing field. Also system migration (i.e., changing from one automated system to another), and networking among libraries, sometimes on a statewide basis such as the OhioLinks project, continued to increase throughout the 1990s, as did interest in the Serial Item and Contribution Identifier (SICI) standard and X12 for Electronic Data Interchange (EDI). Web-based OPACs, with direct links to electronic journal Uniform Resource Locators (URLs), which allow the end user to proceed seamlessly from the catalog to the journal itself, represent a significant trend of the late 1990s. The other major automation developments of the 1990s-the Internet, the World Wide Web (WWW), and electronic journals themselves-have been discussed elsewhere in this book.

According to the International Organisation for Standardisation (ISO), "Standards are documented agreements containing technical specifications or other precise criteria to be used consistently as rules, guidelines, or definitions of characteristics, to ensure that materials, products, processes and services are fit for their purpose. There is not always a clear distinction between an automation and nonautomation standard because a single standard, for example, the International Standard Serial Number (ISSN), can be used in both an automated or nonautomated environment. Yet standards are especially critical to automation because they promote compatibility among different hardware, software, and systems. Accordingly, this section discusses the major organisations and standards that affect serials automation.

The major automation standards pertinent to serials are discussed below.

International Standard Serial Number: Although not exclusively an automation standard, ISSNs contribute to the handling of serials in automated systems by allowing unique identification of a particular title and differentiating between serials with similar titles.

MARC: The MARC formats are standards for the representation and communication of bibliographic and related information in machine-readable form. MARC was adopted by ANSI as a national standard in 1971 and as an international standard by ISO in 1973.MARC-S was initially published in 1970, and the Library of Congress began distributing MARC serials records in 1973. In 1974 a second edition of the MARC serials format was issued, and in 1977 it was implemented by OCLC. Especially significant for serials is the MARC standard for holdings data. By the end of the 1980s, there were nine types of MARC records, for holdings data, authority records, and seven bibliographic formats: books, serials, maps, computer files, music, visual materials, and manuscripts. The *USMARC* Format for Classification Data and the *USMARC* Format for Community Information were issued during the early 1990s. Detailed examination of the MARC record's structure is beyond this chapter's scope, but the four basic components will be briefly outlined. The "leader," the first 25 characters, contains information about the record itself rather than the bibliographic item being described and allows the computer program to read the record.

Next, the "directory" indicates the position of each MARC field within the record, thus allowing the program to quickly locate specific information. The first 9 fields or "tags" of a MARC record (001 through 009) comprise the "variable control fields." These generally use fixed-field codes (i.e., one, two, or three place numerals or characters) to present data about both the record itself and the bibliographic item.

The major benefit of MARC is the creation of a uniform standard for machine readable cataloguing records. It thus promotes the exchange of records among libraries and the use of bibliographic utilities. Moreover, it renders a library's database independent of specific hardware or software, thus supporting system migration. Yet, MARC may not be necessary for every automation objective. Crawford notes that "MARC is not the answer" for projects such as a small library's current periodicals list. MARC "format integration" has recently received considerable attention within the serials community.

For well over a decade, the system of different MARC record structures for seven separate bibliographic formats was clearly creating problems, especially for serials. Ostensibly, such nonserial items as maps, videocassettes, sound recordings, and computer files can simultaneously assume a serial form. MARC-S, developed for print serials, did not fully provide for describing the characteristics of nonprint materials. Further difficulties were presented by mixed media items, such as a map or datafile accompanying a periodical. Format integration's practical implication for serials cataloguing is that the nontextual format of nonprint serials will be their primary aspect, and seriality will be noted in the 006 field as a secondary characteristic. In other words, a serial computer file will be catalogued primarily as a computer file and secondarily as a serial.

X12 for Electronic Data Interchange (EDI): EDI refers to the electronic exchange of business data, such as purchase orders, invoices, etc. EDI offers some advantages over paper communication, including rapid transmission, verification that the message has been received, and reduction of both labour and the possibility of error because trading partners do not have to rekey paper messages into their system.

In the United States, EDI was first used in the transportation, pharmaceutical, and electronics industries, as well as in warehousing. In 1979 ANSI established the ASC X12 for the purpose of developing the EDI standard, which is now referred to by that committee's name-ASC X12 or simply X12. Although Frederick E. Schwartz wrote in 1991 that "in North America and much of the rest of the world, ANSI X12 is synonymous with EDI' a European standard, the Electronic Data Interchange for Administration, Commerce, and Transport (EDIFACT), promoted by the United Nations Economic Commission for Europe, does exist. Although a scheduled convergence of ANSI X12 and EDIFACT in 1997 was reported in the literature, such an event has not taken place. Because X12 is a general standard for business shipping, receiving, and invoicing, it does not explicitly address specific needs of the serials industry, such as claiming.

The applications of EDI to librarianship were, according to Linda Richter and Joan Roca, "proprietary," that is, developed by specific organisations for communication with their customers. Because these early proprietary systems did not conform to a uniform national standard, a system used to communicate with one vendor would not work for other vendors. The first serials vendor to use EDI was Faxon, which decided in the summer of 1989 to experiment with ANSI X12 instead of the ANSI/NISO Z39.55-199X *Electronic Orders and Claims* standard. It began a pilot project involving six publishers plus the Welch Medical Library of Johns Hopkins University, the University of Minnesota library, and the Miles Laboratories Library in Indianapolis.

X12 standard for EDI offers the opportunity for speedier and more-efficient communications among libraries, publishers, and serials vendors. Unlike ISSN and MARC, its full potential has yet to be realized.

Serial Item and Contribution Identifier and the SISAC Bar Code Symbol: The SICI standard was developed by SISAC for uniquely identifying specific serial issues and articles and has been officially adopted as ANSI/NISO X39.56 (1991). Version 2 was submitted by the SICI Revision Committee to NISO on January 1, 1996. SICI, when encoded in machine readable form, is known as the SISAC Bar Code Symbol. Because it can be read by a bar code wand, the SISAC Bar Code Symbol would allow more rapid serials check-in of issues marked with it. The SISAC bar code has received considerable support within the serials community.

As of the mid-1990s many major publishers, automated library system vendors, and serial subscription agents were committed to supporting the

SISAC Bar Code Symbol. SISAC asserts that SICI has possible application to document delivery, interlibrary loan (ILL), copyright payments, and electronic reserve room use, among other functions. Arnold Hirshon and Barbara Winters conjecture that SICI might eventually allow serial issues to arrive in libraries already checked-in and that in has potential application to other automated serials functions.

Bibliographic access to serials

Provision of bibliographic access to serials could be viewed as a subset of serials control, yet it is important enough to warrant a separate discussion. In the broadest terms, this heading includes access to

1. serial titles;
2. serial issues, which are often termed "holdings"; and
3. specific articles, which are generally accessed through "indexing."

CDROM products such as Ulrich's Plus or EBSCO's Serials Directory offer bibliographic access to serial titles. Beginning in 1992 the International Serials Data System (ISDS) database has been available in CDROM format as *ISDN* Compact. Bibliographic control at the article level has long been provided by online access to indexes and abstracts through such services as DIALOG.

Beginning in the mid-1980s an ever-increasing number of indexing and abstracting services have been issued as CDROMs.

In the mid-1990s libraries often have three automation options for accessing indexes and abstracts:

online access, CDROM, or local mounting of the database. In the past OPACs have provided much better access to monographic holdings than to serials.

Basic questions on serials access and the OPAC follow: Are serial titles included in the OPAC? Is holdings information included? Are indexes available through the OPAC? Is dial-in access available? Is a password required for dial-in access? Serials access will be a major component of an ongoing project, the CIC Virtual Electronic Library. Using the Internet and OCLC WebZ software, the project will eventually allow end users at the CIC institutions to seamlessly search the OPACs of the 12 CIC libraries along with numerous databases.

Bibliographical access will be provided to 550,000 serials (along with 60 million books), and end users will be able to initiate ILL and commercial document delivery requests. Although not traditionally thought of as part of bibliographic control, access to serial collections could be considered a fourth level.

Record keeping represents a major component of serials processing. Indeed, some serials textbooks devote an entire chapter to the discussion of serials records. A group of records organized together constitutes a file. Important files for serials automation include bibliographic, holdings, order, vendor, binding, claims, check-in, and fund accounting records, and currency conversion. For a useful discussion of file integration in a serials control system.

A similar annual automation survey has appeared since the mid-1980s in the *Library Systems Newsletter*, published by *Library Technology Reports*. This survey is usually divided into two segments covering (i) PC or

MAC-based systems and (ii) all others. Market trends and profiles of leading vendors are included. In 1989 John Corbin offered a comparative summary of the serials control functions in automated systems, and in 1992 Richard W. Boss offered a similar functional summary of 26 systems. Davis and Huesmann's *Serials Control Systems for Libraries,* published in 1994, compares five microcomputer-based serials control systems in terms of local files, functionality, and systems requirements.

An automated serials system offers the advantages of greater speed, accuracy, efficiency, and the ability to provide new services. An early impetus to library automation was the desire to reduce staff and increase savings, although it is doubtful that automation results in either. An automated serials system can generate data that are quite useful in collection management, especially in the areas of macroevaluation and budgeting.

A report of serials expenditures by subject or department in a series of previous fiscal years can assist in reaching or evaluating such budgeting issues as the overall serial budget's division among subject areas, the proportion of departmental materials' expenditures devoted to serials, and the projection of budgetary requirements for forthcoming fiscal year.

As a downside, it can sometimes be difficult to extract the needed data from the system or customize it to your library's particular needs. Data from a serials subscription agent may be limited to the library's subscriptions with that agent.

Many librarians feel that automated systems have not lived up to their full potential in providing collection management data. An automated system can be quite expensive, and considerable staff time and effort is required to implement it. Vendors may advertise automated products that are not fully developed. An automated system has a finite life expectancy—often estimated at five to seven years.

Most present serials control systems are tied to the traditional ownership paradigm and are geared to ordering, claiming, checking-in, etc. serial titles that will be housed in the library's collection rather than handling electronic journals or document delivery of articles. There may be unforeseen and unintended consequences.

The basic steps in implementing an automated system are outlined below. These steps would apply to the automation of any library function, but the discussion addresses issues pertaining to serials. In the current automation environment, a library usually purchases a system rather than developing one in-house. For a library implementing the serials module of its integrated system, several of the steps would be skipped or abbreviated.

Establishing a timetable: The initial step should entail outlining the tasks that must be accomplished and setting a deadline for each. Various types of planning charts, such as a Gantt chart, can be used. However, as the library proceeds through the project's various stages, revision of the deadlines and addition of new tasks may be required.

Staffing: Staffing arrangements for serials automation should be made fairly early in the planning process, if for no other reason than it is staff who implement the project. Use of a committee or task force represents a standard approach. A large project might use a complex set of task forces and subcommittees covering each module as well as such specific tasks as database content, site preparation, screen design and so forth. The serials control automation task force would typically be chaired by the serials department head or team leader or another key professional staff member. In larger libraries, representatives from other departments with an interest in serials, such as public services, cataloguing, or acquisitions, should be included on this task force.

The serials staff, both professional and nonprofessional, should be involved in planning the system implementation from an early stage. Although the staff may not have computer expertise, they should certainly understand the processes to be automated. Staff involvement will also contribute to their psychological acceptance of the automated system. A strategy for staff training should be a necessary part of any automation project. Because the serials module of an integrated system is often the last to be implemented, it is likely that serials staff will already have experience using the other modules, thus reducing the required training. Unlike for the OPAC, user education would not be an issue for a serials control system.

Analysis of the library's needs: This critical step involves analysis of the library's present situation and what it wishes to achieve through automation. One should examine such fundamental factors as the available hardware, library size, financial resources for the project, and the extent of retrospective conversion of serial titles. Based on these considerations, the first decisions concern the basic approach to be used: a stand-alone system versus a module of an integrated system; upgrading the present system or migrating to a different one. The level of automation already achieved will affect serials automation decision making.

Identification of candidate systems: This step, which logically follows from the needs analysis, might be conceptualized as a two-stage process:

1. identification of the available systems that meet the library's basic specifications; and
2. from the set of systems identified in stage one, selection of a small number of leading candidates.

A possible starting point for gathering the information necessary for this process would be AcqWeb's "Guide to Automated Library Systems, Library Software, Hardware and Consulting Companies," on the WWW. Other tactics include surveying the literature, informal contacts with colleagues, and visiting the exhibition booths at ALA conferences. Sometimes the investigation may reveal that only a few systems meet the library's requirements, so further winnowing of candidates as depicted in stage two is unnecessary.

Selecting a system: An approach to selecting an automated system that has received considerable attention is the Request for Proposal (RFP)—a legalistic document that concisely outlines a library's specifications, Vendor RFP responses can be used to evaluate a candidate system, make a final selection, and to begin negotiations on a contract with the selected vendor. It should be noted, however, that many libraries do not use the RFP approach. Numerous strategies are available for gathering information to assess candidate systems. A literature review would be advisable. One can request on-site demonstrations by vendors. Informal contact with other librarians using the system can be quite helpful.

Many systems have organized user groups that could be a source of information. User listservs for several major systems-including NOTIS-L (for NOTIS), VTLSLIST (for the Virginia Tech Library system), MULTLIS (for MULTILIS), and ADVANC-L (for the GEAC Advance Library System) and their subscription addresses are included in the *Directory of Electronic Journals, Newsletters and Academic Discussion Lists*. Not infrequently, postings appear on *SERIALST* requesting evaluative comments about a particular automated serials system. Basic criteria for evaluating a system include functionality, cost, vendor reputation, vendor support, support of standards, documentation, degree of computer expertise and staff training required.

Depending on a library's situation, the ability to interface with other systems could also be a criterion. Most textbooks advocate the development of "decision rules" for system selection. Joseph R. Matthews outlines five specific evaluation methodologies. "Subjective judgement" uses opinion rather than an objective method.

The "Cost-only technique" selects the least-expensive system meeting all the library's requirements. In the "Weighted-scoring technique," the library assigns point values to desired system features and selects the system scoring the most points, based on its features.

The "Cost-effectiveness ratio" approach uses the weighted-scoring technique but divides each system's total costs by the number of points received to select the most cost-effective vendor.

Contract or purchase agreement: Vendors' standard contracts are written to their advantage rather than the library's. A library can sometimes negotiate more favourable terms with a vendor. If a library has used an RFP, its provisions might be incorporated into the contract. Most textbooks advise that the library have an attorney review any documents before they are signed. In implementing the serials module of an integrated system already in the library, this step would already have been applied.

Site preparation: The two most critical components of implementing an automated system are "people preparation" and "site preparation," which involve "the physical aspects of installing and running a computer-based library system." Site preparation addresses such issues as determining where terminals and printers will be placed; locating power sources; preparing the floor layout; and adding such communications channels as phone lines and port access. Several other major automation issues, including security, file backups, and ergonomics are often considered part of site preparation. Site preparation issues would normally be addressed on a librarywide basis for the entire automation system, but serials automation would entail site preparation for the serials department or work area and possibly for a current periodicals reading room.

Database preparation: Database creation can be one of the most expensive and time-consuming aspects of serials automation, especially for larger libraries. Two interconnected tasks are involved: retrospective conversion of records and loading the records into the automated system. Retrospective conversion has been defined as "the process 'whereby records only humans can read are transformed so that computers can read them, too."

Converting records from one format to another is termed conversion, and retrospective refers to the conversion of preexisting records. A recent search in the Library Literature CDROM indicates that 35 articles have been published on serials retrospective conversion since 1984, so a lengthy discussion is unnecessary. Many of the articles published in the 1980s commented on the poor quality of the converted," records. If a library is Implementing an integrated system's serials module, the retrospective conversion of bibliographic records for serials will probably already be completed.

According to Chen, "the main work" of serials automation is entering the records needed for acquisitions into the system's database. She lists four types of records as the most critical for this function and discusses the problems associated with file creation for each: bibliographic, order, invoice and payment, and check-in.

Sometimes a library's subscription agents can electronically load order, invoice, and payment records into the system; otherwise, records must be entered manually-an obviously labour-intensive process. Of the four, loading serials check-in records can be the most difficult and was once compared to growing bananas in Greenland.

Jean Walter Farrington notes that loading the serials database is often a two-step process: first the bibliographic records, then order, invoice, and check-in data. She warns, "Be prepared for a more difficult and more time-consuming task than originally anticipated." Marlene Clayton and Chris Batt list six major issues in database creation: record content, adherence to standards, the source of records, the input method and staff resources allocated to the project, cost, and timing and sequencing logistics." A particularly crucial issue for serials concerns whether records are entered for inactive as well as active titles. After the records are loaded, cleanup of problems and continued maintenance work are required. The importance of entering and maintaining accurate records can not be overemphasized. Inaccurate automated records are still inaccurate, despite the mystique computers enjoy.

Activating the system: This step entails putting the automated system into operation in place of the previous system. Corbin lists four basic strategies for activating an automated system: total, pilot, phased, and parallel. The total approach completely begins the new system while shutting down the old at a single time. In the pilot method, the serials control module would be tested in one branch or location prior to activation in the entire library system. The phased approach activates one function at a time. For example, serials check-in, ordering, routing, fund accounting, and other functions, would be brought up separately, In the parallel approach, the most conservative and expensive method, the new and old systems are operated simultaneously until one is confident the new system is functioning properly.

Acceptance tests: The final step involves verification that the automated system is operating correctly. Corbin outlines three types of acceptance tests: reliability, response time, and functionality. Arguably, the functionality test is the most critical for serials. One works down a list of functions advertised by the vendor or included in the vender's RFP response, ascertaining that each is performing correctly. By the late-1990s many libraries were migrating to their second or even third automated systems.

Some case studies of serials system migration have been reported in the literature, for example, from MicroLinx to NOTIS at City University Of New York's (CUNY) Queens College, by Belinda Chiang; and from an in-house system to Innopac at the University of Massachusetts at Amherst, by Patricia Banach. Margaret Bell Hentz has described the conversion of serials bibliographic and holdings information from Faxon's SC-10 system to a Techlib/Plus OPAC at Boehringer Ingelheim Pharmaceuticals, Inc., in Ridgefield, Connecticut.

System migration entails unique problems, but the steps depicted above should remain essentially the same whether a library is moving from a manual to an automated system or migrating from one automated system to another.

As William W. Wan observes, "system migration is much more complicated than automating one or two manual procedures." Major migration problems include staff training for the new system and transfer of data from one system to the other. Carol Pitts Hawks has noted the problem involved in transferring payment history records as welt as frequency and publication pattern data for specific serial titles. Wan, in analysing the Texas Woman's University library's migration from the GEAC GLIS 8000 to GEAC ADVANCE, comments that serials encountered the most problems, as enumeration and frequency information necessary for check-in was not transferred correctly. It is advisable, if feasible, to begin the new system at the beginning of the fiscal year to simplify fund accounting.

8

Online Acquisition

Today, the computer capabilities have become less expensive, less energy-consuming and more reliable than ever before. The silicon chip or the microprocessor unit has increased enormously the potentiality for data storage and processing, as well as the same for memory capability. It has been possible to store data of information independently for each such unit, and random access has been possible where any item of a set of data can be independently stored and retrieved without affecting another set of data. The sophisticated computer hardware capability has contributed to the online connection between input/output peripheral and the computer mainframe, the central processor unit

Online processing is the input/output peripheral, usually a visual display unit with a connecting link operated by a typewriter-like keyboard, is directly connected to the computer unit at the time of operation. Such a connection allows the interactive facility which means the ability to set up a dialogue with the computer system, so that, searches can be modified or adapted according to the user's specific need as he proceeds to communicate with the computer. In online operation, the computer waits to receive a series of interrogations before proceeding with the job. Online operation provides the intimate human-computer relationship having a two-way interactive communication.

Offline processing is the user is not directly connected with the computer at the time of operation. Most offline operations are conducted in batch mode which is a method of processing data in blocks or batches and a stack of searches are run in a single unit. Online output or display is made by the visual display terminal looking like a small television set equipped with a manual keyboard.

Since it is interactive, input can be made by means of the same keyboard which may not be faster than ordinary typing. But the output display is very fast and silent. The cathode-ray tube makes the screen line, and the characters of displayed information become visible by an electronic device. The terminal displays alphanumeric characters.

The output or the answers flash on the screen one after another, as they are registered in the memory. If an interrogation is made in the wrong way, it flashes an asking mark. The visual display unit is easy to use and read. It may be continuously used for a long time.

The creation of the permanent record is not possible by the visual display unit unless the matter is printed by the connecting printer. In case of long data or information, the matter which the screen can accommodate is displayed on the screen, and when the matter continues to be displayed, the lines at the top disappear one after another as the display continues. The display terminal is well-suited for obtaining quick response to inquiries. It provides a window to the computer's database. All data or information kept in random access storage is instantaneously available for display on inquiry. In human-machine interaction, the user can carry on dialogue with a properly programmed computer system by supplying data and key phrases. While the system responds with results on display or intermediate results or questions, the user can get his data with a multiple choice format.

Online computer systems are usually 'real time' systems. Such a real time computer interacts with processes external to its system in real time, which means 'as they occur'. The intake data are processed on arrival at the computer system and summarised instantaneously on the display screen as output.

The real time processing operation is in a parallel time relationship with the on-going activity and producing information instantaneously to be useful in controlling the current activity. Since non-perceptible time is the only factor in the real time operation, a real time operation is made in the online system. But all online operations need not be real time ones. In the real time system, answers are instantaneously to be used in influencing the process underway.

In the real time operation, parallel time relationship is essential with ongoing activities. Thus, information retrieval is instantaneous by controlling the dynamic activities. In real time processing, many remote stations may be connected directly by the high-speed communication system with the central processor, and several stations may be operating simultaneously. In modern computer system, 'remote computing' is possible. In such a system, input facilities can be located at a long distance from the main processor of a computer system.

Communications in between the input and the output peripherals and the main computer can be maintained by a telephone or microwave transmission. In this system, several widely separated units located at different places can utilise the central computer facility.

Usually, in such a system, appropriate programming is made, so that a computer can handle both local and remote demands. The data entered at a remote online terminal are stored in the main computer memory and processed according to programmes designed for the particular purpose. In this case, all remote users get the service instantaneously at different locations at the same time, as and when required.

When the central computer system pays attention to each remote terminal, all or several, in a specified time and operates simultaneously in a specified sequence instantaneously, it is called the 'time sharing' system. Each remote terminal gets the output in turn but considering the computer speed, a very small fraction of a second not perceptible by human sense, it is felt that the output is instantaneous.

In a time sharing system, each user has access to the computer whenever he wants it. He can have access to a part of or the total storage of the main computer memory. He may even be assigned a storage area in the main computer and there he can keep his own programme for future use.

In a time sharing system, a number of independent terminals located at various places is provided direct access to the central processor or the main computer. The system allows multiprogramming at a very high speed with one or more terminals. Special purpose time sharing computer systems are more and more being used in libraries both for library and information services so that a large number of users can use the system in various ways for different purposes. Either the housekeeping jobs performed by the library staff or storage of data for information retrieval or current awareness service for the information scientist, or browsing over the library catalogue for information retrieval by users—any of or all such services can be rendered simultaneously by a time sharing computer system.

Several terms are used to mean such a system. These are remote access, multi-processing, multi-programming, multi-access and the like. The term 'multiprocessing computer system' is specifically used where the computer becomes an integral part of a complex operation rather than an instrument used for computation or processing.

In the multiprocessing computer system, a single central processing unit having several input/output terminals is not used, but two or more central processing units are interconnected that serve all the input/output terminals of the system. In such a system, many programmes may be operated simultaneously and complex jobs may be performed.

Online access may be available to local databases or external databases across geographical barriers. The searching is made through an online terminal connected, via the telecommunication network, to a host computer or a series of computers. Within a locality, a terminal can be hardware to the computer.

For distant communications, a telecommunication network is required via either leased or dial-up lines. When a database is needed through an international telecommunication network, access is made through a local node of network using a telephone. The local node is usually a minicomputer that transmits messages through a large computer network. Within a country, the ground communication is made via coaxial cables and microwave communication channels suitable for the computerised data network. The satellite-earth stations are used for satellite telecommunication.

The satellite control earth stations, equipped with the ground communication equipment, such as, the antennae, the tracking and telecommand equipment, communicate via the ground-satellite-ground communication via a satellite is the recent speediest channel of communication. There are many online system networks for access to many databases over the telecommunication network both for current information and retrospective databases.

Millions of document abstracts, serial titles, indexed data and information contained in thousands of documents may be available through a telephone call and a tele-typewriter, which is a device almost identical to an ordinary typewriter with additional keys for communicating with a computer.

The electrical signals from the tele-typewriter are converted to audible signals that move through the telephone line and then the process is reversed for the messages on their way back. These simple communication media have a profound impact on the communication technology, and tremendous progress has been made in respect of rapid access to any quantum of information. The earliest attempt for access to the computerised database was made in the mid-sixties by the US National Library of Medicine with the introduction of the batch processed database on medical science known as MEDLARS. The provision to MEDLATS online is known as MEDLINE. The provision for access to online databases on a commercial basis was introduced by Lockheed under the name DIALOG and by the system Development Corporation under the name ORBIT Online Retrieval of Bibliographic Information Time. Both Lockheed and SDC provide an enormous range of materials with a large number of data bases.

Another commercial organisation is Bibliographic Retrieval Services started in 1976 in USA. Several other online library systems in the USA are OCLC at Ohio, BALLOTS at Stanford university, WLN at Olympia, RLIN. In Canada, the largest online computerised library system is UTLAS. In Britain, the largest online system is BLAISE. BLAISE offers online services through a large number of databases under various names and styles, such as MEDLINE, SDILINE, TOXLINE, CHEMLINE, CANCERLINE. In Europe, online access is available to ESA and DIMDI. The North American telecommunication networks are TYMNET and TELENET. They have more than 200 nodes in Europe and other parts of the world. The nearest point to India is at Hong Kong.

These networks provide access to almost all the major American online services. EURONET provides online service to EEC countries mainly, but it is begin extended to other countries also buy interconnecting with the host computer systems for such countries. In India, online interconnection with ESA has been made on an experimental basis.

Online searching is performed through an online terminal. The user must have a clear idea of the request, a chosen database and the online system with operational capability. The search comprises a series of keywords together with the Boolean or weighted-term logic. The search strategy of the search statement should be framed before logging-on.

When the communication is made by logging-on, the data of system will be displayed on the screen of the terminal and the user will be requested to select the required database. As the search proceeds, the interaction between the machine and the user goes on, and the user gives a series of commands to which the computer responds. The terminal is the visual display unit which has a cathode-ray tube (CRT) display.

A modern terminal is fitted with a continuous printer because it is necessary to get continuous printed record of searches. The printer is capable of working in parallel with VDU. The terminal is connected with the computer. But in between the terminal and the computer, a telephone connection is essential via a modem. Modem means 'Modulator Demodulator'. The function of a modem is to convert the digital messages, which both the terminal and the computer understand, to messages which are understandable trough the telephone. A similar device is connected with the computer at its end of communication. The computer must be connected with the telephone line like the standard telephone set. The telephone line should be a direct outside line, so that the connection is not interrupted by ordinary telephone calls and other noises in the line.

While in operation, the printer prints the hard copy of the search. If the connection is for long distance international search, the telecommunication networks make the connection with the help of the nearest connection node. When the public telephone lines are used for connecting the computer, it is known as dial-up access. A better but expensive system is the leased-line telephone connection, which connects the computer directly and the lines are used only for the computer connection.

Online selective dissemination of information service has been possible owing to random access searching and random access memory to keep users' profiles. The current information is made input under specific areas as required, and the prepared existing files are updated at regular intervals as and when needed to prepare the data files for SDI.

In libraries and information centres where SDI services are offered, an adequate number of profiles is maintained and online profiles are developed by the input and editing systems. SDI service sets are a series of unique data sets of references of information with each set matching with one profile. These unique data sets may consist of reference numbers only or full bibliographic citations or full bibliographic citations with supplemented abstracts.

These may be from various sources, but are arranged logically. If a user has a terminal, he can get the SDI service directly online. If he does not have a terminal, the online SDI service output may be supplied to him by online printouts. The SDI service is a personalised information service. It is a sophisticated form of current awareness service on a selective area basis, so that the user can get up-to-date information for a specific purpose.

The service requires a tremendous speed for collection, storage and retrieval of information, and an online system is best suited to get the desired result. Computerises SDI service was initiated by H.P. Luhn in the early 1960s, while he was working in the IBM corporation. The titles of the documents used in the chemical abstracts were provide on magnetic tapes in 1962.

The institute for scientific information first started SDI service on a commercial basis known as Automatic subject citation alert. Since then, the computerised online SDI service has been being widely used. Some of the SDI services are: Canadian SDI operated by the Canadian institute for scientific and technical information and used in India; computer assisted information retrieval system used at the Leatherhead food research association; storage and information centre; Agricultural system for the storage and subsequent selection of information used at ICI.

In the mid-sixties, the National Library of MEDILINE in the USA produced the printed Index Medicus. The data were kept in the computer-readable form and the files were known as Medlars. These databases were generated files of computer-readable bibliographic description in the batch process for access to offline searching.

The database of Medlars is available on online search service and the service is known as Medline which was wet up in 1973. The software is known as Elhill. The national library of medicine offers online bibliographic search service now with more sophisticated software. It has also several online search services on medical information in several specific areas besides medicine in general. Sdiline contains the latest month's references to be used primarily for current awareness.

Toxline consists of ten separate collections of secondary information in the fields of toxicology and environmental pollution. CHEMLINE is an online dictionary file which enables the users of TOXLINE to describe chemical substances before beginning a search. The mesh vocabulary file contains information on all terms in the mesh thesaurus and it can be searched online.

The online system with the search language DIALOG is a commercially accessible online database operated by Lockheed information services at Palo alto in California, USA. It uses an IBM 360/65 computer with the software DIALOG. The software was prepared from the Recon software developed by lockheed for the national aeronautics and space agency, USA.

The online services of dialog comprise more than seventy databases on a wide range of human knowledge from agriculture, engineering, technology to humanities, social sciences, the arts, public affairs, management, economics and information science. It has databases, both bibliographic and non-bibliographic, American and European. It charges access fee, telecommunication charges and prices for printouts of retrieved references. Some of the databases are AGRICOLA, LISA, METADEX, SCISEARCH, SOCIAL SCISEARCH, condensates, COMPENDEX, ERIC, etc. DIALOG is an outstanding, successful online system and a principal leader in the online service.

With wide publicity in Europe it created a tremendous impact on computerised library and information services in Europe, and it has made significant contribution to online service in Europe. It has consultation facilities and it offers a wide range of boolean search options according to the requirements of users. DIALOG contains over 16 million bibliographic citations available online, and these are constantly being reviewed and updated.

A dialog search is expressed through search words or thesaurus terms with the commands like EXAPAND, SELECT, COMNINE and TYPE. The command or instruction is made input through an online terminal keyboard for processing by the computer. The output is displayed on the screen and then the searcher can proceed can proceed with the next command or can modify his search by the interactive method.

The system development corporation is also a pioneer like lockheed for commercially accessible online services. It is located at Santa Monica, California, USA. SDC and lockheed are the two largest online database organisations in the world. Both of them prepare purpose-built software and render online services through international telecommunication networks to many countries. SDC prepared a software package for online searching in 1968 known as orbit. It has over fifty databases. It uses and IBM 370/158 computer.

Orbit facilities and capabilities are constantly being reviewed and improved for purpose-oriented user needs. Some of the databases available through ORBIT are ACCOUNTANTS, AGRICOLA, BIOSIS, CAS 77, CHEMDEX, ENERGYLINE, ENVIROLINE, ERIC, INSPEC, NTIS, TITUS, etc. For user orientation ORBIT user manual and orbit quick reference guide are most useful.

The European Space Agency (ESA) operates network links with many computer installations in various European countries. Its UK node is located at the technology reports centre of the department of industry in Kent. It offers access to the space documentation service of esa. ESA formerly used the software package known as RECON, and the online database was known as ESA/RECON.

The information retrieval service of the European space agency used ESA/RECON.At present, the version of recon has been revised and the software package is now known as QUEST. The ESA/IRS database system provides access via online process to more than twenty databases mainly on nuclear and space sciences. IRS uses and IBM 360/65 computer located at Frascati near Rome. IRD can be used through the linking of leased line network by member countries.

The department of Industry, U.K., provided a dial-up technical information service known as DIALTECH introduced by the Technology report centre in 1976. This service extended facilities to any user in the UK to dial the node at TRC and be connected to the ESA network having headquarters in Frascati. The node at trc in kent is a minicomputer and the search method is QUEST.

The information retrieval service at Frascati can be accessed online from various locations via telecommunication networks like TIMESHARE ESANET and others. The database includes INSDEC, CONPENDEX, NASA, POLLUTION and the like. The simple access through the ordinary telephone lines to large databases in computer-readable from has been possible, and can be used online. The operational information retrieval service network of the European space agency is the largest European network. It is now known as ESAANET. It serves usually the west European countries. ESANET is planning to provide ready and equal access to scientific and technical information for all member countries of the European economic community through international telecommunication networks.

EURONET is a European online information service operating to offer access to a large number of databases and the sharing of resources among the member countries of the European economic community. It envisages generation of databases in the member countries, as well as access to online databases across geographical boundaries of the member countries.

The countries are interconnected by the online system for sharing of information and online information retrieval. A system has been devised known as DIANE which offers online search service using the packet-switching data transmission network, with such latest technology, information is transmitted in 'packets' by switching operation. It is fast, reliable and effective on available lines, and it makes automatic corrections of transmission errors.

A large number of databases created in the member countries and other online agencies, such as MEDLINE, DIALOG, ORBIT, CANCERLINE, INIS, ISDS, NASA, etc., is available in EURONET. A common command language has been devised that will help the existing sophisticated language as an alternative. The system of packet switching ensures more efficient use of available lines, a large range of terminals compatible with the network and the most effective and efficient service transmission errors are corrected automatically and the network provides alternative routes. It is also inexpensive.

EURONET is interconnected by a large number of European host computers and makes them accessible from any part of the continent. Many host online computer networks are interconnected in EURONET, such as BLAISE, INFOLINE, ESA IRS, information retrieval service, DIMDI, and online host systems of other member countries.

TELENET is an online network operated by bolt, Baranek and Newman in north America. Lockheed and the system development corporation databases can be accessed via this network in the European countries through trans-Atlantic tele-communications.

TYMNET is a network operated by timeshare inc. The network having online services is based in north America, but it has telecommunication access to several nodes in Europe. Lockheed and sdc databases can be accessed also by this online network to European countries. Both the online networks, telenet and tymnet, were implemented in the early seventies in north America and were accessible to Europe and other counties of the world. They have more than 200 nodes in north America and several nodes in Europe in London, Paris, Rome, Viennna, Geneva, the hague, breussels, Frankfurt and other cities, as well as in other cities in Asia and south America like hong kong, manila, Singapore, San Juan etc. When a number of libraries, as a group of participating institutions, work for organised collection of resources and for rendering planned, coordinated services to a wider section of users interconnected by communication channels it is said to form a library network.

The network is formed to achieve better sharing of resources, both acquisition and collection of library materials, as well as bibliographic data recordings. Library automation, growth of computer technology and advances in communication technology have facilitated library networks to render better services.

In online information retrieval the searcher uses a computer terminal usually linked by telephone to a remote computer. The computer stores the database of bibliographic records on rotating magnetic disks always available for immediate access. The database can be searched and researched using special computer programs which allow the searcher to carry out a two-way conversation or dialogue with the computer.

Online retrieval offers many advantages, the following being particularly noteworthy:

— In-depth searches of computer-held files can be carried out at a speed which no human can hope to match.

— The user is an active participant and can instantly adapt his request to the reality of what is actually in the reference file-perhaps very different from what he expects-and also readily recover from errors in the formulation of queries.

— Databases can easily be researched, using new clues.

— The user has easy access to an extremely wide range of indexes and databases, many of which may not be available locally.

— Databases searchable online often offer a far greater number of access points than the corresponding printed indexes.

— There is almost no need for the irksome note-taking so typical of many conventional searches.

There is continuing growth in availability of SDI services from most online suppliers. Generally, the user's interest profile is held in an online file and matched against the incoming information. The resulting list of current references matching the user's profile can as an admirable way to keep up-to-date.

Developments in the supply of SDI services are taking place so rapidly that this Directory makes no attempt to provide details since they would be misleading by the time this text reaches the reader. Up-to-date details can easily be obtained from the main suppliers. However, some idea of the wide range of databases from which SDI service can be drawn can be seen which shows a selection of DIALOG files with automatic SDI capability.

The word "database" is often used outside the library and information field to describe any set of computer-held structured records which can be approached using search keys, and that the word "databank" is sometimes used synonymously. In the field of library and information science the words database and databank are now usually taken to have the following meanings: a database generally provides details of bibliographic references which the searcher uses as keys in order to consult the original source literature to obtain the detailed knowledge he is seeking.

The online record will contain an abstract, or indeed full-text detail, which answers the enquirer's question without reference to other documentation; a databank, on the other hand, concentrates on factual information and generally gives a direct answer without further reference to original source documents. For example, a statistical tabulation of the output from British coal mines over the last century can easily be loaded into an online file; at a later time a question concerning the output in a specific year produces a specific numerical quantity which the enquirer can immediately use as a "fact".

Online databases are usually a by-product arising from the computer-production of conventional printed indexes. Typically, the databases producer/owner makes available magnetic tapes for lease or for sale, usually in a format based on, or deriving from, the producer's, in-house requirements for the production of the printed abstracting journal. Generally, these tapes contain a set of complete bibliographic records, each record being described by the contents of a number of data "fields. The fields used, and the order in which they appear, will vary from producer to producer but may contain some or all of the following:

A = Inter-record gap

B = Start-of-record marker

C = In-house header handling details

D = Database producer's accession number

E = Name of author

F = Corporate author

G = Title

H = Abstract

I = Section heading

J = Controlled thesaurus terms

K = Uncontrolled free-indexing terms

l = Notes

M = Additional in-house handling details

N = Extra field for the specific database

O = End-of-record marker

P = Inter-record gap

The above listing is for the purposes of illustration only; it is not intended as the profile for an average database. The magnetic tapes supplied by database producers are often leased/sold at prices which in terms of a unit-record are very cheap indeed. For example, the METADEX tapes are available at \$5-\$20 per record. But of course the in-house record can be expected to be nearly 100% germane to the interests of the creating body; bought-in tapes will clearly contain much redundant material. "Downloading" from a service supplier's online database, having selected wanted references, clearly has many cost and effort advantages in cases where it is legal to download.

The immense size of producers' production costs is little appreciated by users; VINKEN estimated the global costs of abstracting and indexing publications for eventual storage on databases at \$80 million per year. An online service supplier on receiving such tapes will generally use an in-house reformatting computer program to read the tape and reformat the data-elements as received into a new format appropriate to the online inverted file and retrieval programs used by that specific online service. The reformatted records are then loaded into the online service supplier's retrieval system. A "standard" record sent out on a magnetic tape will thus be handled differently on different online service suppliers' systems. For example, the following variants show some different handling style for a straightforward author's name:

Smith, J. T	Printed index
Smith-j-t	BRS and DATA-STAR
Smith jt	CAN/OLE

Smith, jt INKA-STN

Smith, j.t DIALOG, IRS and ORBIT.

Given the autonomy of online service suppliers it is very unlikely that any great degree of standardization will evolve, and in practice human searchers very quickly learn to cope with the different output formats.

The retrieval systems used by all the major online service suppliers are based on inverted files, the contents of each documents of each document surrogate being posted to index-terms held within the computer thus allowing post-coordinate searching. For example, a document dealing with the adverse reactions of everyday medicines might easily have upwards of 50 keyword terms.

In such a case, the document's unique handling number need only be posted to each relevant term in the master index. Search terms can be coordinated in any desired combination at a later time, hence the phrase pest-coordination. A later search for, say, aspirin effects on children can be carried out simply by comparing the two lists for Aspirin and Child; document numbers common to both lists may contain information useful to the searcher. The concept of post-coordinate searching allows very great freedom and flexibility in searching, particularly when used in computer-based systems with their truly amazing speed-of-search of immense files.

Terminal software

Integrated software comes as part of a larger package, which may also include a word processor, a spreadsheet, a database management system, and moire. This type of arrangement makes it easy to transmit a document once it has been word processed. Sometimes, as in the case of Apple Works, the basic package does not contain telecommunications but may be added on by a purchase from a third-party vendor. Some software such as Word Perfect Corporation's Word Perfect Library, allows you to add your favourite programs to a master menu. Such software is not fully integrated in every sense, but it does make it easy to continue to use packages that have worked without having to start over with a total system. Specific features that should be considered with standalone packages include the following.

— Protocol (file transfer) support is especially important if we plan to send large or important files through the phone lines.

— The system should either come present for major systems or should be programmable. That is, once you enter a system's phone number, it should be able to dial it from then on with just the push of a button. Parameter settings, passwords, and other logon information should be stored as well, making logon totally automated.

— Screensave is very handy to be able to save what is coming across the screen to a buffer or to disk for future recall or print out. It should also automatically save a full buffer to disk.

— DOS commands should be available from within the program.

— It should be possible to activate the printer from within the program.

— Many systems offer timed logons and programmability. If you wish to have your computer logon at 3 a.m when the phone rates or online charges are less, a macro, program, or script, language will be required. This many require something similar to computer programming.

— Ease of use. Some people are willing to spend more time learning how to use a difficult system. Usually, a difficult to learn system offers more in the long run. This is because once learned there are fewer if any menus to go through. Even so, many people would rather have to go through menus than take the time to learn a new system. The time it takes to learn and how easy it is to get up and running, or set up macros, etc., can be important ingredients in the software selection process.

— Auto-dial. While common in most software, just make sure that it is there. It may have some perks as well, such as redial, continuous redial. Redial a specified number of times, etc. Not all software is the same in the way auto-dial is handled.

— Baud rate support: The minimum is now 1200, with 2400 close behind. No one settles for 300 any more.

There are dozens of terminal or telecommunications software packages available to microcomputer users. Those packages listed below represent the most popular for a variety of important microcomputers, including the IBM and compatibles, the Macintosh and the Apple II family. Most will work with any email system and all provide a variety of features.

ACCESS II provides full support for the Apple II series of microcomputer and Hayes compatible modems, as well as the AT & T 103 and 212 modems. ACSP supports PC to host, PC to PC terminal emulation and TTY function.

For use with IBM PC AT. XT, and MS-or PC-DOS machines. Only 64k required. This is a rather marginal packages, since no text editor, programmability, or security is provided. For the price however it is a good bargain providing 300 to 9600 bps, full duplex, ASC II code, 8 bit binary files 60.

Around supports IBM PC, XT, AT and compatible at 600, 1200, 2400, 4800, 9600 and 12,400 baud. Comes equipped with logons built in for most of the major services such as Compuserve news Net, the source MCI Mail GTE mail Dow Jones, etc. $149. ASCII pro comes in several versions including versions for MS-DOS machines and Apple pro DOS. Xmodem, Kermit and Top View protocols are used for error checking.

This has along been a reliable and popular system and easy to use once configured. Inquire for the price. Blast an acronym from Blocked asynchronous Transmission comes in the versions for most micro-computers and even mainframes, and is preconfigured by the manufacture. Features include full-function editor programmability, baud rates from 300 to 19.2 K.

Uses Xmodem, CRC, for error checking password and encryption of data during transmission are provided for security. Compatible with various local area networks. Inquire for the price.

Commx-PAC has transfer speed from 300 to 19.2k, full or half duplex, Xmodem kermit, CRC, and batch transfer protocols, and contains its own telephone directory. It has auto-dial, autotimed dial dialing pauses, redial and auto-answer. No text editor is available. Comes configured for Compuserve, Dow Jones, news/ retrieval, and the Source for logon. Password and encryption of data during transmission are provided for security. Cross Talk supports IBM and compatibles and provides emulation of TTY, IBM 3101, DEC VT52/100, ADDS Viewpoint, Tele Video 912, 920, TI 940. It has upload and download capability assigns, user password, and 128K is required.

Supports LAN netbios and compatibles. It provides 300 to 115.2K bps, is full duplex and Hayes compatible. Uses Kermit, Xmodem, check sum, and Crosstalk for error checking. Comes with many preset logons such as CompuServe, the source, NewsNet, MCI, mail, etc. Macros and other mechanisms provide for programmability. 195. George supports IBM AT, XT and compatibles, and Hayes compatible modems. It is menu-driven, has auto-dial, autotimed dial, and auto-answer, a line editor for online editing, and single level password protection.

Provides 300 to 9600 baud. Uses Xmodem for error checking and has full duplex support. Lync supports IBM AT, Xt, and compatibles. Modems include Hayes-compatible, AT&T, and others. Numerous LANs supported as well. Inquire for the price. MacGeorge supports the Apple Macintosh, Macintosh Finder, and Hayes compatible modems. The minimum required is 512K. Provides a call history log and audit trail. Baud from 300 to 9600. Supports full duplex.

Xmodem and Macbinary for error checking price 79.MacTerminal made for the Apple Macintosh, supports AT&T 103, 212 and is Hayes-compatible. Baud from 300 to 19.2K. Half or full duplex, ASCII code. Uses Xmodem for error checking. Cost: $125. Mail-Com is for the IBM PC and compatibles, and operates under either MS-or PC-DOS.

Modems can use CCITT V.22 or Hayes compatible. Requires 320K. Uses all Xmodem versions and batch transfer protocols X. PC. This menu-drive program will auto dial and redial, as well as provide some fairly powerful editing features. 189.95. Mastercom supports Apple II family, IBM, and compatibles using MS-or PC-DOS. Hayes compatible BPS of 300 to 9600. Uses Xmodem versions, CRC and batch transfer protocols for error checking. Requires 128K.

These are no security features and there is no way to program this system which may explain its low price. 49. Micro Link II supports IBM and compatibles and a variety of modems and local area networks. Requires 32K minimum memory, but 64K recommended. Supports Xmodem for error checking. Auto-dial and auto-answer. $99. Microphone II is a very popular package for the macintosh and provides complete telecommunications including programming for automatic sessions 149.

Microsoft Access a package for IBM PC and compatibles, requires 256K, and is AT&T and Hayes compatible with speeds from 300 to 960 bps. There are no programmable features, but it has a telephone directory, auto-dial and auto-answer, redial and is menu-driven 250. Mite has several versions available, including Dyna-Mite which supports IBM PC AT, XT, and compatibles. It has a menu-driven interface. Transmission speeds up to 38.4K bps. Half duplex. Uses kermit Xmodem, and Mite protocols.

Programmable and includes telephone number editor. Present configurations for Compuserve, The source, Dow Jones. Price is $99.95. Other versions include Maxi-Mite, which has fewer features for 49.95, and Maxi-Mite plus, which appears to be an-between model, but sells for 95. Move-It is a PC or MS-DOS program as well as CP/M.

Most public domain or popular error checking protocols are not supported. Move it has its own proprietary system for error correction. Supports Hayes compatible modems up to 19.2 K bps. Inquire for the price. PC-Dial is for IBM AT, XT and MS-DOS compatibles. It is Hayes compatible, requires 164K minimum Ram. Features include auto dial, auto timed dial auto redial text editor, baud speed up to 9600 &59.95. P/C Privacy takes email messages, spreadsheets, and database management files and makes them unreadable without a password.

Such files are changed into ASCII files when they are to be sent over the telephone as electronic mail. Will work with PC and MS-DOS machines, as well as with apple DOS. PC-TALK III is for use with IBM and clones. This is freeware which may be distributed to anyone. Those who wish to continue using it after looking it over and trying it out are required to send in a registration fee to the programmer. It is low cost, in any case, and packs many features.

A directory of names and numbers will store more than 60 listings, including the parameters for each. It comes ready for the Hayes Smartmodem. Perfect Link is available for PC-or MS-DOS, Apple II series, and even CP/m 80. The system has no programming capability but does support keyboard command macrofiles.

A unique features is its "Wireless File Transfer", a utility that will work locally to translate diskette formats. PFS Access will be familiar home turf to those who use the PFS serics to software packages. Offering bps up to 1200, it provides several additional perks beyond just communicating, dialing out, and sending files. These include data encryption and TTY terminal emulation. Macros can also be used for automatic logon. It is easy to use, like most of the other PFS packages. Inquire for the price. PostPlus supports telecommunications and word processing for CP/M or TRS DOS systems. This menu-driven system provides auto-log for up to 25 different in formation online utilities, and can even be used as a telex station it set to the proper receive mode.

A data encryption mode also provides some security for those in need of such a feature. Procomm Plus is a popular system for MS-DOS computers. It has substantial features, including 12 error-correcting protocols for file transfer, 16 asynchronous terminal emulations a directory that is completely automated, and a script command language. Requires 192K. QModem is a shareware package for the IBM PC.

It is programmable with a script language and it supports error checking protocols of Xmodem, kermit, and others. Reachout is a menu-driven CP/M based program. Contains a number directory that will dial automatically or can be manually dialed.

Features such as auto-redial, error checking protocols, and auto-answer are included. Inquire for the price. Red Ryder is for use with Macintosh II, Plus, and SE with 512 and modem. The Host package requires hard disk drive. This is a simple program to use providing most macintosh users with that they require to link up with other systems. Two separate versions provide different services.

Version 10.3 provides a communications program, but the Host Version 1.4A provides a bulletin board system construction set. Setup and operation of this telecommunications package is not difficult. Smartcom II is for use with IBM and compatibles, and macintoshes at speeds from 300 to 9600 baud. Though there are no programmability and no security arrangements, this is still an outstanding program.

Users will find it easy to learn and operate. The user created directory makes one-finger operation and directory management a reality. Logons can be made automatic with passwords, etc. Top half of screen presents menu and selections, bottom half of screen presents menu and selections, bottom half presents directory.

Toggling between local menu and online screen is easy 149. Xmodem is for use with IBM and clones. This public domain product has long been popular with Cp/M used and is now available in many forms and through PC-SIG for the IBM PC for only 6 per disk. With it, error correcting is much more precise than that which is provide by the modem alone.

9
Acquisition Competencies

A concern with acqusuiton competency has been with us for a long time. Much of the current interest in competencies was generated from a 1990 Harvard Business Review article entitled "The Core Competence of the Corporation". Taking an organizational approach rather than an individual approach, the authors of the article defined core competencies as sets of integrated skills and technologies unique to a particular organization. These core competencies are valued by the organization's clients and allow the organization to differentiate itself from other organizations and there by provide goods or services that other organizations cannot provide. The authors point out that organizational competencies develop from the combined competencies of the people within the organization. Since that article was published, organizations of all types have been trying to identify the current and future competencies of their members.

A quick search of Wilson Web in mid-May, 2000 demonstrates continual interest in the competencies issues in a number of disciplines throughout the decade of the 1990s. If nothing else, this has left us with a variety of definitions of competencies to consider. In 1991, Marcy Murphy, then on the faculty at Indiana University's Jib M, school, writing in the preface of Future Competencies of the Information Professional, defined competencies as the interplay of knowledge, understanding, skills, and attitudes to do a job effectively.

Table 1. Number of Wilson Web artilces in the 1990s

Applied science & technology	Library literature	Omnifile
1990-94:16	1990-94:25	1990-94: 434
1995-99:98	1995-99:42	1995-99:1285

Competencies have been a topic of great interest within the special library environment as evidenced by a 1993 article, 'Core Competencies of Special Librarians of the Future' and a 1996 report entitled Competencies for Special Librarians of the 21st Century. The former work looked at both information management competencies and organization admini-stration competencies as being needed. The latter work defined competencies as a combination of skills, knowledge, and behaviours important for organizational success, personal performance, and career development. While there are any number of ways to approach the competencies issues, much of the work that has been done in this area looks at both professional competencies and personal competencies. A third competency, educational competency, should be added to the mix.

Professional competencies are occupation-related knowledge and skills that make one technically proficient at the tasks that comprise one's job and are needed for success in a particular work setting. These competencies change over time as one's job changes; they also change over time as technology and other factors impact one's work.

Table 2. 25 most frequently cited competencies

Competency	Rank	1975 n=15	1987 n=71	1999 n=75	total n=161	Type of library academic	Type of library public
acquisition work	1	9	31	52	92	76	16
employee supervision	2	5	41	46	92	80	12
communication skills	3	1	42	47	90	84	6
automated libr skills	4	4	43	39	86	74	8
interpersonalskills	5	1	34	46	81	74	7
unit management	6	4	34	31	69	59	10
collection development	7	3	30	34	67	59	8
budgeting	8	2	26	32	60	57	3
serials	9	6	12	33	51	50	1
other duties	10	4	21	25	50	38	12
planning	11	1	19	27	47	45	2
work with vendors	12	1	12	33	46	45	1
cataloguing	13	4	11	29	44	34	10
automated libr systems	14	1	11	27	39	33	6
bibliographic tools	15	0	20	17	37	34	3
policy procedures	16	1	18	16	35	32	3
publishing industry	17	0	19	16	35	33	2
represent unit	18	1	13	20	34	34	0
2nd graduate degree	19	3	14	17	34	34	0
yr of acq exper	20	1	18	13	32	29	1
foreign language	21	2	14	14	30	29	1
problem solving	22	0	9	29	29	27	2
electronic pub.	23	0	1	28	29	28	1
prof contributions	24	0	11	16	27	27	0
materials selection	25	2	11	14	27	18	9

Personal competencies are individual traits, attitudes, and behaviours needed for success in almost any venue. These competencies change as one gets older and acquires more experience within organizational settings dealing with a variety of people in different situations. Educational competencies are those skills, traits, and attitudes that result from studying a body of knowledge on a given topic as one learns how to learn.

All these competency areas change over time, it is important to emphasize continuous or lifelong learning in the acquisition and development of competencies. While this does not relieve our professional education programs from being concerned with competencies, it does require the profession to look at an array of options for developing and maintaining competencies.

Tom Shaughnessy of the University of Minnesota wrote that the role of MLIS programs is to prepare people for entry into the profession, and the competencies needed to progress beyond that point need to be achieved through practice and other developmental activities, including advanced study, continuing education workshops, attending conferences and institutes, and monitoring opportunities. The study described here is based upon two assumptions.

First, work-related competencies are a combination of knowledge, skills, and attitudes needed to be successful at a certain job now and into the future. Second, no organization wants to hire incompetent people —regardless of how well someone may "work out" or "fit in" with an organization, the person would have been hired because he/she was believed to be competent based upon written documentation and/or an interview.

If these assumptions are valid, then one possible way to determine how similar organizations define competencies is to study job announcements for certain positions that the organizations are trying to fill. This is what was done to gather data to identify the core competencies for acquisitions librarians. The job announcements appearing in American Libraries form the basis for the data gathered, and calendar year 1999 was used as the current time-frame.

In an effort to determine if those competencies have changed over time, job announcements from 1987 and 1975 were also analysed, again using the announcements found in American Libraries for those years. These 12 year intervals were used for two reasons. First, the entire range of 1975-1999 covers a period of significant change in the profession and it should be interesting to see how this change is reflected in position announcements for acquisitions librarians. Second, the intervals were selected because the author had access to complete runs of American Libraries for the years 1975, 1987, and 1999.

In addition to the American Libraries data, during the last four months of calendar 1999 (the period of active data gathering), print and web-based announcements from the Chronicle of Higher Education were also used, as well as job announcements posted to a variety of professional-oriented listserves, Acqnet being the most notable of this group.

When an announcement appeared both electronically and in American Libraries, the print version was used for consistency of wording, although few differences were found between print and electronic versions of the same announcements. It was noted, however, that a number of the announcements that appeared electronically in late 1999 did not appear at all in American Libraries. If an announcement was repeated in more than one issue of American Libraries, the initial version of the announcement was the one used. Both the position title and the contents of the announcement were scanned to determine if a job posting would be included in the study and analysed further.

Position announcements for acquisitions librarians were easy enough to identify, however, having acquisitions responsibilities and having "acquisitions" in one's job title are two different things. Accordingly, if the announcement included acquisitions-related activities in either the duties/responsibilities section of the announcement or in the qualifications section of the announcement, the announcement was included for analysis regardless of the position title.

While there were a variety of position titles represented for purposes of further analysis the position announcements were put into one of four categories: acquisitions, collection development, serials, and technical services; with "other" used as a catch-all category for those positions not in one of the first four groups.

The original position titles are provided to allow the reader to see the variety of positions that included acquisitions-related functions. For those positions with dual tides and responsibilities, the position was classified under the first part of the job title. For example, a position listed as collection development/acquisitions librarian went into the collection development category not the acquisitions group; while the position monographic/serials librarian went into the acquisitions category not the serials group. For the three years used for data gathering, 1999, 1987, and 1975, there were 161 positions analysed.

Table 3. 25 most frequently cited competencies

Competency	Rank	Nature of competency du.	qu.	both	Category of position acq	CD	serails	Ts	other
acquisition work	1	55	15	22	26	18	16	27	5
employee supervision	2	42	17	33	30	14	17	22	9
communication skills	3	2	88	0	22	31	15	15	7
automated libr skills	4	14	63	9	23	16	14	26	7
interpersonalskills	5	2	79	0	17	25	12	20	2
unit management	6	45	11	13	18	8	11	24	8
collection development	7	31	7	29	11	36	5	9	6
budgeting	8	42	5	13	25	19	5	9	6
serials	9	22	10	19	8	4	22	14	3
other duties	10	40	3	7	11	8	7	15	9
planning	11	35	9	3	10	11	9	14	3
work with vendors	12	25	11	10	21	12	8	3	2
cataloguing	13	24	9	11	3	3	8	27	3
automated libr systems	14	13	25	1	16	4	6	12	1
bibliographic tools	15	2	34	1	10	3	9	12	3
policy procedures	16	33	0	2	7	16	5	5	2
publishing industry	17	4	29	2	14	16	1	2	2
represent unit	18	31	0	3	7	20	2	4	1
2nd graduate degree	19	0	34	0	9	17	0	6	2
yr of acq exper	20	0	32	0	20	8	1	1	2
foreign language	21	0	30	0	13	7	4	3	3
problem solving	22	4	23	2	8	6	7	6	2
electronic pub.	23	6	10	13	7	8	9	2	3
prof contributions	24	4	23	0	8	8	5	3	3
materials selection	25	22	0	5	4	15	2	0	6

The number of positions increased each year: 1975-15 positions; 1987-71 positions and 1999-75 positions. For those interested in acquisitions-related work, the job market appears to be somewhat steady over the last, 10-12 years.

However, if one wanted to do acquisitions-related work in a public library environment the opportunities are scarce. Of the 161 positions analysed here, only 26 were from public libraries, while the other 135 positions were in academic libraries. As previously mentioned, the positions were identified by both position title and by the terminology used in the job announcements themselves. This lead to most of the announcements analysed for this study falling into one of four categories: acquisitions, collection development, serials, and technical services. The 45 positions that fall into the acquisitions category were the primary focus of the study.

However, as the positions were screened, 38 positions titled collection development or collection management were found to be using terminology similar to the acquisitions positions regarding duties to be performed and qualifications needed to hold the position. This was not surprising as acquisitions and collection development are often seen as two sides of the same coin. Another 24 positions that dealt with the serials function in libraries identified duties and qualifications related to those for the acquisitions positions. This is a result of separating the acquisitions function for serials publications from the acquisition of monograph material.

An additional 39 positions were found in the technical services category. These were usually at smaller institutions which combined functions like acquisitions, cataloguing, and serials into one position or at institutions where the acquisitions function was supervised by someone in a technical services position. The technical services positions were included to see if the competencies needed to "do" acquisitions would be similar to the competencies needed to "supervise" acquisitions. Finally, 15 positions did not fall into any of the four categories above and were placed in a separate category labelled of other.

The wording from the position announcements was used as much as possible, however, if two announcements used different wording to describe essentially the same function, they were grouped together. If the competency appeared as both a duty of the position and as a qualification for the position, it was counted once for that position. However, if things were phrased differently enough, they were counted as two separate categories. For example if a position listed experience with acquisitions work, that was counted under the general "acquisitions" competency as a qualification. However, if the position indicated a specified number of years of experience of acquisitions work that went under a specific category of "years of experience acquisitions." Altogether, there were eight such "years of experience" categories.This resulted in some 60 areas of competency being identified at least once in one position announcement.

For purposes of further analysis, the 25 most consistently mentioned areas will be discussed. The range of total responses for these 25 areas goes from a high of 92 positions mentioning a competency area to a low of 27 positions including a competency area. The competency could have been cited as a duty or responsibility associated with a given position, a qualification needed to obtain the position, or cited as both. The number of positions from 1975 is too small to make many comparisons, however, it is interesting to note that there is a reasonable amount of uniformity between those competencies needed in 1987 and those needed in 1999, the largest difference coming in knowledge of electronic publishing which is understandable as the emergence of electronic publishing really began during the 1990s.

One of the most often mentioned competencies was acquisitions work itself so the job announcements analysed wanted this type of work to be performed and/or wanted some knowledge of experience with acquisitions work, the next five competencies mentioned are not related specifically to the acquisitions function. Most of these competency areas have been viewed as requirements to hold an acquisitions-related position. With regard to the 45 positions that were primarily acquisitions oriented, beyond acquisitions work itself, one especially needs to be able to supervise others, communicate well, work with vendors, and have some knowledge of fiscal management and automated library systems according to the information obtained from the job announcements. Furthermore, it is somewhat reassuring that 27 of the 39 technical services positions in this study indicated a need to know something about acquisitions work, whether it is a "jack-of-all-trades" position or a supervisory position. These results derived from the position announcements, were further supported by people working in acquisitions and related areas.

Specifically, the participants at the Acquisitions Institute at Timberline (20-23 May 2000) were divided into five groups of approximately 15 people each and asked to list what they felt were the core competencies for acquisitions librarians. The individual groups came up with lists of eight items (on the low end) to 23 items (on the high end); when duplication among the groups is removed, the Timberline participants collectively came up with a list of 31 competencies.

Each group did come up with at least one new competency not found in the position announcements or mentioned by another group. These new areas include: awareness of end user needs; ability to see things from a systemwide perspective: ability to multi-task; a sense of humour; awareness of emerging trends/paying attention to what is happening; willingness to share information with others; and awareness of trends in higher education. One thing that clearly stands out from all five groups is the need for some level of knowledge, skills, and/or ability in four areas: the publishing industry; budgeting/financial management; management skills; and working with vendors/negotiating contracts.

From the perspective of the Acquisitions Institute participants these are four core areas needed for success in the acquisitions arena. How do these results compare with other perspectives on the competencies needed for acquisitions librarians? There are two fairly recent works that provide good comparisons. In early 1998, Karen Schmidt wrote an introduction to four essays that depict what those authors saw as the future directions of acquisitions work. In her remarks, Schmidt highlighted five areas of competency:

a) financial resources management;

b) acquisition and delivery of both non-disposable and disposable materials;

c) negotiation and standardization of contracts and licenses;

d) service sector and records management initiatives; and

e) personnel management.

Acquisitions and personnel management are clearly covered by the two most frequently mentioned competencies identified form the position announcements analysed. Financial resources are covered under budgeting. Vendor negotiations find knowledge of the publishing arena were also mentioned by Schmidt under financial resources, and both of these areas are represented among the 25 competencies from the current study.

Negotiation of contracts is also part of the "working with vendors" competency. Schmidt includes electronic resources in her category, which comprises part of the electronic publishing competency from the current study. At first glance, the service sector category appears to be something of a stretch, however, Schmidt explains this as acquisitions records becoming more public information through the use of automated library systems.

The competencies concerning knowledge and use of automated library systems cover this area. It appears that the areas of competency identified by Karen Schmidt are also included in the position announcements analysed in this study. In 1997, Carol Diedrichs looked at skills needed by acquisitions librarians. She began by anticipating the current study and reviewed the job duties and qualifications for the head of acquisitions at the Ohio State University, as they existed in 1987. Briefly, the duties included:

a) administering the operation of the department;

b) formulating policies and developing procedures;

c) supervising staff,

d) serving as a member of the Administrative Staff Conference;

e) working closely with other appropriate department heads; and

f) representing the library in relevant activities.

The first three competencies, as well as the last one mentioned, are clearly included among the competencies found in the current study. Serving on the Administrative Staff Conference can be seen as a component of being a departmental manager and as part of representing your unit to the larger organization. Working closely with others can be included as an aspect of having good interpersonal skills. In addition to the duties of the position, Diedrichs also included six qualifications needed to be OSU's acquisitions head. Those qualifications were:

a) an accredited MLS degree;

b) relevant acquisitions experience;

c) leadership; problem solving skills;

d) analysis and planing skills; and

e) communication skills.

The requirement of an accredited MLS was not specifically counted in analysing the position announcements, as it appeared to be a universal qualification. Rather, it was noted that 23 positions did not mention the requirement of an accredited degree and/or indicated an equivalent degree was acceptable. Of the remaining five qualifications mentioned above, all were found in the position announcements analysed, however, leadership was only mentioned 16 times and not among the top 25 competencies.

Diedrichs further identifies three areas of competencies that acquisitions librarians will need in the future: management skills, business skills, and personal skills. The managerial skills identified were:

a) having a vision and setting goals;

b) creativity and innovation;

c) leadership;

d) problem management; and

e) change management.

In the positions analysed goal setting was seen as part of the planning competency. The term problem management was not used, however, problem solving was identified as a major competency. Leadership has already been addressed; while creativity and innovation were also mentioned in the position announcements, they were cited even fewer times than leadership.

Change management and having a vision were not specificatly mentioned as either a job responsibility or qualification, however, a number of the positions analysed contained information about the institution undergoing change as an overarching environmental factor. The business skills identified by Diedrichs were:

a) financial and contract administration;

b) publishing expertise;

c) automation and technical skills; and

d) negotiation skills.

All of these areas are covered by the competencies identified in the current study.

The personal skills needed for the future were defined as self-leadership attributes:

a) good attitude;

b) making good first impressions;

c) stress management;

d) assessing one's performance; and

e) using power effectively.

There does not appear to be any direct connection to any of these areas and the competencies identified from the position announcements. One could, however, make the case that strong communication and interpersonal skills help in making a good first impression.

Institutions in the process of revising position descriptions may wish to look more closely at these aspects of self-leadership, as they will no doubt become more and more important for successful professionals in virtually any line of work. Expanding the focus beyond acquisitions work somewhat, Peggy Johnson has recently addressed the competencies needed in collection development.

Competencies mentioned in this chapter included those that should be learned in library school and those that are developed beyond formal study. While the areas suggested as competencies developed in library school are much more collection development oriented than the position announcements analysed, the major differences found deal with knowing the library's community/users and understanding collection policy and procedures within the context of library operations. Vision was specifically mentioned as a post-library school competency to develop, and as seen above, this area was not found among the position announcements analysed.

Collection parameters

Collection development librarians face a formidable challenge when attempting to acquire information resources for students in emerging, rapidly growing, non-traditional disciplines. Unable to rely on a literary canon or scholarly infrastructure that has been developed over centuries, bibliographers are often hard pressed to identify and collect relevant materials. The law enforcement or criminal justice field is a prime example of such a discipline. In addition to being a relatively new field, it has experienced exploding undergraduate enrollments during the past twenty-five years. Bachelor's degrees conferred in the general field of protective services have increased from 2,045 in 1971 to 25,165 in 1997.

Collecting sufficient materials in an area experiencing an 800 per cent increase in enrollment is challenging, especially when resources in the field are scattered across disciplines as varied as cniminology, economics, public administration, social work, policy studies, sociology, urban planning, psychology, and legal studies. How can librarians determine the resource needs of professionals and students in an emerging discipline? Studying citations from scholarly journals is an accepted method of identifying important resources for scholars, but undergraduates require different resources than those utilized by the erudite and the initiated.

An overview of the materials considered necessary for college students is an essential component of effective collection development. One method of determining such an overview of resources for undergraduates in a developing field is to examine textbook citations. Carefully examined, these citations indicate the characteristics of the resources that experts recommend to beginners in the discipline.

Textbook authors refer to resources that introduce and summarize established research for newcomers rather than those that expand the boundaries of the discipline for practitioners and professionals. Textbook authors discuss the contribution of historical figures more often than authors of journal articles. They identify publications in which important concepts in the discipline originated or were discussed in full. They identify leading scholars and best works.

Since students frequently seek out materials cited in their textbooks to complete assignments or to complement lectures, studying cited references in textbooks can provide librarians with a concrete collection development formula. Empowered with an understanding of the distribution of resources across the range of subjects, formats, and publication dates.

Book selection responsibilities

Reference librarians typically serve as selectors of books and other library material. However reference librarians for the most part are hired to perform public service duties revolving around busy reference desk. In the past few years, additional responsibilities have been added to the reference librarians' workload, making it difficult to perform collection development duties. Acquisitions collection development librarians are frequently frustrated at how reference librarians seemingly off or defer their collection development responsibilities.

During 1991, as the new Collection Development Librarian, Robert Sorgenfrei walked into situation where a great deal of unspent money had been allowed to roll over for a couple of years. In addition, the library collection was in desperate need of updating and enhancing. So, soon after starting work, he announced to the head of reference that she could have a virtual carte blanche to buy what she needed to get the reference collection up to speed. He assumed her reaction would be one of elation. To his surprise, the opposite occurred. She threw up her arm in despair over how she or the other librarians in reference would ever find the time to determine what should be ordered. This was a shock, but then the author thought back to when he had worked as an acquisitions librarian.

It had been hard enough to get some of the selectors who were reference librarians to come in on a regular basis and to make simple decisions about which approval plan books to keep. This was no different. It was just that as a collection development librarian he was facing this problem from a new perspective. Even though he faced some problems on his new job, the author was fortunate in many ways.

Book selectors had not been given much guidance or leadership in collection development. Indeed, hardly a new book title had been ordered for a number of years. Faced with this situation, the author that he had to get books and other material coming into the library as soon as possible. To accomplish this goal, he put together a collection development team with reference librarians who have a number of responsibilities, only one of which was collection development.

The response given by the head of reference is not at all surprising for those who work behind a busy reference desk. Although utilizing reference librarians for collection development activities is quite common, reference librarians often feel burdened by these responsibilities. Discussions with librarians and a review of the literature reveal that five concerns restrict reference librarians from fully engaging in and enjoying their collection development responsibilities.

1) *Time*: Few would disagree that the central concern is simply the lack of time. Going back a decade or so, reference librarians were involved with four or five distinct tasks such as staffing the reference desk, bibliographic instruction, online searching, and preparing instructional materials and handouts. However, the inception and rise of the Internet along with decreases in library budgets and staff sizes have resulted in an expansion of responsibilities handled by a reference librarian.

   Many new tasks have been added in addition to the ones we traditionally perform. Some of those new tasks are converting instructional and informational materials into web documents, developing and managing access to electronic resources, serving as webmasters for part or all of the library website, and maintaining lines of communication with academic departments. In addition, many reference librarians are asked to contribute in other areas of the library.

2) *Immediacy*: The consequence of the widening scope of reference librarianship is summed up succinctly by David Null in a recent article, "What almost always happens in such situations is that when push comes to shove, collection development gets shoved". Many reference librarians as a result, now spend much of their day in a reactive mode. Responding to patron inquiries, repairing or editing access to a given resource, conducting an online search, giving a library tour or class, and editing a web page are a few of our most common daily tasks. These tasks often have a direct impact on the patrons and their ability to access library resources and cannot be put on the back burner.

3) *Subject field knowledge*: There seems to be some disagreement on whether intelligent selecting requires subject expertise. However, many of us would agree that it is quite difficult to develop a collection without keeping up with the literature in the selecting field. In his text selecting materials for libraries, Robert Broadus makes clear that there is "no fully adequate substitute" for extensive reading on which to base selection decisions.

   In a 1999 survey of chemistry librarians, the author compared the education level in chemistry versus the time spent reading/reviewing literature in the field. He found that librarians armed with a graduate degree spend 2.5 times more time (107 to 45 min/per week) reading the scientific literature than those without a graduate degree in chemistry.

4) *Admistrative support*: Another major problem results from the general lack of administrative support and supervision in the area of collection development.

Jasper Schad suggests that library administrators may send mixed messages about the importance of collection development because they often do not understand the complexities of collection development. Along these lines, Carol Cubberly reported that nearly half of librarians with collection development responsibilities at medium-sized academic libraries agreed that the organizational structure of their library did not support and reward collection development activities.

A reason for this may lie in the fact that librarians often report to the heads of their sections and rarely to a collection development officer. Certainly, any of these deficiencies in the administrative support may lead to discontent on the part of tile selector, and result in deferring selection activities.

5) *Exppertise in collection development*: Another source of frustration among reference librarians stems from an expectation or maybe simply a hope that any librarian will have the background and tools to succeed at selecting. Perhaps we should. However, very few library schools offer adequate classes or training in collection development. Nevertheless, because many times there is no one else to turn to, we are assigned collection development duties.

Faced with the need to have collection development covered, it is often forgotten that first and foremost we are reference librarians, and for many of us, our only formal training came in a single collection development class in library school. These factors have led many reference librarians to feel a bit stressed at the thought of being responsible for developing a collection.

> When dual-responsibility selectors are over-burdened, they become frustrated. When they think that their libraries do not support collection development, nor regard it very highly, they see it as an imposition and something that is not particularly important. When they worry about whether they are doing a good job and derive few rewards from selection work, they develop an illusion of incompetence and the result is low morale and productivity.

The points brought up by the reference librarian are certainly valid. While fully acknowledging that these problems exist, there are ways to set up a workable system where busy reference librarians can fulfil collection development responsibilities. At the Colorado School of Mines (CSM), collection development is entered around the thirteen academic departments on campus.

Librarians act as liaisons to the departments, maintaining lines of communications between the departments and the library. Since most of the departments are fairly distinct in what they teach and research, being a liaison to a department also means that you are responsible for a particular subject. In cases where subjects may be interdepartmental, a librarian usually has liaison responsibilities with both of those departments, for example both Chemistry and Chemical Engineering.

When setting up a program using multi-tasked reference librarians, we had a clean slate on which to map out a strategy and wanted to take advantage of that. We envisioned a team approach to collection development with clearly defined responsibilities and policies. The first thing we did was start an approval plan with the idea of using the plan's profile as the centrepiece for later writing a collection development policy. It would also be the basis for forming the selectors into a team.

As a way of starting a team approach to collection development, the selectors would take part in the selection of an approval plan vendor and be responsible for helping write sub-profiles for each department where they had liaison responsibilities. We felt it was important to have the selectors invest time and effort in the approval plan so that they would take some ownership of it, and go the extra mile to make it work.

At the 1999 Feather River Conference, Martin Cohen and James Galbraith gave a presentation describing the differing perceptions at McGill University over starting an approval plan and the initial resistance they encountered in the beginning among bibliographers.

We encountered little resistance to starting an approval plan. There was no talk among the selectors that we were "outsourcing" selection. What we did encounter were doubts among certain librarians at other institutions and on the part of at least one vendor representative over whether an approval plan would work at a library of a small school with an enrollment of around 3,000 students.

Some simply thought we were too small to do one successfully. We did not see it that way. We would be spending well over a $ 100,000 a year on books and would be buying in very focused engineering fields such as mining engineering and chemical engineering, and in the applied sciences such as applied mathematics, applied physics, geochemistry, materials science, metallurgy, etc.

A committee composed of selectors and the author chose Blackwell North America for their approval plan vendor. As soon as the plan was in operation, they made the overall collection development expectations clear:

— Look at the new book shelves weekly.

— Monitor approval plan sub-profiles to be sure that the appropriate books are being sent.

— Monitor sub-profile form selections electronically.

— Understand the limits of the approval plan (i.e., it cannot bring in everything)

— Make sure the books that the approval plan cannot bring in are acquired.

— Maintain lines of communication with departments.

— Spend time keeping current with subject areas by perusing major review sources weekly.

Some of the expectations such as "look at the new book shelves weekly" seem obvious, but it is sometimes difficult to get people out of reference areas and down to technical services even once a week. Efforts to aid reference librarians in their collection development duties were enhanced by new technical innovations such as Blackwell North America's Collection Manager. Blackwell began to develop Collection Manager in 1996 as a web application designed to facilitate the identification, evaluation, selection and acquisition of books of interest to a library. We immediately embraced Collection Manager when we saw its potential. As it developed we began to use it as a tool to ease the collection development burden.

Collection manager helped us in the following ways:

— It made requesting and ordering of books easier.

— The extensive bibliographic database gave selectors a better idea of what had been and was being published in their subject areas.

— It took some of the guesswork out of whether a book would come on approval or not since books could now be "forced" to come to using collection manager since anything in the database could be ordered and sent on approval.

— Selectors could now gain easy access to their profiles and understand them better.

• It gave selectors a broader understanding of the approval process as a whole.

When Blackwell offered the option of shifting from getting form selections in paper format, and instead receiving them electronically via collection manager, we immediately jumped at the opportunity. This was well received by the selectors and we saw an increase in ordering activity.

The use of collection manager markedly helped selectors more effectively utilize the approval plan as a collection development tool. Our collection development program has been in place now for almost nine years, and we believe it has proved to be an effective way of utilizing busy reference librarians as part-time selectors.

Based on the literature and our experiences from opposite sides of this issue, we have agreed on seven recommendations to ensure a successful collection development program using part-time selectors:

1) Implement a matrix organizational structure, that is, the traditional library hierarchy overlaid by a lateral authority. This allows for a collection development officer to utilize the diverse expertise of the staff, while remaining the central authority on collection development activities.

2) Develop a clearly written collection development policy that states the library's overall vision with a broad general foundation and a definite plan, including selecting criteria with examples of materials that should be collected.

3) Center collection development responsibilities around a well-designed approval plan. The voluminous amount of literature published in any one subject makes it improbable, if not impossible, for the part-time selector to keep on top of the literature in a subject. For example, there are 700,000 documents published annually in the field of chemistry alone. Approval plans, by and large, take a large weight off the selector's shoulders by systematically and automatically providing books from the major publishers in any one field. The selector can then focus on the more peripheral material such as conference proceedings, interdisciplinary materials, popular titles, and gray literature.

4) Create an atmosphere in which the selectors take ownership in the approval plan.

5) Spend time formally and informally training the part-time selectors thoroughly on the techniques of collection development and the procedures specific to the library and the approval plan.

6) Periodically evaluate the work of the selectors, not necessarily to grade their performance, but to provide a formal platform for discussion or guidance. The evaluation process will also act to give the reference librarian a degree of accountability as part of the collection development team.

7) Give selectors the time to do their work. Library administrators and heads of reference, in this case, need to realize that collection development activities cannot always be completed while staffing the reference desk. Selectors need to set aside routinely at least weekly a sufficient amount of time designated to collection development.

Putting collection development in the hands of the reference librarians is quite beneficial. Elizabeth Futas states that public services librarians are particularly suited to this task because they have the closest ties to the clientele and are, therefore, able to attain "knowledge of the trends, goals, and objectives of the users". It is just this relationship with the library users, according to George Bonn, that works as "a good barometer of the adequacy of a library's collection". This reasons along with the obvious cost savings of not hiring full-time bibliographers; make this model very attractive to library administrators

Having collection development in our position descriptions in many ways makes us better reference librarians by:

— Strengthening our grasp of a given field by allowing routine perusal of the literature, which is essential when communicating with the faculty and students and in our never-ending efforts to gain respect.

— Heightening our understanding of the strengths and weaknesses of the collection, while providing a way to do something about the weaknesses.

— Providing insight into material costs and value to the collection.

— Strengthening the lines of communication between the disparate sections within the library and reducing or eliminating the isolated department syndrome.

— And finally, giving us a sense of pride in the library collection.

Index